THE
HORIZONTAL EVEREST

Extreme Journeys on Ellesmere Island

THE
HORIZONTAL EVEREST

Extreme Journeys on Ellesmere Island

JERRY KOBALENKO

Copyright © 2002 by Jerry Kobalenko

First published in Canada in 2002 by
Penguin Books Canada
First published in the US in 2002 by
Soho Press

Published in 2010 by
BPS Books
Toronto and New York
www.bpsbooks.com
A division of
Bastian Publishing Services Ltd.

ISBN 978-1-926645-17-9

Cataloguing in Publication data available
from Library and Archives Canada.

Cover design: Kirill Lysenko
Cover photo: Jerry Kobalenko

Maps are by Alexandra Kobalenko. Used with permission.

To Alexandra, with whom the sun shines
twenty-four hours a day

and to the memory of my mother, an explorer
of the farthest regions of grace

Contents

Acknowledgments

It takes the help of many people to complete such solitary pursuits as writing a book or sledding across Ellesmere.

I'd like to single out: In Norway, Kåre Berg, Per Egil Hegge, and especially Susan Barr for their hospitality and for offering their thoughts on Otto Sverdrup. In England, the great Geoffrey Hattersley-Smith and also William Mills and Shirley Sawtell of the Scott Polar Research Institute. In Sweden, Sven-Åke Jonasson for so freely sharing his Björling material. In Poland, crustacean researcher Jan-Marcin Weslawski. In Russia, the late Valery Kondratkov. In Greenland, Torben Diklev, Inalunguaq Joelsen and David Qaavigaq. In the United States, Janet Baldwin at the Explorers Club library in New York, Len Bruno at the Library of Congress, Philip N. Cronenwett and John Schwoerke at Dartmouth College, Genevieve LeMoine and the librarians at Bowdoin College, Leonard Guttridge, Tom and Kathy Hornbein, Mary Kunzler-Larmann, David Mech, Paul Schurke, and John Tierney. I'd like to thank Bowdoin College Library for permission to quote from the journal of Fitzhugh Green, and Dartmouth College Library for permission to quote from George Rice's journal. A special thanks to W.L. Gore & Associates for the Shipton-Tilman grant that allowed me to reach Krüger country on southwestern Axel Heiberg.

The Canadian list is particularly daunting, but I'd like to say a word about three generous people. Lory James and her hardworking crew at Banff Designs provided the clothing that has allowed me to travel Ellesmere without a single case of frostbite. Bob Davies, formerly of Canadian Airlines and now with First Air, took a personal interest and has been essential in helping me fly north every year, sometimes with twelve pieces of baggage. And in conversation after conversation, Renee Wissink, former Chief Park Warden of Quttinirpaaq National Park, dazzled me with his knowledge and understanding of the island. Truly, a warden of the old school.

Others who gave of their stories and time, or with whom I enjoyed Ellesmere moments, include: Seeglook Akeeagok, Scott Akin, Jim Allan, Larry Audaluk, William Barr, Carolyn Bateman, Lyle Dick, Miles Ecclestone, John England, David Gray, Anne Gunn, Richard Harington, Vicki Hurst, Peter Jess, Terry Jesudason, Aziz Kheraj, Tom Kitchin, Peter Kobalenko, Janis Kraulis, Waldemar Lehn, Graeme Magor, Karen McCullough, Al McDonald, John McDonald, Doug McLeod, Elaine Mellor, Frank Miller, Jeffrey Qanaq, Peter Schledermann, Martin Silverstone, Josef Svoboda, Ray Thorsteinsson, Cameron Treleaven, Barry Troke, Karl Z'berg, and all of the Royal Canadian Mounted Police officers in Grise Fiord over the last fourteen years.

The charismatic Boyce Partridge of Operation Hurricane in Eureka gave good company, a flight to the fossil forest, and a surprise care package of ham sandwiches that showed up in Alexandra Fiord just as I had OD'd on peanut butter. Major Stéphane Marcoux hosted Alexandra and me in Alert, and the Honorable Art Eggleton, Canada's Minister of National Defence, gave us the rare privilege of visiting the station. James Little, the editor of *Explore* magazine, picked up the substantial tab for my Björling adventure. Martin Fortier of the North Water project and Richard Dubois, captain of the *Pierre Radisson*, allowed me to experience Ellesmere by ship.

I'd never applied for a writing grant before, but as this project stretched into a marathon trek, anything short of robbing banks became fair game. The Canada Council and the Writer's Reserve program of the Ontario Arts Council helped at critical junctures. The Leighton Studios program at The Banff Centre provided a little cabin in the woods where some of these chapters were written. Denise Bukowski convinced publishers in North America to believe in a project without an obvious "overarching narrative." My photography agents, First Light in Toronto and Stone/Getty Images in Seattle, sold enough of my wilderness imagery to buy me that most important research tool, time.

A note on spelling: Explorers rendered the names of their Inuit companions in a variety of creative ways. Today there are accepted orthographies, but they sometimes make these historic figures unrecognizable. For clarity, I've opted for traditional spellings: Peeawahto instead of Piuaatsoq, Kudlooktoo rather than Qilluttooq, and so on.

Finally, I'd like to thank my editors, Melanie Fleishman and Kathy Beyer. And most of all, my partner in daily life and in extreme journeys, Alexandra.

"No climate can rightly be considered good, though bananas and yams may flourish, if men decay."

—Vilhjalmur Stefansson

"Like land of mystery in a dream or gateway to a forbidden world of untrodded wonder."

—H. P. Lovecraft

Greely   Rice   Peary   Cook

Nares   Sverdrup   Stein   Green

Björling   Krüger   Nukapinguaq   Joy

Stallworthy   Wissink   Hattersley-Smith   Akeeagok

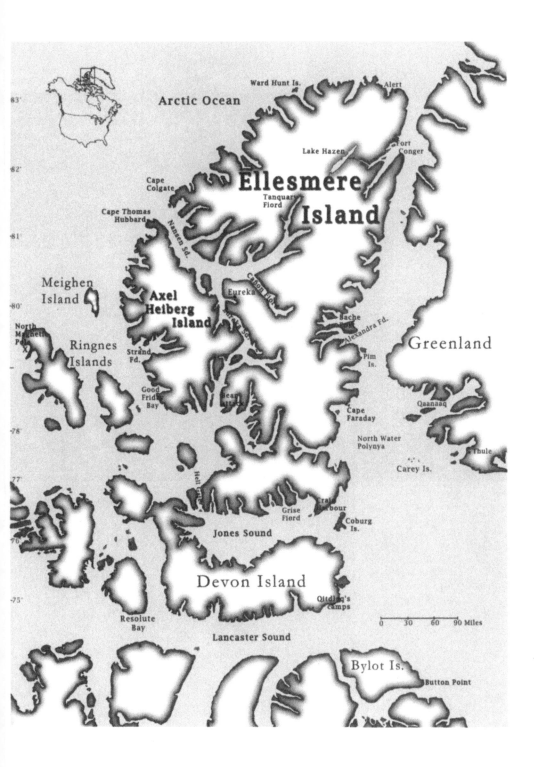

Prologue

The pack ice ground together with a comforting shriek. Crashing waves snapped an antenna near the bow, and sparks flew from a wire. I clung with both hands to the railing above the wheelhouse as the snow flailed. To the east winked the low specks of the Carey Islands, where two young explorers vanished in 1892. To the west, the maw of Makinson Inlet, where Inuit migrants endured a winter of starvation and murder. All along Ellesmere Island's austere coast, glaciers never trodden covered land never seen, framing stories never told.

Home at last.

Home is not where you live, it's where you belong. To me, the cold of Ellesmere Island was invigorating, its solitude lyrical. Its historic tragedies had a reality that current events did not. Here, the ice age still lived, shaggy relics called muskoxen pawed for dark lichen, and the last camps of explorers stood as if freshly abandoned, the inhabitants swallowed up moments before by some arctic Bermuda Triangle.

Where is Ellesmere Island? Think of the little metal disk that sits on top of a globe: Ellesmere is under that. Over the past fifteen years, I have put in some 3,500 human-powered miles here—more than any known traveler except the great Greenlander, Nukapinguaq. But I was not on foot now. I was on the *Pierre Radisson,* a Canadian Coast Guard icebreaker helping scientists from Canada, the United States, and Japan study the North Water polynya. Ellesmere science fascinated me as much as Ellesmere history but ships are terrible conveyances. I sympathized with those Inuit who left an explorer's ship after a single day because they found life on board oppressive and its comforts upsetting.

Space was liberal on this 105-yard behemoth, privacy adequate, food excellent. The captain was a gentlemanly French-Canadian who let off steam by giving tango lessons in the officers' lounge, and passengers and crew alike were bright and friendly. Still, I understood why so many naval arctic expeditions had ended in disaster. Ships were societies of the sedentary. Nightly dancing in a smoky bar was the only physical relief; the least active ones, it seemed, danced the best. I put in polite appearances but always felt like a wallflower at the prom and soon slunk away to pace the outside decks in the deepening polar night. Now and then, as on this stormy afternoon, I glimpsed the world I sought. Onshore lay a life of perpetual motion across a gloriously agoraphilic landscape. Here on the *Pierre Radisson,* I had never felt so close to home, yet so far away.

Every day, researchers lowered a large circular framework called a rosette into the ocean. Tubes with radio-controlled lids collected water and plankton at various depths. After dividing the samples, the mostly postgraduate chemists retreated to their sheet-metal trailers that had been temporarily soldered onto the *Radisson's* deck and hurriedly processed their data before the next rosette cast. "People back in Quebec said to me, 'You're lucky, you're going to the Arctic,'" declared a marvelously obsessed expatriate Iranian named Behzad. "I told them, 'We see nothing. We work.'"

Indeed, most spent their days in darkened labs cluttered with flasks and laptop computers and pails of what looked like tiny shrimp and wriggling grains of rice. I'd studied science at university but had given it up, feeling that, as Rimbaud put it, "I know what work is, and science does not move quickly enough." Behzad had zeal and urgency and a razor-sharp mind, but many others seemed to be methodically stockpiling data that was only tenuously connected to the Big Picture, any Big Picture.

I'd heard of extremophiles before this journey. Magnificent word, denoting microscopic creatures, usually bacteria, that not only survived under extreme conditions but needed extreme conditions to survive. Not for them, the beguiling comfort of room temperature. They sought the extremes of pressure, salinity, or temperature that other creatures avoided. Tissues laced with natural antifreeze, they could be frozen solid without their cells rupturing. They thrived in the superheated steam baths beside volcanic vents. Ocean pressures that could crush nuclear submarines were feather kisses to them.

They were the metaphor of Ellesmere. Here, the explorers, the animals, the plants, the very rocks were extremophiles. In this topsy-turvy world, the compass pointed west. For much of the year, the sun shone either twenty-four hours a day or not at all. No middle road. It was cold or hot; it was night or day; it was stunningly calm or terrifyingly violent.

Home.

The sort of place you either loved or hated. Lukewarm feelings were for tepid climes.

There are many such places. "This desert, all deserts, any desert," declared Edward Abbey. His true love was the vast American Southwest. I had felt the pull of this desert as well, but Ellesmere was special. Over the last two centuries many had heard its siren call.

No, Ellesmere was not just one of a hundred interchangeable deserts. It's easy to fall in love with a place, but it's what you have in common that sustains the relationship. Ellesmere's physical beauty, its cold, its nontechnical terrain, its isolation, its tolerant wildlife, its twenty-four hour sunshine, its unwalked expanses, its alien flavor, all felt like a purer form of my own inner geography.

Jody Deming was the chief U.S. scientist on the *Radisson*. She specialized in extremophiles and had come to investigate whether cold-loving bacteria, or their enzymes, functioned in Baffin Bay's 30°F sea water. She too was an extremophile and she came to symbolize for me the people who were drawn here.

Like her microscopic subjects, she sent out enzymes that broke down the barriers of everyone on board. At forty-seven, she was as open with us as a young woman sharing her deepest feelings with her best friends. Deming was at a convulsive time in her life. She was exploring aspects of her womanhood as exuberantly as she investigated her benthic microbes. ("Maybe microbiologists are so immersed in biology that we're not afraid to explore our own.") She had dyed her hair and pierced her ears for the first time. She confessed to enjoying the novel sensation of PMS.

Deming was so talented and successful that she'd overcome most of her early low self-esteem. But a sweet vulnerability remained. After a conversation which spanned everything from the Texas ranch where she grew up to jealousy among scientists of the highest caliber, I felt deeply privileged, until I spotted Deming, half an hour later, in an equally intense discussion with the ship's chief engineer. Many of us, it turned out, enjoyed at least one such remarkable tête-à-tête with her during the voyage.

Most of the time, Deming remained in her lab, monitoring bacteria on a rickety fluorometer and lost in grand thoughts. But when she emerged, the extremophile in her came out. If she was not having lively conversations about visits to old Hawaiian strip clubs, where the dancers performed amazing feats with their vaginas (Deming went backstage to ask for pointers) she was taking dancing lessons from the captain, or attending the nightly lectures, during which she invariably pointed out some universal application of the most seemingly limited data. She reminded me of Kierkegaard's knight of faith, who effortlessly found eternity in the commonplace and who, through the most commonplace actions, embodied eternity.

But I was not a knight of faith, and could not make ordinary environments extreme. I needed the wild landscape under my feet. Most of all, I needed to walk. While Behzad and Deming stalked about the ship with the all-consumed air of those for whom every second has meaning, I gazed through binoculars at the distant coast of Ellesmere and recalled the many times its extremes had gripped me with a similar magnificent obsession.

Chapter One

Into the Void

One day, years earlier, I had come home with a new backpack, the largest I could find. "What's that for?" my girlfriend of the time had asked.

"Not sure," I replied. But its size made it look serious, which seemed important.

My one previous attempt at winter camping had been in high school, when four of us shivered all night in cheap sleeping bags lined with Space Blankets. As soon as dawn broke, we hurried back to the car with a new-found understanding of Napoleon's retreat from Moscow.

This time I decided that if I were going to do something crazy, I would do it intelligently. I stopped reading fiction and began to study outdoor equipment catalogs, how-to books and naturalists' musings. The writing was unintentionally entertaining: Bjorn Kjellstrom's *Be Expert With Map and Compass*, with its illustrations of smiling figures in beanie caps finding their way hither and thither with the aid of their trusty compass and Kjellstrom's pointers; John Rowland's *Cache Lake Country*, with its thumbs-in-the-suspenders prose: "Sam was plumb scared to death . . . he was in a fix and no mistake"; *Backpacking*, by R. C. Rethmel, with its appendix on winter camping provided by the author's "good friend," James (Gil) Phillips, who used polyurethane foam to the absolute exclusion of all other insulation. Snapshots of Gil in full regalia showed him looking warm enough, but he was standing in what was evidently a sunny yard in New Mexico. A dog in the background panted from heat.

Only rarely did a kindred spirit appear in this wasteland. Calvin Rutstrum first won my heart as the only winter guru not to solemnly intone, "If your feet are cold, put on your hat." Although his way of the wilderness was more traditional than what I envisioned following, his workable ideas were timeless. Rutstrum also had a love of solitude rather than a dislike of mankind. He was didactic, like most self-educated men, but his noble character tempered the pontificating. He wrote into old age, long after he should have put the pen down, but this octogenarian's last words, in his last book, were a touching thanks for the life he had lived.

I took to naturalists for whiffs of the good writing I missed in how-to manuals. The early Edwin Way Teale was distinguished by some of his fine lyric passages; Aldo Leopold by his tang; Jean Henri Fabre by his sense of wonder; Rachel Carson by her passionate use of facts; and Thoreau by the depth of his reflections, and by his eyeballs. His eyes had that mixture of sadness and purity that is sometimes found in the faces of the truly great. They were as magnificent as August Strindberg's forehead. One would never find those eyes in the sockets of a clod.

Gradually, I became aware that I wanted to do an extreme wilderness trip, which seemed to include winter camping. I worked from three principles. First, since gear "used on Everest" was readily available, while gear "used at the North Pole" was not, I assumed that high-altitude mountaineering and extreme arctic travel required similar equipment— bombproof tents, five-pound down bags, offset-baffled parkas. Second, traditional equipment was for those who had mastered field repair and general woodsmanship; ignoramuses such as myself were safer with modern stuff. Third, I chose the best of everything—lightest, warmest, toughest, biggest—and only from what I perceived to be A-list companies. When you get to know equipment, you can make item-by-item judgments, but from the armchair it's impossible to tell the necessary from the overkill. So I erred on the side of caution, reducing the cost of these Rolls Royce packs and Lamborghini bags by presenting myself to companies as an outdoor writer. Most were happy to offer me wholesale prices which, in this industry, usually meant forty percent off. Soon I was equipped for the Worst Journey in the World.

I had no idea how much food to bring on this theoretical trek, but I had recently trained as a marathon swimmer, logging six miles a day in the pool. That much exercise leaves you free to eat as much as you can, and I discovered that I simply could not hoover in more than 7,000 calories a day. My jaw ached from chewing, I got hemorrhoids from all the activity of a supercharged metabolism, and I ran out of things I wanted to eat. Even a whole strawberry shortcake every day palls after a while.

By default then, 7,000 calories seemed like a good dietary target for an extreme cold-weather expedition. Hard spring sledding, I learned later, only burns about 5,000 calories, but during the midwinter cold of my first expeditions I needed the extra 2,000 calories to stay warm. In the end, making the most extreme choices in food and equipment worked.

■

Although I originally fixated on Labrador as my wilderness ideal, a chance trip to Ellesmere Island turned my world upside-down. This was the most extreme place in North America. It drew extreme people, nurtured extreme plants, harbored extreme animals, and showcased extreme phenomena. It was everything I wanted. I forgot about Labrador.

I soon learned that the difficulty of traveling on Ellesmere is nothing compared with the difficulty of getting there. There are no roads, no boats and only one scheduled flight, twice weekly, to the lone village of Grise Fiord on the south coast.

The quest to reach Ellesmere begins two hundred and fifty miles to the south, in Resolute Bay on Cornwallis Island, "perhaps the most dreary and desolate place that can well be conceived," according to one early description. The town of Resolute lies two thousand miles due north of Winnipeg, in a part of the Arctic known as the Barren Wedge. Northern plants can endure almost anything, as long as they get one month of decent weather in which to grow. But summer in the Barren Wedge is typically windy, dank, and foggy, so Cornwallis Island has the lushness of a gravel pit. First-time visitors are astonished when they fly another five hundred miles north and step into Ellesmere's alpine meadows and warm sunshine.

Resolute is actually two villages: an "unlovely huddle" of interconnected government buildings near the airport, and the Inuit village. The two are connected by a four-mile gravel road of excruciating dullness that the truly desperate sometimes hike to kill time.

As the last stop of jets and the staging area for science and adventure in the High Arctic, Resolute has a certain character. Visitors have plenty of time to explore this when bad weather grounds all aircraft for days. Six days is my record, but this is by no means exceptional. One weatherman in the Barren Wedge was stranded for a month and lost his entire vacation.

A passion for Ellesmere is like an addiction to heroin: You have to subsidize the craving through humiliating pursuits. Hitchhiking on half-empty planes used to be a respectable means of northern travel, and early arctic obsessees—including such notables as photographer Fred Bruemmer—rarely paid their own way. Communities put them up until they found a charter flight to hop on. Today it is sometimes possible to hitchhike back from Ellesmere, but planes to the island are usually full, and to show up in Resolute without firm plans is to risk never getting out.

In recent years, travel has become a little easier for me because I can barter my knowledge about the island. But just how does someone, for whom two thousand dollars is a lot of money, accumulate twenty journeys to the most expensive wilderness destination in North America?

My first trip was a magazine assignment, covered partly by an outfitter and partly by tourism agencies. More wealthy magazines, to ensure objective coverage, send their writers as paying clients, but smaller publications rely on outfitters to cover the cost, which is negligible if the tour is already going and there is space. Smart outfitters also give photographers the occasional freebie, because good photos are vital for trade show exhibits where they find new customers and for brochures which tantalize repeat clientele. My love of photography, which was born and developed on Ellesmere, is partly to credit for four of those twenty trips.

Another Ellesmere stratagem is to buy a piece of someone else's charter. Sometimes there is enough space left over for one or two people and their gear. In the spring, adventurers attempting the North Pole need periodic resupplies, and their expedition managers in Resolute are always open to recouping part of their costs. The difficulty is that you never know the dates of the resupply flights ahead of time or whether they will have room. You show up in Resolute and take your chances.

In summer, tour operators may also sell a place on their flights. This is a better arrangement because their dates are fixed. However, most tours are full or almost full, and it's hard to confirm your spot until shortly before the trip leaves. Outfitters understandably prefer to fill their planes with customers paying five thousand dollars for the full service rather than with independents tagging along for a few hundred bucks.

If flights don't go exactly where you want to go, you may sometimes side charter. Most travelers aren't aware of this option. It's as if, flying from New York to Chicago, you paid an additional small amount to be dropped in Detroit, just off the flight path. Twice I've side chartered the "sked" to Grise Fiord. The regularly scheduled flight to Grise is cheap, and it's not far from there to interesting places. Once, a charter to Eureka made a ten-minute detour to drop us on western Axel Heiberg Island, a remote destination that would have cost four thousand dollars to reach on our own. Cost, including detour and our share of the charter, eight hundred dollars.

These little finesses, when they work, make Ellesmere accessible. But sometimes all options fall through. You sit in Resolute for a week, camping behind the airport or watching your dollars fly away at one of the local hotels. The charms of Resolute wear thin. You have worn thin on Resolute's citizens. The airline managers stop looking up when you walk into their office for news. The Polar Continental Shelf Project, with its many Ellesmere charters, will not accept your offers of good coin, leading you to be somewhat cynical about that science agency's well-publicized financial straits. The resupply flights of the North Pole adventurers are full with sponsors and friends. "There's another resupply in two weeks, though." A promising flight falls through: Weather delays have allowed two groups to combine their charters, so instead of two half-empty planes, there is now one full one. Steel doors clang shut. At least two more days in Resolute before the next ray of hope.

You accept the ancient wilderness principle—travelers need either lots of time or lots of money. You have come prepared to serve time, but once in a while, time is not enough. The only way out is with a credit card.

When I first went to Resolute hoping to extend the north's hitchhiking tradition by another few years, it was understandable that I should feel like a moocher. I was. My partners in crime likewise commented on how they felt like "stray cats" or "bag ladies" in Resolute. Sometimes we came prepared to spend substantial amounts of money and still felt like second-class citizens. Resolute's icy heart had seen too much. Too many foreign polar bear hunters willing to drop $20,000 in four days, leaving thousand-dollar tips in their wake. Too many North Pole expeditions with half-million dollar budgets. Too many planeloads of doctors and stockbrokers. Too many cruise ships disgorging ladies in furs (mink, not caribou) and men with glaring, corporate eyes who plunk down two thousand dollars for a narwhal tusk during their one hour on shore. Resolute is like Las Vegas: impossible to impress, no matter how much money you throw away.

Once, using airline frequent-flyer points and hooking rides, I traveled from Toronto to Ellesmere and back for two hundred dollars. But, at worst, Resolute could be so disheartening and humiliating that I would return home never wanting to go north again. Yet, like cold, fatigue, soft snow, high winds, and partners from hell, I soon forgot Resolute and remembered only Ellesmere.

■

Ellesmere's most extreme time of the year begins in September, when the sun sets after four thousand consecutive hours of daylight. By late October, Ellesmere is locked "in the black coffin of the Polar Night." Of all ordeals, explorers most dreaded the next three months. "A world without sun is like a life without love," wrote Nansen.

During these months, expeditions continued their skeleton scientific programs, but mainly everyone read, smoked, played cards, argued, and slept twelve hours a night. The length of journal entries typically plummeted from one or two pages a day to three or four lines. At Christmas and New Year's, much ado was made of the special menus, usually written in mock French, with such delicacies as Salmon à la Paleocrystic or Muskox Tongue in Arctic Sauce.

Lectures, singalongs, and weekly theater helped break up the monotony; the reason that prospective arctic volunteers were asked at their interviews, "Can you sing or play an instrument?" Officers tried to teach some of the illiterate men to read. Short walks, half a mile to a mile a day along a trampled route, prevented total physical decrepitude. Most groups put out a weekly newspaper, full of gossip, line drawings and bad inside jokes. Usually, these newspapers died quickly. "We, the editors, found it interesting," reported one.

Snow magnified the reflected starlight so that even without a moon, it was possible to see a little. "The line below will give an idea of the size of type

LEGIBLE AT MID-DAY

"wrote one explorer. Another claimed that the full moon equaled the light of a candle at forty-nine inches. Reducing the darkness to numbers was one way to cope with it.

The darkness was not nearly as trying as the social friction of this confined life. Once, even two members of the fabled Royal Canadian Mounted Police lost their poise. "I told him to pay attention to his own affairs," reported one. "Immediately he invited me to take off my hat and fight. I refrained from this method as long as possible, but in December he carried it into personal affairs and it came to blows."

Intense pastel colors wash the frigid February sky, making this the most beautiful time of year. For the Inuit in neighboring Greenland, this is the end of the winter depression called *perlerorneq*, literally, "to feel the weight of life." Custom dictates that the first time the Inuit see the sun, they take off one mitt and hold their bare hand in the air. The more devout also smile with half their face. Traditionally, all lamps in the community are put out and relit with fresh oil and new wicks. The world is reborn, and for Inuit and explorers alike, the exciting sledding season is about to begin.

■

I didn't know exactly how cold it was that night, but I knew it was cold. It was as if the thermometer were in freefall. Sleep was impossible. I couldn't stop shivering inside my sleeping bag. My breath formed delicate catkins of frost on the tent ceiling over my head. These fairy chandeliers, indicators of at least −30°F, can't be touched, however gently, without disintegrating. Sometimes I marveled at their loveliness, but now I just tried to blow them off before they became so heavy that they dropped by themselves and hit some small uncovered part of my face like a spritz of frozen carbon dioxide. Because moisture from breathing gums up insulation, I couldn't bury my face in the sleeping bag.

It was a long night. As soon as the dark purpled, I got up. Movement was the only antidote for this cold. I stomped around outside to warm up, then checked the thermometer. Fifty-eight below. A surge of pride overcame the fatigue. I'd had plenty of minus forty nights, and except for the periodic frost spritzes, I had slept pretty well. But -58°F was another dimension. The experience was so alien, so extreme, that I enjoyed it despite my misery, and it awakened a curiosity about the cold.

By arctic standards, most of my trips have not been particularly cold. Minus thirty sounds bad, but it isn't really, except in a stiff wind. A good sleeping bag can handle –30°F, just like a good backpack can handle eighty pounds but not a hundred and twenty pounds. Life only becomes difficult after about –44°F. Thanks to the moderating influence of the sea, mostly frozen though it is, –44°F is sometimes the winter minimum on Ellesmere.

Extreme cold has occurred. In 1963, scientists at Tanquary Fiord experienced –77°F, just 4 degrees shy of the North American record set at Snag, Yukon. On March 4, 1876, explorer George Nares reported –74°F on Ellesmere's northeast coast. Whisky placed outside froze after a few minutes, "so a few of us had the rare opportunity of eating it in a solid state." No doubt there were many quips that night about hard liquor.

Sledding below –30°F is difficult because of the friction on such cold snow. At –77°F, it would be like trying to drag a Volkswagen with no wheels down the street. During the day, perpetual movement, four layers of clothing and 7,000 calories can overcome most any cold. But sleep would be hard.

On their winter quest for emperor penguin eggs in Antarctica, Apsley Cherry-Gerrard and his two companions survived –76°F, the record low for camping. "Dante was right when he placed circles of ice below circles of fire," Cherry-Gerrard commented in his Antarctic classic, *The Worst Journey in the World*. On Ellesmere, North Pole adventurers occasionally experience –72°F at Ward Hunt Island in early March, but they usually linger in the camp's heated weatherhavens until it warms up.

I've done two trips where the evening temperature was –40°F or less about half of the time. Strange things happen then. Beard growth on my exposed face slowed to a crawl, while hair under my turtleneck grew at a normal rate. Once I couldn't feel my left foot for several days, but it was not frostbitten. I eventually discovered that my sock had slipped down and was subtly restricting circulation. I pulled the sock up and feeling returned to the foot a few hours later. As the weeks wore on, however, my perpetually cold toes went numb and the nerves didn't reawaken for a month after I'd returned home.

But the real quirks of cold cannot compare to its imagined powers. Cowley Abraham, whose ship was blown south of Cape Horn into the subantarctic in 1683, found "so extreme cold that we could bear drinking three quarts of Brandy in twenty-four hours each man, and be not at all the worse for it." You have to wonder what drinking records they'd have set had they continued into the Antarctic itself!

An epic tale of frostbite, amputation, and near death appeared in 1894 in *The Strand*, a fashionable London magazine. Written by one G. H. Lees, it was entitled "Lost in a Blizzard" and was introduced by the editors as "an absolutely true narrative of actual facts . . . written down from Mr. Lees' dictation, the loss of both his hands, of course, precluding him from writing."

The incident took place one wintry day near Indian Head, Manitoba, temperature a balmy –30°F. Riding his sleigh along a lonely trail, the narrator "began to feel very sleepy, through the intense cold," and got out to walk a bit. The horses bolted; he had left his gloves momentarily in the sleigh and his hands were bare. Apparently he never thought of putting them inside his coat.

He first "ran some distance, when the cold seemed to make me faint; I lay down an hour before I could recover myself." When he got up, his hands were frozen. He then wandered for hours, tired, but "dared not sleep, knowing it would mean death." It was believed that extreme cold induced a hypnotic drowsiness, and that to fall asleep was to never wake up. However, as any camper knows, to fall asleep without enough insulation is to wake up cold, or not to sleep at all.

Frostbite was also thought to make fingers as brittle as icicles, and Lees next writes, "I crawled on my elbows, for I was now afraid of breaking my hands to pieces." At length, "being famished, I had to bite the snow off trees, though it pulled the skin from my lips." Passing over the fact that snow does not stick to the mouth like cold metal, another common misbelief is that if a civilized person misses a meal or two, he becomes starvation-maddened. This narrator had gone all of twenty hours without food.

Such myths may sound quaint now, but the bogeyman of cold remains a good excuse for dismissing the Arctic as a land of Cain rather than an Eden.

■

When we think of arctic sledding, we usually think of dog teams, but a person can haul too, and that's what I do. A simple harness of seat belt webbing slips across my chest and attaches to a seven-foot fiberglass sled with plastic runners and a nylon cover. The sled holds up to two months of supplies. When towing a sled, walking is faster than skiing, so I only ski in deep snow. Like a dog, I haul with four legs: the two I was born with and a pair of ski poles.

Manhauling has been described as "about the hardest work to which free men have been put in modern times." Victorian geographical societies rightly saw arctic exploration as less dangerous but more arduous than the tropical variety. Arctic travelers didn't die from malaria or native spears but they often had to haul their own gear on foot. This is no more dangerous than walking on a sidewalk. Less so, in fact. The one injury of my Ellesmere career happened when I was bitten by a dog while strolling to the National Archives in Ottawa.

Sledding is a lovely occupation, if you like walking. Coleridge considered a twenty-mile hike in the mountains nothing special. Beethoven composed while trekking in the Alps. Nietzsche wrote that only thoughts reached by walking have value. Bertrand Russell claimed that war would end if every young man walked twenty miles a day.

But not all cultured Europeans understood activity. In *Journey to the Center of the Earth*, Jules Verne's heroes endured "three hours of terrible fatigue, walking incessantly." Jean Malaurie, author of *The Last Kings of Thule*, a wonderful study of the Polar Inuit, makes much of walking six miles per day and "penetrating inland to a depth of nineteen miles." Even Mark Twain, that vigorous traveler from the vigorous New World, believed that walking was "merely a lubricant" for good conversation.

In his essay on walking, Thoreau writes that the origin of the word "saunter" may derive from the medieval peripatetics who claimed to be going to the Holy Land, "la Sainte Terre." Sledding is, in this sense, a lot like sauntering. An imitation of Christ whose Golgotha is healthy exhaustion. For the Western soul, exertion may do what fasting does for the Eastern one.

Of nineteenth-century explorers, only John Rae had the walking gene. This first polar athlete snowshoed a total of 6,500 miles in the Central

Arctic. Those who met him described him as "full of animal spirits" or "active as a squirrel." As for the Ellesmere pioneers, American Adolphus Greely disliked exercise so much that he couldn't bring himself to order a fitness routine for others. George Nares was typical of British leaders. Rather than a swashbuckling star ship captain who was always first in line for dangerous missions, Nares remained in the stateroom, pushing his miniature battalions across the field of war with a shuffleboard cue.

Many of these early expeditions came to grief on Ellesmere, for which *The New York Times* credited the island with the highest misery-per-visitor ratio on earth. However, all the scholarly analyses of expeditions-gone-wrong, all the excuses and the crowing, fail to acknowledge the role of luck in arctic sledding. When I landed in Churchill Falls, Labrador, to begin my first winter trek, I had no idea whether I would be able to pull 250 pounds for ten miles a day. But by chance, the route I had blindly picked followed the wind-blasted lakes of the interior plateau. Superb conditions.

A few years later, a Toronto lawyer named Pat Lewtas embarked on a similar solo quest. Unluckily for him, he chose a stretch of Yukon wilderness where he quickly became bogged down in the impossible snows of the timberland. A couple of years later he went to Baffin Island, but, due to his bad-luck route, faltered again in the rough ice of shallow inlets. On his third try, over the hard snows of the Barren Lands, he accomplished a flawless six hundred mile hike from Cambridge Bay to Arviat in central Nunavut.

Many early British sledding experiences happened to occur in the same idyllic snows as Lewtas's third journey. In the windswept Central Arctic, snowshoes are unnecessary. So, when Nares explored northern Ellesmere in 1875, only one or two men brought them. After their miserable sledding mileage, Nares endured unflattering comparisons with those earlier, glory days of British sledging. Even in modern times, one armchair expert dissected several expeditions and concluded that 208 pounds per sledger was the maximum sustainable load. Nares's men averaged 240 pounds. Therein, he says, they erred.

But the Arctic is not all the same. Conditions vary over large areas and from bay to bay, hill to hill. One freak snowfall can ruin a trip. Thus, a 208-pound limit is meaningless. In good snow, 300 pounds is easy; in bad snow, 100 pounds is murder. The best windpacked snow is so hard that even ski poles make little impression, and a sled of almost any weight will glide effortlessly; hauling through powder snow is one of the Arctic's worst ordeals, or best cardiovascular workouts. The Nares expedition had to drag their one-ton sleds through powder, over the worst pressure ice in the world.

Since snow conditions make all the difference between an easy thirty-mile day and a hard three-mile day, it was disappointing to discover that the supposedly many Inuit words for snow is a myth. The myth began in 1940, when a talented amateur linguist named Benjamin Whorf misinterpreted an old anthropology text which stated that Inuktitut has four root words for snow. Whorf had never been to the Arctic, but he seemed to understand that for northern peoples, snow types are important enough to deserve their own nouns. In a somewhat casual vein and with no good reason, he wrote an article claiming that, "To an Eskimo, this all-inclusive word [snow] would be almost unthinkable; he would say that falling snow, slushy snow, and so on, are sensuously and operationally different, different things to contend with; he uses different words for them and for other kinds of snow."

Whorf's article was picked up by the mainstream media and soon lodged in the public consciousness. Since then, the "many" Inuit words for snow have taken on a life of their own as a clever cultural symbol. "Many" became fifty, fifty became a hundred, one hundred became two hundred. I recently saw three hundred on a public television spot about Inuit culture. The record hyperbole is currently four hundred, proffered some years ago by a magazine writer in need of a juicy metaphor.

Since Whorf, scholars have tried to debunk the myth, but without much success. It is, in the words of pop linguist Geoffrey Pullum, "too good to be false."

Finding out exactly how many Inuktitut words there are for snow is a thankless task that bogs down in philological hair-splitting about the definitions of "word," "snow," and "Inuktitut." Suffice it to say that English has as many or almost as many, if you count such terms as corn snow, powder, slush, and windpack. Moreover, the two or four or dozen Inuit snow words differentiate not between fine gradations of traveling snow, so wonderfully useful, but to more mundane concepts such as snow on the ground versus falling snow. Apparently, like us, they just refer to traveling snow as great, pretty good or crappy.

Digging into the myth did leave me with one small reward. A California professor informed me that the Chamorro language of Guam has thirty-seven words for coconut. I haven't dug further into it, preferring to believe that the truth behind the myth is alive in the Tropics, if not in the Arctic.

■

A sledder's day begins in low gear. The nights in the sleeping bag are too sweet to abandon easily. They have an infant's reassuring lack of responsibility. Legs are tight from the previous day's exertions and must be periodically stretched with cat-like luxuriance. If you have been disciplined the night before, leaving two hours between supper and bedtime and not overdoing the fluids, the need to pee will not wake you prematurely.

The eternal daylight eliminates the need for a rigid schedule. It doesn't matter whether the traveling day finishes at six in the evening or one in the morning; it all looks the same. As long as the miles get done, you can indulge yourself as much as your limited resources allow.

After a good sleep, I sometimes spend a defiant extra hour in the sack, stretching and savoring the uterine warmth. Finally, bracing myself like a swimmer diving into a cold lake, I unzip the sleeping bag, ignoring the ripe odors, put on puffy camp clothing, step outside, pee, get the stove going for hot chocolate and melt snow for cereal. While lingering over breakfast, I melt one and a half quarts of water for the trail. Iceberg ice tastes the best, and as it melts, it sometimes sizzles like bacon frying.

For the first few days, breaking camp takes three hours. Once the routine becomes automatic, it's down to two hours. With no dawdling, it can be done in one. On every trip, efficiency has to be relearned.

The first three hours of sledding are the hardest of the day. It's not that sledding is pain but you have to put the comfort of camp behind you. Only then does sledding feel natural. The stiffness in your legs has disappeared by then, the rhythm kicks in, the mind dances, the hours fly.

Apsley Cherry-Garrard's sledders in Antarctica claimed to spend their time thinking of "grouse moors and pretty girls," but that is hard to believe. Even when the girl you love is waiting for you at home, even when you stare at her picture every night, she seems impossibly far away, like a half-remembered dream, too distant to dominate the stern arctic horizon. More likely, Cherry-Garrard's moors and lassies were topics of conversation in the tent, not mental company on the trail.

On his 1906 trek across Ellesmere's north coast, Robert Peary grimly spent whole days counting his footsteps, presumably to measure distance. "My brain is numb with the incessant 'one, two, three,'" he complained. Why he didn't use a sled wheel odometer, like other explorers of his era, is hard to understand, unless driving himself bananas was part of his peculiarly bitter form of discipline.

Every sledder counts some of the time, though; the metronomic regularity of one's steps is soothing, and it's helpful and entertaining to graph the relation between miles per hour and steps per minute. With my stride, 112 steps per minute—a typical sledding pace in good snow—covers 2.4 miles per hour; 90 steps per minute, 1.5 miles per hour. Seventy-three steps per minute means I'm on skis in bad snow and making about a mile an hour. That pace traps you in the dreary present. It does not let the mind soar with the detachment that effortlessly devours miles. I seem to need at least 85 steps per minute to achieve escape velocity.

I usually have one or two special hours each day, when a stimulated brain invents jokes or feelingly recites old poems or catches a whiff of childhood sensations so alien and fleeting that they "tend toward the outermost limit of communicable thought." Other hours feature blank staring at the landscape or scanning for wildlife, broken only by random thoughts caroming around the skull: "Will she get used to living without me? Will my left knee give out? Are those muskoxen or just rocks? I'll take off my sunglasses at five p.m. today. I don't like chocolate-covered peanuts any more. If I make fifteen miles, I'll have the potato casserole for dinner as a reward. Slight pain in right side, maybe that couple who removed their appendices before overwintering in Antarctica were right. I . . . did . . . it . . . my . . . way . . . tra la la."

Many an hour is dominated by some idiotic song that the brain, like some scratched old record, repeats obsessively. The songs come out of the blue, but the words usually have a dreamlike connection to what's beneath the surface of the mind. Once, the old Rolling Stones' song *Ruby Tuesday* just wouldn't go away. That was in polar bear country and anxiety was high. Ruby's need to be free at whatever cost seemed ridiculously meaningful. Hour after hour, day after day, the damned song played. A year later, with storm clouds gathering on several fronts in my personal life, I couldn't seem to free myself from *Bring Him Home*, the plaintive *Les Misérables* tune.

After the first hour on the trail, it's time for a quick drink. Before the invention of waterproof bottles, chronically dehydrated sledgers drank only at the noonday stop. Nowadays, many sledders use a big Thermos that keeps fluids hot all day, but my journeys began partly as ascetic exercises in self-denial. Take enough away, and how you appreciate the little that remains! Although my camp luxuries have increased, plain Nalgene bottles are one of those spartan regimes that I affectionately hang onto. The bottles lie on the sled, insulated in my down parka, and I space the day's drinking so that only the last couple of mouthfuls are slushy.

After two hours, the 1,000-calorie breakfast has lightened. Out come high-energy snacks: chocolate, chocolate peanuts, fatty cheeses. The more water in the cheese, the harder it freezes. Until late April, even asiago has to be "cut" with violent swings of an ice ax. Sometimes I can avoid these time-consuming reenactments of the murder of Trotsky by finding a grocer at home who will vacuum pack it in pre-cut chunks.

And so it goes. Midday hikes break up the sledding rhythm too much, so I push all day and try to camp in interesting spots. In early spring it's too cold for long lunches, anyway. By mid-May, heat, not cold, is the problem. You can still get frostbite in a wind, but on calm days the sun is so strong that even an undershirt feels too warm. Sledders then begin "sleeping upside-down," traveling during the cooler night. There is a fierce, unconventional satisfaction to having breakfast at eight in the evening, sledding all night and bedding down at noon.

The changing snow conditions provoke never-ending mental arithmetic about how far you'll make that day. Of all arctic skills, learning to relinquish expectations is the most important. Since you are not in control, every camp, every stop along the trail, every type of weather, should be equally accepted. Much-anticipated sites are often disappointing; minor destinations, marvellous. Because the magic moments are so unpredictable, you live in what one traveler calls "a constant state of optimistic expectation."

In particularly optimistic states, I sometimes tried to build a snow house, but the architecture was beyond me. It is hard to say which was more difficult, building an igloo or understanding its theory. An igloo, according to scholars, is not a hemisphere but a "catenoid of revolution with an optimum height-to-diameter ratio." This shape, apparently, eliminates "ring tension and shell moments." It gets worse. The best snow for block-cutting "has a density of about 0.30 to 0.35 gm/cm^3 and a hardness of about 150 to 200 gm/cm^3."

In igloo construction, as in other arts, a thousand cutaway diagrams can never replace the master-apprentice relationship. I know the principles, but my walls never lean inward enough. So my end product is not a catenoid of revolution but a cone whose narrow end tapers upward toward infinity.

Igloo, language purists point out, means house, any kind of house, so it is the wrong word for a domed catenary of snow blocks. But that's a losing effort, like insisting on using Himalaya instead of Himalayas because Himalaya is already plural, or like the explorer who insisted on calling muskoxen exclusively by their genus name *ovibos*, because they are neither oxen nor musky.

Using an igloo is like traveling with dogs: The mystique cannot be denied. It is redolent of seal oil lamps, polar bear skin pants, and sleeping mats of caribou fur. Old, infirm Inuit walking nobly off into the blizzard without spoiling it by saying, "I may be some time." Those were the days. Sometimes, those are still the days, although most Inuit just bring canvas tents on their snowmobile-drawn komatiks.

Unlike dinosaurs, igloos leave no trace of their passing ("But where are the snows of yesteryear?") so their origin is lost. One archaeologist speculates that the artistic Dorset people may have passed the knowledge of igloo building on to the Thule. There is at least an aesthetic link between the Dorsets' exquisite carvings and the thing of beauty that is a well-built igloo. "Maybe there are so many artists among the Inuit because of the traditional need to build igloos and carve harpoon heads," suggests another scholar. "Their small groups were so spread out, they couldn't rely on one craftsman per community." There might have been some selection pressure for spatial intelligence.

Explorers quickly discovered the benefits of snow houses, and ignored or embraced them, depending on temperament. John Rae and Leopold McClintock used igloos during their journeys in the 1850s, for which they were disdained by the British establishment of the time. "Anyone can go native," sniffed Sir Clements Markham. The American explorer Charles Francis Hall occasionally built snow shelters but after spending two hours and forty minutes on one in 1871, he remarked, "This is a long time to keep tired men exposed to severe weather after dragging a heavy sledge for ten or eleven hours." Three hours is actually a typical novice time; an experienced pair of hands can build one in an hour. And once in Iqaluit, I saw a man complete an igloo in an astonishing twenty-nine minutes. In the end, however, I had to resign myself to that nylon igloo known as a dome tent, for which no spatial intelligence is required.

■

Extreme endeavors, such as manhauling four hundred miles across the Arctic, puzzle most people. Many are just curious, but occasionally some old sobersides will ask Why? when what is clearly meant is, Why do you want to do something stupid like that?

The big Why dangles over all our heads, but adventurers seem to be fairer game for the question. Yet, one might just as properly ask: Why run marathons? Why birdwatch? Why work at a job you don't like? Why believe in God? Why help the under-privileged? Why get up every morning?

Now and then I come across a line that seems to buzz around the Why of adventure. "To circle or cross a place meaningful to you is a reverential act." "The difference between vice and virtue depends on whether the pleasure precedes or follows the pain." That Ellesmere travel is a pursuit of virtue sounds a lot more impressive than, "I like it."

British poet and mountaineer Wilfrid Noyce identified thirteen adventure motives (comments mine):

1. *The ascetic streak.* Hard travel teaches self-control and gives a purifying glimpse of life as a hair shirt. Refreshing for pampered Westerners.

2. *Enjoying the contrast of civilized and primitive.* Meeting a little ship after months of living on raw seal meat, Knud Rasmussen describes with pure joy how, "Ten minutes later I was on board, with my teeth deep in an Orange. A little later, I sat staring with wide eyes at a real cup of actual steaming coffee. There were such things as Bread, and Cheese, and Butter . . . " Unless you eat the seal meat, you can't fully experience the Orange.

3. *The spice of danger.* Unlike mountains, the Arctic presents little danger from falling, avalanches, rockfall, and deadly winds. Arctic travel is more an endorphin high than an adrenaline rush.

4. *Pleasures of technique, pursuit of excellence, physical movement.* You feel like a sorcerer's apprentice every time you sleep comfortably at 40 degrees below. Also, trekking twelve hours a day is very different than exercising for an hour: The physical being awakes.

5. *Lure of wild country.* High altitudes are more extreme than high latitudes, but how many mountains are three hundred miles from the nearest village?

6. *Lure of the unknown.* A powerful motive during the first few trips, when the Arctic looms as strange and compelling as Mars.

7. *Escape.* Those who are ill-at-ease in their own culture look for home in distant places. Most travelers eventually find their personal Ellesmere.

8. *Fame, fortune.* "Most nonfamous people," writes essayist Cintra Wilson, "are frequently in a state of dull torture from the lack of boundless international adoration in their lives." Because adventure seems so dashing and difficult and arouses our Walter Mitty longings, it is one of the roads to celebrity in which no outstanding talent is required.

9. *Conquest and competition (nationalism).* A little out-of-date now, but the first Brazilians to the North Pole would still create a stir in their own country.

10. *Knowledge (science).* Often simply a ruse adventurers use to clothe, as Bill Tilman puts it, "their more or less frivolous aims with a thin mantle of science." Self-knowledge, on the other hand, is a driving force. Under extreme circumstances you quickly learn how much you're the person you want to be, and how much you're not.

11. *Fascination with machines (especially the airplane).* Around-the-World-in-Eighty-Days types continue to flock to the northern skies in putt-putts of all kinds.
12. *Curiosity about people, places.* This refers largely to less extreme adventures. One can be curious about Morocco; it's too weak a term for Ellesmere. People-curious adventurers usually go where there are more people, although a few grand arctic figures, such as Frederick Cook, Jean Malaurie, and Charles Francis Hall, fell under the spell of Inuit culture.
13. *Sense of purpose.* For some of us, what the Inuit call a journey in pursuit of its tail—one that has no purpose other than its own completion—holds more meaning than practical goals.

Noyce's forty-five year old list remains the closest anyone has come to encapsulating the Why. However, it does not address the basic mystery of why some people crave adventure while others avoid it. In particular, why go to extremes?

During one trek, I developed a crackpot theory that helped pass a lot of hours. It tries to explain the thirst for adventure and at the same time answer the basic question, What made Beethoven different?

There is such a thing as genetic energy. Scientists may suspect that it exists but they do not yet have a yardstick to measure it. Nevertheless, we are all born with different amounts. It doesn't make us everything we are—there's personality too—but it determines how exaggerated these personality traits are. When our pride is stung, do we cringe slightly or conquer nations in revenge?

Genetic energy can be squandered or fully used. As with height, a good environment takes us only so far. Beyond this, we can't make giants of ourselves through "the omnipotence of unyielding human will." At a certain level of excellence, everyone is dedicated, but the higher the energy, the further you can push without hitting the ceiling or breaking down.

Energy is not the same as talent. Talent is the ability to do things easily. The sharpness of a lumberjack's ax is talent; energy determines whether he swings that ax a thousand times a day, or a hundred.

We can consciously channel some of this energy, but it tends to flow according to our predispositions. There are five channels for genetic energy:

spiritual, physical, intellectual, sexual, and practical. While renowned French author Honoré de Balzac funneled great spiritual and intellectual energy through his talent for writing, it would be hard to find someone with less physical energy. In his few moments away from his desk, all this brilliant walrus did was sit.

Great individuals all have prodigious amounts of genetic energy. This is the basic gift that sets the Beethovens of this world apart. Some seem able to focus it all in one area; with others, it "runs madly off in all directions." Some fields of endeavor require more energy than others. Intuitively, it takes more to found a religion than to establish a business empire. A ranking of great figures by energy level would be Prophet, Leader, Poet, Writer, and Intellectual. Finally, genetic energy in an individual, and in a species, decreases over time.

I inherited my genetic energy from my mother and her high-spirited family. It seems to have been just enough to glimpse, at times, how ordinary I normally was. But I had always been physically and spiritually restless, and this restlessness was enough to shape my life. It may have been what prompted me, for instance, to buy that huge pack when I hadn't camped since high school.

The more genetic energy, the farther and more often we need to go. Much of the year, I pace endlessly, barely able to sit down. The few days or weeks after a hard Ellesmere trip are the only times I feel physically at peace. Soon the restlessness begins again. I pace and plot. Without some strange project to work toward, my days feel empty. Perhaps it's personal style, to expend energy in floods rather than in measured daily doses. Perhaps it's discontent with adult life. Not enough wonder.

If I had to walk ten miles to work, then carry backbreaking sacks of potatoes all day, voluntarily sledding across Ellesmere would be incomprehensible. But not for everyone. I once hiked the Karakum Desert of Turkmenistan with a Russian named Andrei Ilyachov. He was one of the poorest Russians I'd ever met, which is saying a lot. In a frustrating country which grinds down the strong and crushes the weak, Ilyachov spent his vacations biking hundreds of miles—without food or water. He had done this for years in Siberia, southern Russia, and Central Asia. He was not only able to adapt to the hard conditions of his everyday life, but he had so much energy left over that he devoted all his free time to making his life even harder. A holy fool.

How does this relate to adventure? Today, survival in the West requires little energy. Sometimes, the ache of unused energy drives us to tilt at windmills. Then, we discover that the happiest state lies near the edge of our capabilities, and extreme journeys take us to that edge.

Chapter Two

Raw Fear

Most extreme travelers do not begin their careers by gradually acquiring skills in outdoor courses or by five years of easy backpacking. It doesn't fit the personality. Instead, most of us learn either by apprenticing on someone else's expedition, or by taking risks. I took risks.

On my first expedition, I set out to ski three hundred and fifty miles alone across Labrador in mid-winter, no caches, no radio, no air support. It was as extreme an expedition as I could conceive at the time, in the most extreme place that I knew about. Labrador is the coldest place in the world for its latitude.

I prepared for the journey meticulously, and for two weeks all went well. Then one afternoon in early February, near the headwaters of the George River, I was crossing a frozen lake when I came across some wet ice. It was late in the day, and I was tired and impatient to reach the other side. I assumed that the moisture was just slush that wells up through cracks and rests on firm ice. A little sloppy to wade through, but perfectly safe. However, I hadn't skied many steps when the ice beneath my feet began to give way. Attached by rigid poles to the sled behind, I couldn't back up. I tried racing ahead but couldn't ski fast enough. I fell through. Only the fiberglass poles lying on the rotten ice held me up and prevented the sled from joining me in the water, where it would have dragged me to the bottom of the lake like an anchor.

For some reason, my mind stayed calm. I scrambled back onto the rotten ice and managed to remove my skis and unhitch myself from the sled harness. Then, distributing my weight, I crawled on my belly toward the sled. I was a hundred and twenty miles from anyone, and all my gear and supplies were on that sled. If it broke through, I too was sunk.

The ice was so bad that as I shimmied forward, my hands and elbows created holes wherever they rested. I removed a minimum of gear from the sled, flung it toward shore, then crawled after it till we both reached safe ice. I was afraid to spend too much time near the sled because my maneuvers were visibly saturating the ice around it.

That night in the tent, with just a crumb to eat for supper, I took stock of my situation. At any moment, the lake could swallow up my sled. My ski boots were hopeless blocks of ice. Night temperatures often dropped below minus forty. During the day, I had Labrador's terrible northwest wind in my face.

The clear-headedness that had guided me through the accident had evaporated. I was deeply shaken. Convinced that this was still a survival situation and that time was critical, I flipped on the emergency transmitter that I carried with me. It would beam my location to search-and-rescue authorities and request pick-up. As far as I was concerned, the expedition was over.

Unknown to me, the transmitter was defective and the signal never reached them. To my horror, no one came the following morning. No one came that afternoon. I kept the transmitter on till the battery died, but no one ever came. This failure of my one security measure hit me harder than the accident. I really was on my own, and it was terrifying.

At least the sled was still on the ice. I crawled out to it, surprised to find that the ice had firmed up in the clear, cold weather. I was able to retrieve everything.

Theoretically, I could have continued as if nothing had happened, but I was in no state to go on. A deep fear, such as I had never felt before, gnawed at my belly. It made me spontaneously burst out sobbing several times a day. I'd read about the paralyzing fear that occasionally gripped front-line soldiers. This was it.

I decided to diverge from my route to an empty outfitter's camp forty-five miles away. I'd spoken to the outfitter the previous summer and he'd promised to leave a two-way radio for me as an emergency measure. Shaken though I was, forty-five miles was not far to go.

The fear held me for several days until finally I became so disgusted with it, and with myself, that I shook it off by defiantly skiing on bad ice. After that, it left me alone—although when the outfitter's camp came into view, I burst into sobs one last time, crying, "My life, my life." I'd made it. I'd survived.

Then another shock. The outfitter had forgotten to leave the radio. Naïve as it sounds, I hadn't realized that some people are reliable and need to be told something only once while others are well-meaning but forgetful, busy or just sloppy. I hadn't followed up.

Now I could only wait helplessly until my family notified search-and-rescue officials on the agreed-upon day. I had filed my route with the Royal Canadian Mounted Police and even mentioned the existence of this camp, but again, I had not pounded the point home. Although the camp was established enough to appear on the topo maps, no one noticed. It was three days and about $100,000 before the search-and-rescue aircraft, flying grids, happened over my camp.

My trek was novel enough to have attracted a little attention before I left, but my disappearance, of course, was a much better story. A few, who regarded such ventures as frivolous, wrote huffy letters to newspapers complaining about their tax dollars going to my rescue. "Don't worry, if we hadn't spent it on you, we would have spent it flying practice rescues," one official told me, but that hardly helped. It was a pitiful and embarrassing end to a first expedition. Although I returned to Labrador the following winter and did the complete trek with no problems, and although it's now seventeen years and 4,000 trouble-free arctic miles later, I still feel foolish about it.

That first expedition did, however, show me a great deal. I felt as if those forty intense days had taught me the equivalent of two thousand days of ordinary backpacking. Also, despite the later fear, my calm and clarity at the time of the accident gave me confidence that I could rely on myself to act coolly when seconds counted. Since then, I have carried neither a radio nor a satellite transmitter, preferring to make conservative decisions in the field than to rely on a contrivance that might fail me when I needed it most.

I eventually discovered that the Arctic is not a dangerous place. What is dangerous is acquiring the experience to minimize the few dangers that do exist. And as I studied arctic history, I came to notice an intriguing fact: Most famous arctic disasters had relative novices at the helm. You learn so quickly in that environment that after the first trip or two, most people are no longer capable of screwing up in grand style. The timeless adventures are created by rookies.

■

On my fourth expedition to Ellesmere I was sledding along the first-year sea ice of Eureka Sound—flat as a lake, for the most part. Ring seals birth their young under the snow of first-year ice, beside breathing holes they keep open with the claws on their flippers. Polar bears eat mainly ring seals. You're pretty safe from bears over much of Ellesmere Island, but they like Eureka Sound, especially the lower part. The explorers recognized this and names such as Great Bear Cape, Little Bear Cape, Bear Corner, Bear Strait and Bear Peninsula cover the maps.

On my first evening I camped at Depot Point, on the Axel Heiberg shore. Nowadays I would explore such an historic spot. At the time it was just another campsite. Following the precise routine of wilderness travel, I threw my sleeping bag in the rear of the tent, placed the stove in the left front corner and the shotgun beside it. Every day of every trip, each item goes in the same place, in the same sequence.

I wandered over to collect some tidal ice to guy down the tent. Suddenly a polar bear rounded a piece of ice, and we found ourselves face to face. The shotgun was in the tent, twenty long yards away. It was hard to tell which of us was more surprised, myself or the bear. We just looked at each other. The bear lifted its nose and sniffed and then—I could see it make a sudden decision—started nonchalantly sniffing the ice at its feet. "You look into a caribou's eyes and not much is going on," a friend once pointed out, "but bears have a psychology." This bear just wanted to escape with its dignity intact.

I edged back to the tent with the same pretence of unconcern and brought out the shotgun, but the bear was already wandering off over Eureka Sound, nosing for seal holes. The whole charade à deux had been an exercise in neither of us showing fear.

Despite the eyeball-to-eyeball encounter, I wasn't too worried about polar bears. My camp had been invisible in the shore ice, and we'd simply surprised each other. Eureka Sound was so flat that I could usually see five miles in every direction. I had long cultivated the habit of glancing over my shoulder every so often. Polar bears do not blend into a snowscape. They appear yellowish in sunshine and greyish in overcast weather. Even from a distance, a moving object is impossible to miss in this stillness.

■

A poem in the outhouse of a botanists' camp on nearby Devon Island advises,

> *Though you may be enthralled*
> *by a passion for flora*
> *Do not ever forget*
> *the Order Carnivora.*

Globally, polar bears kill an average of one person a year. Most incidents involve young bears that haven't yet mastered seal hunting. The encounters usually take place in camp. Every fall, one or two foolish bears wander into Resolute, where they end up as rugs or pants. In 1987, a polar bear hung around the weather station at Eureka. It rested its paws on the window sill of the lounge and stared inside, like Dickensian orphans press their noses to the windows of candy stores. This made going outside a little too adventurous for the average meteorologist, and they eventually shot it.

On Somerset Island, south of Resolute, three scientists were sleeping in a tent when their dog started barking. They looked out to see a polar bear in camp. One scientist ran to the nearby quonset for their rifle. He tried to chamber a bullet but he didn't pull the bolt back far enough and the bear knocked him down. When a second scientist tried to intervene, it seized him by the neck and was dragging him to a creek bed when the third man shot the bear. Both victims recovered.

More recently, some biologists were studying thick-billed murres on wind-battered Coburg Island, off the southeastern coast of Ellesmere. Coburg's cliffs and nearby open water make it a paradise for nesting sea birds but "not very interesting as a place of residence for human beings," as explorer Otto Sverdrup put it. Only thirty-six species of flowering plants, huddled behind windbreaks, have gained a toehold on this blasted heath.

"We were into a deep sleep when a polar bear took our tent vestibule in its mouth and started shaking it," said one of the researchers. "It had bypassed all the other tents and made straight for our yellow dome, which was the farthest tent from the sea." She escaped out the back door while her partner shot the bear.

In the last twenty years, several adventurers skiing to the North Pole or the North Magnetic Pole have had close calls with bears. None of the skiers have died, but some incidents led to the deaths of bears. It is not always clear whether the adventurers were too quick on the draw.

In 1990, a lone Swiss dogsledder named Markus Bischoff was working his way across the Arctic. In southern Eureka Sound, a bear approached his camp. Eager for pictures, Bischoff photographed the bear until it broke into his sled and began eating the seal meat for his dogs. At this, Bischoff shot the bear. When he reached Eureka, he reported the incident.

Although he had been protecting his property, his seized film suggested that he had let the bear come too close before trying to chase it away. Wildlife officials charged him, but the case never reached court. That fall, Bischoff was boating with his dogs to a camp on Great Slave Lake in the western Arctic, where he planned to spend the winter. A sudden wind capsized the overloaded sixteen-footer. Bischoff managed to swim to shore, but he died of hypothermia and was eaten by his dogs. "All that was left of him was his head, guarded by the lead dog," recalls Mitch Taylor, Nunavut's polar bear biologist.

■

Several days after my first encounter, I was sleeping blissfully on southern Eureka Sound when a strange sound woke me. Sounds, like smells, are few on Ellesmere Island and can be counted on the fingers of one hand. Most are wind sounds. The wind roars; hard grains of snow scratch along the surface; loose strings on the tent beat a little tattoo on the drum-tight fly; cooking pots and fuel cans creak as they expand or contract. That's about it. In such a simple world, a new sound is very disturbing. I don't remember what it was, but it startled me out of my exhausted sleep.

I sat upright, grabbed the shotgun and flipped the safety off. No wind. There are only so many things a new sound can be. I was familiar with the scratchings of the arctic fox and this was different. I peeked out of the zippered crack in the tent door toward my sled, which I kept several yards away in the hope that a polar bear might prefer the food in the sled to the gamey odors of unwashed manhauler within. The sled was gone.

The next two minutes seemed like hours. I glanced left and saw the sled forty yards away, upside-down, its contents scattered on the snow. A polar bear was lying down beside it eating my food. "God, this is it," I thought.

Before the expedition, I'd had recurring nightmares about this. Wish fulfilments, these dreams were not. They seemed to be playing out different scenarios. I'd shoot the bear, but the bullets had no effect. Or I'd try to escape by climbing a tall chest of drawers. Or I'd dive away at the last instant: An Inuit hunter with a feel for physics had once pointed out to me that a charging bear's speed and weight meant it couldn't change direction quickly. But can you keep pirouetting away like a matador when the bear wheels around and charges again? In their surrealistic way, the dreams probed these tactics but always ended inconclusively.

"I wonder if the bears are also discussing you," my running partner had joked, when I shared the latest installment. "'Last night I dreamt I ate him.'"

I had, at least, mentally rehearsed the situation, so I followed the plan. First, make sure the shotgun is at hand, safety off. Check.

Next, put on clothes. I slept in my underwear, and I didn't want to confront a polar bear in the middle of the Arctic wearing only socks and long johns.

Third, stuff spare ammunition into pockets. Although the gun held six one-ounce slugs, I was no hunter and didn't want to die for want of ammunition.

Finally, get out of the tent and chase the bear away.

When I stepped out of the tent, I entered the full-blown nightmare. The bear had heard the nylon rustling as I dressed. It had left the sled and was striding resolutely at me, head lowered, eyes raised. It was within fifteen yards. No doubt about this bear's intent.

Next to being killed or maimed yourself, the worst nightmare is having to kill a bear on one of these expeditions. A generation ago, no one thought twice. Bear presents danger; man removes danger. One old arctic geologist shot seven nuisance bears in his career. Maybe he was a little trigger-happy, but who can judge until they've stared into the eyes of a threatening bear?

Nowadays, shooting a polar bear in self-defence is more than tragic, it's a bureaucratic ordeal. Every polar bear killed comes out of the quota of the nearest Inuit village. Since a skin sells for two thousand dollars and a sanctioned big-game hunt may earn over ten thousand dollars for the guide, a wasted bear is bad business and the Inuit don't like it. Some communities want scientists to have to post ten-thousand dollar bonds against the possibility of a defence kill. Technically, on shooting a polar bear, you must immediately contact the local wildlife officer by radio, who then comes to investigate the incident. For a modern expedition, shooting a polar bear is as bad form as eating your dogs.

The polar bear was within a few yards of me, too close for just a warning blast. I raised the shotgun and sighted down the barrel at the vulnerable hump behind the bear's neck. The shotgun was a borrowed stockless model and I hadn't fired it before. I hoped it would work.

The blast set my ears ringing and flung the barrel in the air as the pistol-grip handle slammed into my mouth. I had missed completely, but the bear wheeled in its tracks and ran away. It disappeared behind some ice and I never saw it again.

Blood trickled into my mouth from where the recoil had split my upper lip. A dawning realization: You're supposed to fire a pistol-grip shotgun from the hip. Nevertheless, my ignorance had been a blessing in disguise. Had I fired riot-cop style, I might have actually hit the bear. As it turned out, we had escaped the usual no-win outcome of such encounters: "A polar bear attack on a human ends only when one of them is dead," writes Ian Stirling, the world's foremost polar bear researcher.

The crisis was over but I was a hundred and fifty miles from anyone and I could still be in trouble if my gear was wrecked. I went to inspect the sled. The bear had cracked the hull, but not badly. Luckily, the sweeping north winds of the day before had died, or the stuff would have been blown halfway to Baffin Island. I rounded everything up. I smelled gasoline vaporizing through a hairline crack in the fuel can and I sealed it with duct tape. The bear had eaten a half-finished peanut butter sandwich and crunched open my mug to lick the frozen cocoa dregs. It had given my hardshell sunglasses case an experimental nip but had not liked the taste. All fine. But where was the big nylon duffle with most of the food?

I followed the bear's tracks for seventy-five yards to a ravine. Here lay the duffle, open and rummaged through but intact. The bear had carried it in its jaws. Rather than rip it open, it had delicately unzipped the bag by hooking a claw through one of the loops that I keep on zippers to make them easier to pull with mitts on. It had ignored the dried sausage and gone straight for the box of Belgian chocolates I was bringing as a gift to friends in Grise Fiord. Then it had wandered back to the sled to clean up the loose ends, no doubt planning to return later.

My mind had stayed clear during the attack, but as often happens, the fear hit afterward. I realized that I had no control over when a polar bear might strike. This was the High Arctic's one freak hazard, a kind of four-legged avalanche. The near-infinite visibility made me safe during the day, but for years afterward I slept like a seal on Ellesmere, waking every hour to look out the tent for something off-white and moving.

Chapter Three

Getting Away with Murder

The Ellesmere obsession began, perhaps, with murder. In the middle of August, 1986, as slanting light signaled the last days of the High Arctic summer, a few of us were tramping the meadows along Ellesmere's Buchanan Bay when Mike Watts, an Ontario surgeon, spotted an open grave among the rocks. Inside lay an ancient human skull, four teeth still clinging to the upper jaw. One of us took the skull out and turned it around in his hand as if musing on the way of all flesh.

"What's that cut above the ear?" asked Mike.

On the side of the skull was a deep horizontal gash that looked as if it had been made by a small ax. The bone below the gash projected slightly: The blow had come from above.

"This injury was fatal," said Mike, thoughtfully tracing the cut with his fingernail.

We put the skull back in the grave and continued our hike. That night in my journal, I droned on for page after page about muskoxen and sculptured ice floes and the one-liners of my companions, but never even mentioned the skull. So much went on during these twenty-four hour days that the discovery of a murder victim was, evidently, not noteworthy.

■

That original trip to Ellesmere planted many seeds, but it was the skull that haunted me. What was the story behind this violent end? How long ago did it happen? Was the killing community-sanctioned? After all, the body had not been dumped through a hole in the ice but placed in the open for all to see.

In some ways, the skull came to symbolize a dark corner of this island, where stress could drive men to murder. Seeking to compensate for my lack of interest at the time, I tried to find the skull again ten years later, but without success. I then took to delving into the Ellesmere region's other homicides. These were, after all, the northernmost murders in the world.

Eventually, murdered ghosts rattled their chains everywhere I traveled in the High Arctic. Murder prompted the flight of Qitdlarssuaq, the great shaman, from Baffin Island to Ellesmere. There, on a small lake in Makinson Inlet, more murder. Further north, at Pim Island, Adolphus Greely's execution of thief and murderer Charles Henry. Three hundred miles further north, in Greenland waters, Charles Francis Hall collapsed within view of Ellesmere, supposedly of apoplexy, but it is now believed that his doctor poisoned him. Often a cloud of uncertainty played around the corpses. Was it murder? An accident?

In 1970, the world's northernmost murder took place on the drifting ice island T-3, two hundred twenty miles northwest of Ellesmere. Ice islands are big, flat pans of ice that break off from the 3,000-year-old ice shelves that cling to parts of northern Ellesmere. The pieces drift around the Arctic Ocean for a couple of decades and are ideal platforms for ocean science. The first one, discovered in 1946 off Barrow, Alaska by a U.S. spy plane, was classified top-secret because of its value as a base. Ice islands are like large soda crackers floating in a loose polar soup. During their lifespan, they can cover marathon distances from Ellesmere to Alaska and back to Greenland. Eventually, they reach open water or break up.

T-3 was discovered in 1947. It was the third such "target" sighted, hence its name. Since 1952, researchers under the U.S. Air Force had occupied it almost continuously. At first, it was thirty-one miles across and two hundred feet thick, but by the time of the murder, it had shrunk to seven miles long, four miles wide and one hundred feet thick.

Researchers on T-3 lived in comfortable trailers and spoke by radio with the outside world. But planes could not land on the puddly summer ice and T-3 was well beyond the range of helicopters, so the nineteen men were on their own for months. In that era, such outposts were not today's politically correct environments. Even in the mid-1980s, towns like Resolute drew a lot of freewheeling, hard-drinking misfits. Porn videos blared nonstop in the background like arctic elevator muzak. Bush pilots routinely dented aircraft in seat-of-the-pants landings. T-3 was like a university dorm full of engineering students.

"Porky" Leavitt was one of these ungrounded wires. He had already attacked three people on T-3 in his quest for alcohol. On July 16, 1970, Mario Escamilla heard that Porky had just broken into his trailer and stolen some homemade raisin wine. Escamilla had been attacked by Porky before so he brought along one of the camp rifles for protection.

He found Porky next door with the station manager, Bennie Lightsy, drinking a withering concoction of raisin wine, grape juice, and pure ethanol. Escamilla told Porky to stay away from his wine and was back in his trailer when he heard footsteps. Thinking it was Porky, he picked up the gun, flipped the safety off and pointed it at the door. Bennie Lightsy entered, thoroughly drunk himself. The two argued about the raisin wine. Escamilla ordered Lightsy to get out and continued to brandish the rifle as the argument heated up. The gun went off, and a seriously wounded Lightsy died shortly afterward.

Legally, T-3 was perhaps the most awkward spot in the world for a homicide. An ice island is neither land nor ship. It does not belong to anyone. T-3 had originated in Canada and lay in the so-called Canadian sector, which extends from the coastal edges to the North Pole. But it was a U.S. station, manned by Americans. Although maintained by the Air Force, its civilian personnel were not subject to military law. Ice islands simply did not exist in international law. Lightsy's death had occurred in one of those rare jurisdictional gaps where serious crimes might go untried. "Murder in Legal Limbo," declared the headline in *Time* magazine.

Ultimately, Escamilla was tried as if it had taken place on the high seas. In 1971, he was found not guilty of second-degree murder but guilty of involuntary manslaughter. He was sentenced to three years (with possible parole after three months), but his appeal turned up enough procedural flaws to win a new trial. The retrial never occurred and all mention of the ice island homicide disappeared from legal literature as abruptly as the ice island melted away in the spring of 1984.

At his death, Lightsy had a blood alcohol level of at least .26. Curious to know just how inebriated he was during that conversation with Escamilla, I threw an Ice Island Murder Party. Designated drinkers were given charts to keep track of their drinks and the time between them. The local police agreed to provide the breathalyzer tests. We were warned, of course, that drunken behavior depends less on blood alcohol content than on personality and individual tolerance. Both breathalyzer technicians had seen chronic drinkers who appeared sober despite registering in the high .3s. Death from alcohol toxicity normally occurs at .4, though one of the constables had tested someone with even higher levels who was still ambulatory.

All of us were wine-sippers and naïve in the ways of hard drinking. Nevertheless, the volunteers gamely set to work in the interests of quasi-science. Mark Wold, a slender, fit sales rep, won the Lightsy Award, consuming sixteen shots of vodka in two hours, one every seven minutes. Since the body eliminates one drink an hour, Mark had fourteen drinks in his system when tested. His score of .177, still six or seven drinks away from Lightsy's state, says nothing about the murder on T-3 except just what level of drinking used to occur at isolated arctic outposts.

The only side effects of the Ice Island Murder Party were hangovers and a consuming desire for total abstinence that lasted several weeks.

■

All hard Ellesmere journeys are stressful; that's part of their appeal. Anxiety is high in polar bear regions. When the going is bad, you worry about covering the distance before your food runs out. When the going is good, it can only get worse. If it's cold, the sled glides poorly; if it's warm, the snow may disappear before a land crossing.

In May 1988, my partner and I flew to Copes Bay, forty miles north of Alexandra Fiord, to cross Ellesmere from east to west by a new route. Edward Shackleton, son of the legendary Ernest, had tried it in 1935, but deep snow aborted his attempt. We budgeted three weeks for the two hundred mile trek to Eureka.

The mountain pass follows a river valley beside a huge glacier, then angles west to Cañon Fiord. On our maps the route looked good, but we were soon trapped in a gorge with a glacier wall on one side and a cliff on the other. Overhanging seracs creaked and dripped overhead. Small frozen waterfalls forced us to strap crampons to our sealskin boots, climb eight or twelve feet, then haul the gear up. We were making just five miles for ten hours' work. At this rate, we were not going to make Eureka. We hoped the route would improve when we reached higher ground.

1988 was a hot year on Ellesmere. Day and night, the sun blazed from a cloudless sky. The air was warm. Winds were calm. This made travel pleasant. By mid-May, we sunbathed naked in camp, dipped our water bottles in melt puddles and watched the year's first insects warm themselves on the tent. But the snow was disappearing at an alarming rate. The pile that we banked around the tent at night would be gone by morning.

The twenty-four hour sun usually burns off the snow by early June. Then only the ice caps, the glaciers and the frozen sea remain wintry-looking, while most of the island becomes toast-brown. But this year, summer arrived a month early. Within five days of beginning our journey, every flake of snow was gone. We dragged the sleds over bare land, leaving gelcoat streaks behind us on the rocks like canoes bashing down rapids. The river to Cañon Fiord was in full flood. We needed rafts, not sleds. Eventually, we had to portage our gear overland in three loads and fell further behind our schedule.

Reluctantly, we doubled our travel time. For two days, we marched nonstop for eighteen hours. On the third day, we pressed on for twenty-four hours. The second night, I nodded off with my supper spoon in my mouth. When we finally reached Cañon Fiord, we were so tired that when I broke through some sea ice weakened by the river flow, the jolt of adrenaline nauseated rather than energized me.

Once out on the sea, our troubles were unexpectedly over. The ice was in great shape. We hauled twenty-five to thirty miles a day and managed to reach Eureka in five days.

Some Ellesmere journeys are harder than this, some easier, but every one throws unnerving twists in the traveler's path. Some of us thrive on this insecurity, or at least accept it. Others crack.

■

In 1914, explorer Fitzhugh Green shot and killed his Inuit guide Peea-wahto. Green was a member of the Crocker Land Expedition, which set out to find the snowclad summits of a mysterious island allegedly sighted by Robert Peary off northwestern Ellesmere in 1906.

The expedition leader, Donald MacMillan, had been north only once before, as one of Peary's assistants. An ambitious man, MacMillan expected the discovery of Crocker Land to vault him into the front rank of contemporary explorers. Although Crocker Land proved illusory, Mac-Millan did manage to win a place in the thinning pantheon of polar heroes. What explorers accomplish is often not as important as their knack for self-promotion, and MacMillan always affiliated himself well, in this case, with the American Museum of Natural History. MacMillan later became something of an educator, introducing many students of Bowdoin College to the Arctic through summer excursions by ship.

The published account of the murder had always seemed strange to me. On northern Axel Heiberg, Fitzhugh Green's dogs are buried in a snowstorm and die. Peeawahto won't slow down for Green, who is on foot. Green, convinced that he is being abandoned, shoots Peeawahto in the back, appropriates his team and rejoins the others. MacMillan's one-sentence summary of the event is almost comic: "Green, inexperienced in the handling of Eskimos . . . had felt it necessary to shoot his companion."

To better understand the murder, I walked four hundred miles to the scene of the crime near Cape Thomas Hubbard, then visited Bowdoin College in Maine and the American Museum of Natural History in New York to look over the expedition journals. Bowdoin College, one of those lovely New England campuses full of maple trees and greystone chapels, still basks in the afterglow of its two arctic alumni, Peary and MacMillan. The college's mascot is a polar bear; researchers at its Peary-MacMillan Arctic Museum continue to make ethnographic trips to the pair's old stomping grounds in Greenland. Bowdoin has Green's journal. Between the tattered brown covers, erasures, pemmican stains, and fear lurk between the grandly pencilled lines. MacMillan's journal is in New York. "Not our favorite topic," volunteered the librarian, when I asked for Crocker Land material. "Wasn't someone killed on that expedition under museum auspices?"

Green's journal bears the earmarks of authenticity: pages smudged from where wet mittens gripped them; writing somewhat faint, pencil does not register well in the cold. The words too are authentic. Green would write some forty books in his life, all bad. But the journal is, at its key moments, unaffected. It shows a man overwhelmed with panic.

■

The Crocker Land Expedition floundered from the start. When their ship ran aground off the coast of Newfoundland, MacMillan frantically chartered a second. Eventually they reached Etah, on the Greenland side of Kane Basin, where they spent the winter. The following February, with an army of 19 men, 15 sleds and 165 dogs to lay depots, MacMillan set out for northern Axel Heiberg and the Arctic Ocean.

MacMillan had hoped an early start would minimize open water during their travels over the ocean. But mid-February is a hard time to begin a long trek. The weak sun has just returned from a four-month absence and limps along the horizon, giving light but no heat. It feels like the sun must feel on the surface of Pluto; the slightest wind burns exposed cheeks like liquid nitrogen. In the profound cold, familiar substances acquire unrecognizable properties. Butter shatters. Plastic bags snap like potato chips. Dental fillings drop out. On the coldest days, pee crackles as it arcs through the air and freezes before it hits the ground. Little wonder that when some men fell sick, MacMillan returned to Greenland for a month to regroup.

Mid-March is still cold but feels less like a space walk. MacMillan and a smaller crew retraced their steps across Kane Basin to Hayes Fiord, unknowingly passing the skull of the ancient murder victim we discovered seventy-odd years later. Eager to avoid the sled-destroying gravel of Sverdrup Pass, they followed the fiord to its terminus at the Beitstad Glacier.

The modern Canadian Inuit of Grise Fiord shun glacier travel, but the Polar Inuit who accompanied MacMillan lived in the shadow of the Greenland ice cap and were used to it. Even today, that is the only way for dogsledders to skirt the open water that laps against certain cliffs. Two Greenlanders carved steps in the glacier wall; dramatizing difficulties, MacMillan describes the wall as nearly insurmountable, but his photo shows a relatively minor obstacle that would take just a few patient hours to overcome.

MacMillan unexpectedly lost four of his party here. Minik, who spoke perfect English, may have sensed trouble ahead and quit; a second man, fearing Minik's interest in his wife, followed. The group's geologist frostbit his toes and had to return to Etah with a third Greenlander. That left only MacMillan, Green and four natives, carrying heavy loads with dogs weakened by bad pemmican. MacMillan sent Green and two of the natives back for supplies while he and Etukashu continued ahead. They were to reunite on northern Axel Heiberg.

Fitzhugh Green, a 25-year-old naval ensign, came from good old stock; his great-great-grandfather had been a large Virginia landowner in the 1600s. As a young man, he was talkative and ingratiating, with a tendency to fawn over his betters, and he expected those whom he considered his inferiors to snap a salute when he spoke. This made his dealings with the Inuit condescending at best. Nevertheless, he and his party fetched the extra food and oil and charged back across the glacier to catch up with MacMillan.

MacMillan and Green fancied themselves the dauntless explorers leading the happy-go-lucky, childlike Eskimo. "Their life was a sublimely simple fight for food and clothing," puffed Green later. "Mine was a cruel struggle of such labyrinthine intricacy that only the genius could be rich and none be truly contented save the shrewdest philosophers."

Little did they know that the Greenlanders who accompanied them were really the distinguished ones. It was as if Peary, Nansen, Sverdrup, Amundsen, and Shackleton were all part of the same expedition. Etukashu had joined Frederick Cook on his great 1908 journey that climaxed with wintering in a stone den on Devon Island and a magnificent four hundred mile trek back to Greenland. Peeawahto had also served with Cook, as well as with Peary and Knud Rasmussen, who described him as "a comrade who was ready to make personal sacrifices in order to help and support his companions." Minik was the famous "New York Eskimo," brought south by Peary as a curiosity, raised by a white family, who attempted to reassimilate in Greenland but eventually died in New Hampshire. Akqioq was awarded Denmark's highest medal for his role in Knud Rasmussen's epic Fifth Thule Expedition and later mysteriously disappeared with the German explorer, Hans Krüger. And Nukapinguaq, a young man on his first expedition, evolved into the greatest traveler the High Arctic has ever known.

■

The Canadian arctic islands are the size of Europe, but for nine months a year their territory is doubled, because the sea between all the islands is frozen. For sled travel, the sea is better than land, and the west coast of Ellesmere is particularly good. Surrounding mountains catch most of the snow and make Eureka Sound, the six-mile-wide artery dividing Ellesmere from Axel Heiberg, a true polar desert. Sweeping north winds transform the little powder that does fall into a hard surface resembling squeaky styrofoam. Every explorer recorded a burst of speed on this arctic autobahn. And its muskoxen and polar bears made it a land of plenty for these expeditions, which all depended on hunting.

Spring weather is usually good on Ellesmere, but 1914 featured one gale after another. Fighting the north wind was exhausting; once Green fell asleep chewing his supper, that barometer of a hard day. They couldn't spot wildlife in the blowing snow. Dogs died, and men went hungry. Worried entries about the worn-out dogs recur daily in Green's journal. But eventually the three of them caught up with MacMillan. "How we found them . . . seems now a miracle," wrote Green, adding grandiosely, "I think it was the fiendish intensity of our determination which did it."

■

Except for the Beitstad Glacier, I've covered the Crocker Land Expedition's entire route from Greenland to the northern tip of Axel Heiberg. Little has changed since then. Ellesmere is theoretically easier to reach, but charter flights costing up to $20,000 create a financial barrier as daunting as the ice of old. Tour groups focus on a couple of areas; the rest of the island remains gloriously unwalked.

Hikers in the Lower 48 are never more than twenty miles from a road, but Nunavut has no roads, just isolated Inuit hamlets separated by three hundred miles of Ice-Age wilderness. Ellesmere lies 2,500 miles from the nearest highway and 2,000 miles from the nearest tree. On a map, Ellesmere and Axel Heiberg resemble Britain and Ireland linked by a frozen Irish Sea, what is known as Eureka Sound.

Many of my sledding trips begin at the Eureka weather station, because charter aircraft refuel here and it's easy to reach. A meat locker door one foot thick leads into the main building. Within this oasis, a dozen employees can make phone calls, watch videos, and eat fresh bread every morning. But no one forgets that the High Arctic is just outside. The canine pug marks in the snow belong to wolves. Muskoxen have to be shooed off the airstrip before planes can land. Despite its e-mail access, Eureka is wilderness.

Still, the true sledging experience doesn't begin till six miles out, when the Telesat dish at Skull Point vanishes from sight and you pass through a time portal into Eureka Sound, where everything is just like it was in MacMillan's time. On the near coast, the rolling, muskox-dotted hills of the Fosheim Peninsula. Across the Sound, the mystery and austerity of Axel Heiberg, one of the world's loveliest islands. There resides what John Muir called the "unexplainable mysticism" of glaciers.

Like the polar bear, the spring sledder is a marine mammal. He travels on the sea, camps on it, and sometimes drinks old ice from which the salt has leached. The ice is five feet thick, a secure platform. "White men always think of ice as frozen water, but Eskimos think of water as melted ice," Nukapinguaq would explain to some British explorers years later. "To us, ice is the natural state."

I sometimes feel that this is what I was born to do, haul a sled over Eureka Sound for eight to twelve hours a day, temperature −20°F, snow hard, winds calm, trudging, as Thoreau wrote, "like a camel, which is said to be the only beast which ruminates when walking." In good conditions, the sledder can continue for twelve hours in this vein. Hours eleven and twelve are the most revealing: They are like the final rounds in great championship fights, when all the bullshit and grey areas of the personality slough away, and only strength and weakness remain.

In April 1997, my partner and I set out from Eureka and reached Skraeling Point on Axel Heiberg after seven hours. Here, we camped among the many "tent rings, store houses and traps" that prompted the Norwegian Otto Sverdrup to give the place its name. At the south end of the Schei Peninsula, where MacMillan had camped in a blinding snowstorm, we discovered an ancient Thule settlement, built around the remains of a bowhead whale which they had slaughtered. A bonanza for them. A bonanza for MacMillan too, for Etukashu and Peeawahto killed thirty-five muskoxen nearby. Almost a century later, muskoxen still favor the gentle slopes at this northern terminus of Eureka Sound.

We hurried up shallow Flat Sound, past thirty-two grounded icebergs and toward the lonely form of White Mountain, like a bump on the end of a long stick, "the most conspicuous point on the northern horizon." Thirty miles beyond, the high ice caps of Axel Heiberg taper to low hills. Western storms can now deposit their snow on upper Nansen Sound. The very names reflect the moister climate. Ellesmere's Black Mountains yield to the White Peninsula. The mood changes too. Even in a gale, Eureka Sound feels protected, full of nooks and crannies in which to hide. But as Nansen Sound opens into the Arctic Ocean, there is nothing but exposure. It is a wild and creepy place, a good spot for a murder.

■

On April 14, MacMillan sent Nukapinguaq and Akqioq home from the northern tip of Axel Heiberg. MacMillan, Green, Etukashu, and Peeawahto now struck northwest across the Arctic Ocean toward the hypothetical Crocker Land. The Arctic Ocean is not solid everywhere like fiord ice; it is thick and thin and open by turns. They advanced ten miles before meeting open water; when we were there, these leads appeared just offshore. We tried to imagine picking our way north, but there was too much open water.

MacMillan's party was lucky. The weather turned good, and the full moon, whose high tides break up the ice, had just ended. Day after day, their mileage over the floes was impressive: ten miles, eighteen miles, thirty miles. Yet despite recent feasts of muskoxen and caribou, their dogs struggled. Green and MacMillan walked to lighten their load; Etukashu and Peeawahto rode, as Greenlanders always did.

"I could plainly see that the Eskimos were discouraged," MacMillan confided in his journal. "Peeawahto did not like the looks of so much open water so late in the year." Spring catches hold quickly after mid-April, and open water might block their return to land. Miles from shore, in an Empty Quarter with no game to speak of, the Greenlanders were uncomfortable. Despite the superficial similarity, this was not their world.

By April 23, they had traveled nearly 150 miles northwest of Cape Thomas Hubbard. They should have been standing on Crocker Land, but they saw nothing but ice. Already they had crossed thirty-four leads; it was only going to get worse. MacMillan signaled the turnaround. They hurried to reach Cape Thomas Hubbard before the next full moon. Averaging thirty miles a day, they touched land on April 28.

MacMillan had proven that Crocker Land didn't exist, although belief in it didn't entirely die for another twenty years. In the early twentieth century, the search for the last crumbs of new land was a powerful fund-raising tool, and explorers continued to flog the Crocker Land myth until the public lost interest.

Since their quest for Crocker Land had failed, MacMillan must have felt pressured to bring back as many extras as possible. So although the dogs were exhausted and Peeawahto and Etukashu were impatient to get home, he proposed a four-day split-up: He and Etukashu would cross Nansen Sound to revisit old Ellesmere cairns. Meanwhile, Green and Peeawahto would close the ring on Axel Heiberg by covering its last unexplored section, the thirty miles between Cape Thomas Hubbard and latitude 80°55' on the west coast. Here they were to retrieve Sverdrup's 1900 cairn message. "All the adventurous blood in my veins boiled up at the prospect," wrote Green later.

Sverdrup's elusive *slutvarden*, or end cairn, has escaped all five parties who have looked for it over the last hundred years. It is a great prize; in it, Sverdrup left a note declaring sovereignty over the arctic islands for the King of Norway. As the high point of our 1997 trip, my partner and I scoured that entire coastline for it. We focused on the north side of a small, unnamed bay, which most closely matched Sverdrup's vague description. Sverdrup and one of his men spent hours building the cairn, and even chiseled a hole in the toprock, in which they planted the Norwegian flag. The construction must have been sizeable, but in an open landscape where nothing manmade escapes notice, we found no trace. Assuming that the cairn had collapsed, we walked the hills for a day and a half, investigating every rocky area, before giving up.

Green and Peeawahto never got that far. Shortly after separating from MacMillan on April 29, eight miles southwest of Cape Thomas Hubbard, the worst storm of the year hit. It became so violent that they had to take shelter. Peeawahto quickly built a small igloo near shore, and they crawled in.

For the next two days, Green's journal becomes almost raving. Their stove doesn't work. Drifting snow keeps plugging their igloo's ventilation hole. "I was about done for," he writes. "It was black as night in the hole."

The next day, April 30, the wind dropped a little and they go outside and dig out Peeawahto's sled. Green claims that his own sled and dogteam are "under 15 to 18 feet of hard-packed snow," so he gives them up for lost. "We cannot move yet, although to stay here is almost suicidal," he says.

Retreating to the igloo, they try to melt snow for tea but have more trouble with the stove. "P. refused to make a hole in the roof. . . . The fumes made us both sick and I vomited several times."

In the early hours of May 1, the wind briefly dies and Green wants to continue to Sverdrup's cairn. Peeawahto refuses, saying that MacMillan had instructed them to proceed just one day down the coast. "I told him that I was master now until we got back to Mac," says Green, although the argument becomes academic when the storm rises again and they have to stay in the igloo.

A little later, they begin their retreat with the one dogteam. Green walks to keep his feet warm, but he cannot keep up with Peeawahto, who rides the sled. The storm picks up yet again. A panicking Green orders Peeawahto to slow down. To emphasize his point, he takes the rifle off the sled. But a few minutes later, Peeawahto begins to pull away again.

> *I fired once in the air but he kept on. Then I fired twice, knocking him off his komatik. The dogs stopped. I ran up and found the man unconscious. I lashed him onto the komatik. . . .*
>
> *I must have wandered about for six or eight hours trying to find a familiar landmark. Finally I recognized a rock on the shore and headed for the igloo. . . .*
>
> *I finally got the snow cleared out somewhat [and took] P. in first. When I tried to do something for him, I found that he was dead.*
>
> *The situation is an unhappy one. Here I am in a howling blizzard with a dead Eskimo, a strange team and a few soaking or frozen garments. . . .*

Green's story of those three days sounds mostly true, but certain aspects are puzzling. What happened to his dogs? Fifteen feet of snow does not accumulate overnight in a desert where the average month's snowfall is two inches. (In a later account, Green inflated the already preposterous fifteen feet to thirty feet.) Avalanches are rare in the High Arctic, and the shoreline is flat in that area. On the same day, MacMillan, who was not far away, writes of seeing the outline of his dogs under the snow.

However, if Green parked his dogs behind an ice block, blowing snow might have swirled into the eddy and solidified over their heads. Otto Sverdrup had a similar experience on Ellesmere, when one of his dogs died under a mere eight inches of snow. "It would have been a very easy matter for him to shake it off," wrote a puzzled Sverdrup. "He had not made the slightest attempt to rise from the place where we found him lying."

Much stranger, Green's carbon monoxide troubles. An igloo needs an air hole to vent the poisonous stove fumes, and wind-driven snow could have kept filling the opening. But their stove was out on that first day, and Green's terror of being smothered sounds like an attack of claustrophobia.

Finally, Green's constant criticism of Peeawahto contradicts the Greenlander's unblemished record with earlier expeditions. He had even been one of Peary's favorites—no easy task, for Peary expected blind obedience.

Nevertheless, it is possible that Green's insufferable bossiness exasperated the veteran guide. The young naval lieutenant seemed to imagine that he was Peeawahto's commanding officer. He speaks of "forbidding" the natives to delay, and considered their disquiet on the Arctic Ocean "mutiny." So it's not surprising that he shot Peeawahto for what, in his panicked state, must have seemed like desertion in the face of an enemy.

Green's later accounts fill in some details that his journal omits. The murder weapon was Peeawahto's high-powered .22 Savage. At the first shot, Peeawahto slumped against the sled's upstanders. "As the dogs did not stop, I thought that possibly he might still be alive so I shot again, splitting his head open so that his brains fell out."

With a macabre presence of mind, Green removed Peeawahto's kamiks; his own footwear was falling to pieces. They didn't fit. Green couldn't stand the dead man's eyes staring at him in the igloo, so he dragged the corpse outside and left it behind an ice block. He continues his heroic posturing: "I kept wanting to say, 'Peeawahto, you lucky dog, it's all over for you. For me it's hundreds of miles of hell, with all the pain and misery of hell, and not one degree of its heat!' But I wouldn't let myself say it. I was afraid of being afraid."

Green retreated the next day toward Cape Thomas Hubbard with Peeawahto's team. The storm had also forced MacMillan to abort his journey, so he and Etukashu were camped nearby. "Mac, this is what is left of your southern division," announced an exhausted Green when he pulled up on May 4, driving Peeawahto's team.

"Good God, Green, is Peeawahto dead?" asked MacMillan.

Green sketched out the story. Etukashu knew some English and overheard their conversation, but scared for his own life perhaps, he appeared to accept their explanation that Peeawahto had died in an avalanche. "Etukushu took the news of his friend's death very complacently," wrote Green, "and was pleased with Peeawahto's kamiks, which I brought."

The wind continued to roar over Eureka Sound on their homeward march, but at least now it was at their backs. Green continues to use facts as bladders to be inflated into melodramatic balloons of fantasy. He writes of waist-deep snow in Bay Fiord and of the 200-foot glacier cliff they rappelled down. On May 20, they reached their cache at Pim Island.

"What a wonderful day," writes Green, "all surprises! . . . We found the box of supplies: sweet chocolate, marmalade, canned pears and peaches, hash and a can of corn. My, we were happy!"

Back in Greenland, they continued to maintain that Peeawahto had died during the storm. Thanks to Etukashu, the villagers knew better but said nothing. At least one member of the Crocker Land Expedition was disgusted.

"[Green] did not consider it murder," wrote their doctor, Harrison Hunt. "Peeawahto was just a savage. . . . I would have to live with and care for a man who had killed my friend. . . . I found my anger hard to control."

Even MacMillan was unsympathetic. "[Green's] assertion that if he had permitted the Eskimo to escape with the sledge, dogs, and food, he would have starved, is not a sufficient reason for killing one of the best Eskimos I have ever known. Green knew perfectly well that I would never have left him."

The Crocker Land Expedition remained in the Arctic for three more years. Morale was poor. Hunt, a man of old-fashioned integrity, became disillusioned with MacMillan's self-serving leadership and with the crew's practice of bedding native women. In a *menage-à-quatre* out of Greek mythology, Green himself had spent many nights before the fatal journey with Peeawahto's wife, Allakasinguaq, who, as a teenager, had borne Peary's child. Some Greenlanders considered this, unrealistically, the motive for Peeawahto's murder.

After his return to America, Green continued to show the total lack of shame that was his greatest asset. In a 103-page article for a naval publication, he prefaced the murder with paragraph after paragraph of poetic babble: "Every sense has its pleasurable side. Sight loves beauty. Hearing revels in music. For touch there is sensuous softness and smoothness. . . ." His description of the shooting itself is no less surreal. "He that had loomed hostile and a deceit between me and safety lay now crumpled and inert in the unheeding snow. . . . I had baffled misfortune. The feeling sent red gladness to my anemic humor. . . . The present was perfect, ecstatic. . . . I laughed, not fiendishly, but because I was glad. . . ."

Green never went back to the Arctic after 1917, but his four years in the White North allowed him to affect an explorer's persona for the rest of his life. He lectured widely on his experiences. Many of his books and articles play up those arctic years. After Robert Flaherty's 1921 film, *Nanook of the North*, brought the humanity of the Inuit before a wide public, Green began to write of "my friend Etukashu" and how "I lived with the natives for almost four years, so I know how wonderful they are." At the same time, casual references to "darkies" and "small brown people" (Japanese) continued to make their way into his strutting prose.

Always a talented sycophant, Green was aide to an admiral, to the president of the Naval War College, and to book publisher George Putnam, for whom Green wrote a gushing biography of Robert Peary. He followed with a biography of yet another arctic faker and establishment hero, Richard Byrd.

Now and then, the specter of May 1, 1914 resurfaced. In 1921, for example, Denmark asked the U.S. State Department to support Peeawahto's five children. But personally or professionally, the incident does not seem to have harmed Green. He died in glory and honor, and his jottings and family photographs are now preserved in Washington, D.C.'s

Georgetown University. That, to me, is the real crime, not that a primitive man should panic and commit murder in such an extreme place.

I had only a day at the library of the American Museum of Natural History, and my time was running out. Hurriedly I flipped through drawer after drawer of Crocker Land photographs. A couple of minutes after closing time, at the bottom of the last filing cabinet, I found what I was looking for. It was the collection's one photo of Peeawahto, unpublished and forgotten. It showed a small brown man in furs, crouching on the hard snow of Eureka Sound, and holding the gun that would kill him.

Chapter Four

The Horizontal Everest

It is almost impossible nowadays to like Robert Peary, and for that reason I tried very hard. New Age sentiments dominate the outdoors; only the meek, it seems, are entitled to inherit the wilderness. But I've always preferred curmudgeons to sensitive souls. My own soul, by most accounts, does not brim with gentle fluffiness, so if anyone could sympathize with the explorer everyone now loves to hate, I thought I might.

It's hard to get a fix on Peary, even in his Ellesmere haunts, because his obsession with the Pole limited his explorations to mostly minor detours off one well-worn supply route. It is possible to travel the island for years and never overlap with his journeys. Even at Fort Conger, where Peary showed such steely indifference to losing seven toes to frostbite, he was always somewhere else. It wasn't until I visited Payer Harbour that I began to buttonhole him in the shadows.

Payer Harbour, on Pim Island, was a popular retreat for explorers' ships thanks to its phalanx of protective little islands. As any traveler knows, cartographers are not infallible, and the real Payer Harbour is not the blind little bay indicated on the map but the stretch of protected coastline just south of it.

In 1900, Peary's wife Josephine heard about the loss of his toes and came north to tend to him. While Peary wintered at Fort Conger, Josephine's ship sheltered in Payer Harbour. Here she made the most bitter discovery of her life. Among the visiting Greenlanders was a young mother named Allakasinguaq, who said that she was Peary's wife and innocently showed Josephine the two-year-old son of Peary's whom she carried in her parka.

Perhaps Josephine shouldn't have been surprised. "The presence of women is absolutely necessary to render the men contented," Peary had written revealingly. In one of his books, he had even published a photo of the teenage Allakasinguaq, lying attractively naked and smiling up at the camera. It was presented as one of those anthropological studies of a child of nature that used to make adolescent guys so interested in anthropology. A girlfriend of mine once noted, "You can usually tell when people are sleeping together even if they're trying to hide it—they behave a certain way together." You did not have to know the history of the relationship to recognize the twinkle in Allakasinguaq's eye.

Another small expedition was wintering on land that year in Payer Harbour, and Josephine found a confidant in Julian Warmbath, a Boston taxidermist. "You can believe me when I say these are the darkest days of my life and any kindness shown me now will never be forgotten," she wrote him that winter in one of a series of affectionate little notes that the two exchanged.

Josephine's letter to her husband was more blunt and, for that era, astonishingly candid. "To think she has been in your arms, has received your caresses, has heard your lovecries, I could die at the thought," she wrote.

She could not resist passing on gossip about Allakasinguaq. "She has been Stein's 'companion' almost constantly on the trip . . . if I remember correctly she is Lee's leavings too." But when "Ally" fell gravely ill, Josephine swallowed her feelings and nursed her. In the end, Ally recovered. She eventually married Peeawahto and was attractive enough in her thirties to catch the eye of twenty-five year old Fitzhugh Green.

Peary received Josephine's scathing twenty-nine-page letter from some Greenlanders while sledding south from Fort Conger. Cunning even in domestic matters, he delayed a few days, timing his arrival at Payer Harbour to coincide with his birthday. No doubt he put on a good show of limping as well.

■

The North Pole is not as dangerous a quest as Mount Everest. There are no avalanches, no violent winds and—although local outfitters sometimes get calls from confused novices wondering if you need oxygen "that high up"—no altitude sickness. Nevertheless, the Pole has claimed forty-seven victims over the centuries, from starvation, scurvy, carbon monoxide poisoning, and murder. By comparison, over 150 climbers have died on Mount Everest.

In many other ways, the two are similar. The North Pole is no more a good hike than Mount Everest is a good climb. It's like walking across an immense frozen lake for two months, except that the terrain is worse.

Adventurers also go to the North Pole for the same reason that others climb Everest: It is a career move among ambitious outdoor people. The highest mountain and the highest latitude have a mystique shared by no other geographical prize on earth. To walk to the North Pole is, at least, to make a splash in your local newspaper. At best, it can be like winning an Olympic gold medal. You become a celebrity in your own country and, depending on your ambitions, it can earn you a living lecturing corporations on teamwork, or it can be the name recognition to start a successful outfitting business or find sponsors for new adventures. The North Pole has always been a destination for professionals, not amateurs.

Warmbath and Stein, who shared Payer Harbour with Josephine Peary that winter, were classic amateurs. I had always sympathized with Robert Stein because he was a man of ordinary means trying, as I do, to lead a rich explorer's life. Stein was an M.D. but had never practiced, preferring, for reasons beyond understanding, to work as a government clerk. By 1893, he was presenting his plan to explore Ellesmere Island to all the top arctic figures of the day. He offered Baron Nordenskiold and then David Brainard the command, and asked Frederick Cook to be the expedition surgeon. All politely declined. He approached politicians such as Chamberlain and Roosevelt for recognition, explorers such as Nares and Greely for endorsements, and philanthropists such as Carnegie for donations. Then as now, moral support was easy to come by; money was another matter. Anheuser-Busch eventually agreed to donate beer and a hundred dollars. By comparison, the Ringnes brewery in Norway fronted half the $200,900 for the Sverdrup expedition four years later.

Stein humbly approached Peary for passage on one of his ships, but he had chosen the wrong benefactor. Other explorers inspired in Peary only caution and resentment. Nevertheless, Peary's noncommittal replies encouraged Stein; perhaps merely being in correspondence with the great explorer made his projected trip seem more real. Peary wanted $2,500 for the passage north, including $1,000 up front. Stein innocently explained that the most he could raise by mortgaging his farm was $888.25, but that he hoped to bring this close to $900 by withdrawing his life savings of $7.44 from the bank.

Peary led Stein on for six years, half-promising rides, then reneging, while offering a spark of hope for the following year or the year after. Their correspondence leaves the impression that Peary wanted to keep this small fish twisting on the hook for as long as possible. But Stein clung to his dream, and in 1899, he, Warmbath, and Leopold Kann sailed north on Peary's supply vessel. The captain hastily dumped them at Payer Harbour with a promise to return later with walrus meat for their sled dogs. The three novices built their hut in the lee of a small cliff, not realizing that that's where all the blowing snow accumulates. In an attempt to be a good professional explorer, Stein called their camp Fort Magnesia, in honor of the company that had supplied him with inch-thick magnesium insulation.

Peary's support ship never returned with the walrus meat, and only one of Stein's dogs survived the winter. Worse, Stein became aware of the consequences of the six-year delay to his plans: The year before, Otto Sverdrup had wintered nearby in the famous *Fram*, and his large, well-financed expedition had already penetrated parts of western Ellesmere. This event seemed to have made Stein realize that he was out of his league.

His continued dependence on Peary became plaintive at times. When Peary informed him by note that no ship would return south until the summer of 1901, Stein begged Peary to intervene. His life insurance was paid up only till 1900, he fretted. His leave of absence also expired soon and he was afraid of losing his job; couldn't the ship return in the summer of 1900, as originally planned? He sounds here like the clerk he was, not a daring explorer ready to seize new lands and new opportunities.

To his credit, Peary was patient with Stein and even helped him in little ways. Stein eventually passed a second winter at Fort Magnesia, along with Julian Warmbath; their third member sledded to Greenland and caught a whaling ship home. Warmbath busied himself with collecting biological specimens, which, on barren Pim Island, was a task comparable to collecting icicles in Borneo. But Warmbath had taken to the Arctic, as opposed to the idea of the Arctic, in a way that Stein had not. Stein had had a grand notion: get up north cheaply, travel fast, and explore the unknown region to the west. One of his ambitious circles on the map coincides with the position of then-unknown Axel Heiberg Island. But even if Stein had managed to get north before Sverdrup, some other obstacle would likely have come between him and greatness. His legacy is not an enviable one. "Stein's expedition must be rated among the least effectual which had ever crossed the Arctic Circle," writes the great arctic historian William Barr.

The year Stein returned to his government job, Peary overwintered in Payer Harbour, just a few feet from Fort Magnesia. Peary lived in the deck house brought ashore from his ship. Curiously, he did not simply adapt Stein's hut, as he had done with Adolphus Greely's house at Fort Conger.

Only a few scientists had visited this obscure Payer Harbour site before me. The huts are gone, but the number of artifacts on the ground was impressive: pieces of Peary's stove, hundreds of cans, barbed wire, linoleum, dinner plates and the skeletons of six Greenlanders who had died from a disease they caught from Peary's ship.

The foundation posts of Fort Magnesia still exist, but when I was there they were buried under ten feet of snow, thanks to the hut's poorly chosen location. Just a few steps away, the gravel bed where Peary's own winter quarters had stood was completely snow-free.

A storm sent spindrift snaking across the gravel. The wind became so bad that I couldn't find my way back to the tent. But the temperature was mild, so well bundled up, I continued to poke around. A ragged chunk of silver-black metal caught my eye. The metal was soft, and I took a few shavings from it with a penknife. After the wind died down, I went back to camp and made some tea. When I threw Stein's magnesium shavings onto the stove, they flared briefly with a brilliant white light, then died.

■

Although I've read most of the books that dissect, sometimes with a scalpel, and sometimes with a crooked blade, the rival claims of Robert Peary and Frederick Cook, I never really warmed to the debate. Most arctic travelers take it for granted that neither of them came close to the North Pole, so who cares whether Peary made it within one hundred or two hundred miles, or whether Cook ventured twenty-five miles out, or a hundred and twenty-five miles? It had always been a sport for armchair detectives. A few years ago, a Resolute weatherman passionately assured me that Cook had reached the Pole because of the length of the shadows in one of his photographs. Apparently, the ghost of the debate will continue to walk the earth for some time.

Defenders of Cook or Peary can explain away the diary gaps, phony-smelling entries, questionable navigation, suspicious past claims, guilty behavior during the controversy, and remarkable speeds. Some of the defences are even plausible singly, but not all together. Enough modern expeditioners have gone to the Pole in the last fifteen years that we now understand the challenge. Today we are better equipped, more knowledgeable, and more fit, yet no one has ever approached the speeds claimed by those two over the surface of the Arctic Ocean. Some may believe that we live in a time of iron ships and wooden men, and that there were giants on the earth even a hundred years ago, but in the physical domain that's a fallacy. I am no great athlete, but back in 1909 I would hold world records in several Olympic events. Even our dogs are more fit. If something can't be done as quickly today, it wasn't done in the past.

Scientists point out that sea ice was almost twice as thick in those days; thicker sea ice *may* buckle less, making travel easier. But even then, with the private papers of Peary and Cook finally accessible to scholars, the willful fraud is pretty clear. Neither man could bring himself to destroy the doctored papers that in the end invalidates his claim.

Even the prestigious National Geographic Society, whose unflagging support of Peary has prompted ambitious polar trekkers from Vilhjalmur Stefansson to Will Steger to give him the benefit of the doubt, is now taking its first quiet steps back from its historical position. "Join Commander Robert E. Peary in 1909 in his quest for the North Pole," carefully states the introduction to the CD-ROM set of the complete

National Geographic. The attainment has become a "quest." And in their Explorers' Hall in Washington, D.C., the caption to the classic portrait of a droopy-eyed Peary in furs also now skirts the issue of whether or not he succeeded. It simply acknowledges, "Although many have challenged Peary's claim to have reached the North Pole, his exceptional courage and boundless determination remain legendary." A nod to his determination may be Peary's sole eventual legacy.

■

Early books on the controversy were shamelessly partisan. They were for Peary, or they were for Cook. Either one got there, or the other did. Either one was a villain, or the other was. Cook lost the battle for mainstream faith back in 1911. Peary's detractors were eventually silenced after a controversial vote of confidence from Congress, and for the next sixty years, he reigned in history books and encyclopedias as the discoverer of the North Pole. Then in the early 1970s Peary's claims began to be reappraised. All the latest scholarship points to a conclusion that never occurred to earlier writers: Neither of them made it.

Although new books about this eternal debate come out once every ten years, none will surpass Robert Bryce's *Cook and Peary: The Polar Controversy Resolved* for the weight of its arguments, four pounds, 1,133 pages. Bryce, a slender, well-spoken librarian at a community college in Maryland, not only mastered a staggering amount of material, but what was perhaps even more difficult, found a publisher willing to print it.

"I know more about Frederick Cook than I know about my own father," Bryce admitted in his tidy, overheated office, decorated with a photograph of Cook in furs and a full-page reproduction of the *New York Herald* announcement that Cook had reached the Pole. Bryce had amassed data on the controversy with the obsessiveness that a philatelist collects stamps. Although he dismissed Cook's claim, Bryce had a high regard for the explorer himself, whom he regarded as an emblem of humanity, torn between high ideals and low urges. His appraisal of Cook was, I felt, the most sympathetic that would stand up over time, and it was ironic that while Peary's descendents kept mostly silent in the face of his well-documented conclusions, the Cook Society attacked the book.

Peary has never had a populist fan club, the Peary Arctic Club was a
political and corporate entity, but over the years Cook has continued to
attract a small number of nonconformists who believe, as an article of
faith, that he both reached the Pole and climbed Mount McKinley. Some
have even done a great deal of research. It doesn't matter to them that
their conclusions fly in the face of what is now mainstream thinking; didn't
the mainstream used to believe Peary? I'd never met anyone from the
Cook Society, but through their writings I recognized them, because I
have seen them before in other guises. They were the same people who
meticulously collect reports of eastern cougar sightings or who scour logging roads for a glimpse of Bigfoot. Cryptozoologists. They were intelligent and sincere but had an anti-rational side and preferred interesting
long-shot explanations to orthodox likelihoods. Frederick Cook gave people like these something, but Bryce seemed comfortable with the moral
ambiguity of his subject in a way that these admirers generally were not.
For them, it was really The Pole or Bust.

■

Bryce had no love for Peary: "I didn't try to make him mean and petty.
He was mean and petty." The more I reluctantly delved into the details,
the more I had to admit that I wasn't doing a good job of liking Peary either. It was okay when you just walked Ellesmere and marveled at the
single-mindedness of a guy who could say, "The loss of seven toes is a
small price to pay for the Pole." Or who, while recovering from the crude
amputations at Fort Conger, scrawled a quote from Seneca on the wall
of Greely's house, "Find a way or make one." Such bitter determination!
As for the character flaws, what was that worldly-wise saying?—that you
rise only so far on the strength of your merits; after that, you rise on the
strength of your demerits. Those who achieve high status generally leave
dirty laundry and/or personal carnage in their wake. Even Gandhi was no
saint to his wife and children. It's a myth that the great are also great human beings.

The problem was that Peary had more than his share of the weak-
nesses of the great, and few of their genuine accomplishments. It is not
only his North Pole claim that has fallen under suspicion in recent years.
Many of his geographical discoveries were wrong, deliberately, one sus-

pects. He was not trying to be a great explorer, he was trying to be famous, and rewriting failure as success was a necessary part of his master plan. His real motto might have been, "Find a way or fake one."

Peary was thirty-six and on his second arctic expedition when he made his first major discovery, the first of four big question marks in his career. While attempting to reach the north end of Greenland over the interior ice sheet in 1892, he found his way blocked by a narrow inlet. In his journal he confided his disappointment that this "puny" fiord that had thwarted his plans. But back home the dead-end fiord suddenly evolved into the glorious Peary Channel, which separated Greenland from a new land to the north which he called, with typical humility, Peary Land. From a solid but modest journey, his expedition had suddenly become a magnificent geographical achievement. He had proved Greenland was an island, reached its northern tip and discovered new territory beyond it. It made his reputation. When Peary's sole companion on the trip, Eivind Astrup, published a different map and a more accurate conclusion, the spin doctors who now watched over Peary's career stepped in to discredit the young Norwegian. It was a sign of things to come. Some of the most distasteful maneuvering in the years ahead would be masterminded not by Peary, but by his Machiavellian entourage.

It is no coincidence that while most explorers sought concrete objectives such as new land, Peary devoted himself to chasing a mathematical point on the earth's surface. Abstract quest or not, it had sizzle, and Peary recognized that for nearly everyone, the sizzle was what mattered. He was a pro. He pretended that he was merely a patriot striving to bring honor to his country. Like all modern expedition organizers, one of his chief skills was fundraising, "shaking the corporate money tree," as Paul Schurke, co-leader of a 1986 polar trek, puts it. But because the North Pole proved such an elusive target, Peary had to shake that tree for twenty years, so he needed to bring back some lesser sizzle each time to keep interest high for his next attempt.

In 1906, Peary made the third of his four attempts on the Pole. Eleven years earlier, he had written, "I am too old to snowshoe twenty-five to thirty miles a day for weeks, and to carry a heavy load during most of the time. For that work, one should be a trained man, a thorough athlete, and that I am not." He was right, and that was what explorers failed to grasp about the

North Pole. It was only partly a logistical challenge. Mainly, it was an athletic one.

In 1906, Peary was fifty, and surely he must have felt that the expiry date on his dream was approaching. He had achieved fame, but the real prize had eluded him. He must have felt like the star quarterback with a reputation for never winning the Big One, with only one or two seasons left in his career.

His 1906 attempt didn't bring him the Pole, but he still managed to carry away some lesser sizzle, a Farthest North of 87°06', still two hundred miles short. There is some doubt whether he made it quite that far. He may have rounded up to 87°, since no one had broken that milestone before. He must have been discouraged, but rather than wallow in failure, he immediately set out on another hard trek along the north coast of Ellesmere. His refusal to accept defeat showed the admirable side of Peary's character. The steel in his makeup was real, even if Peary Channel and the Farthest North were not.

And then there was Crocker Land.

■

Robert Peary would not have been amused, but I sledded to his haunts on the north coast by way of Nansen Sound, the route favored by his hated rival, Frederick Cook. Fifteen miles across the Sound, obscured by yellowish arctic haze, the Svartevaeg cliffs signaled the approach of northern Axel Heiberg Island. Although Svartevaeg means "black cliffs," they only look dark in the overcast weather Sverdrup had had when he first saw them. Even at this distance, I recognized a distinctive cleft in the rocks from one of Cook's published photos. On his North Pole trek, he had camped at the base of that cleft. This is his last verifiable position. From here, his route is shrouded in mystery and controversy.

With irritating persistence, Peary insisted on calling Axel Heiberg Island "Jesup Land," after his main sponsor. He claimed that he saw it from a distant height two years before Sverdrup set foot on it, a patent falsehood. Even Peary's own map places what he saw as the north coast of Greely Fiord, still Ellesmere. But that was Peary, always minimizing the accomplishments of others while aggrandizing his own, phony or not. He was a master of the sneaky putdown disguised as the casual remark.

My partner on this trip, Graeme Magor, was a long-time Ellesmere colleague. We were not quite friends, but our mutual interests kept us in close touch, and occasionally we shared a trip. Graeme was a Sverdrup enthusiast, and in the past he had dragged me to historical sites when I just wanted to run as quickly as I could through the beautiful wilderness, increasing my receptivity by taxing my body to the limits. A world-class triathlete, Graeme quenched his restlessness in training and competition, so he preferred easier trips than I usually did. After my interest in Ellesmere exploded in all directions, I came to envy some of the quiet shining moments he had had around old Sverdrup sites on the south coast.

This time, we were looking for an undiscovered 1902 Sverdrup cairn at Lands Lokk, at the northwest tip of the island. A photo exists of Sverdrup's camp here, and using the configuration of the hills as a guide, we set our tent in the same spot. This was Sverdrup's farthest north, and he had commemorated the event by leaving a note declaring sovereignty over the High Arctic islands for the King of Norway. (He left a similar note in 1900, the one Green and Peeawahto set out to look for, on northwestern Axel Heiberg.) Although only licensed researchers are supposed to meddle with historic sites, none come to this part of the island, and we hoped to find the note and give it to the appropriate museum before it turned to pulp.

In 1906, Peary had also looked around Lands Lokk for Sverdrup's cairn, but without success. The measly hundred miles from Alert Point to Lands Lokk had been the only virgin Ellesmere coastline Peary had ever trodden, yet he exulted about it as if he had just discovered a new continent: "What I saw before me in all its splendid, sunlit savageness was *mine*, mine by the right of discovery, to be credited to me, and associated with my name, generations after I have ceased to be." You can imagine him rubbing his mittened hands and cackling. As if marking his territory, he built three cairns within fifteen miles of each other.

Through binoculars from the top of Lands Lokk, we could see one of these cairns on a gravel bar to the north—the wondrous visibility of the Arctic, seeing a three-foot pile of stones from four miles away—but of Sverdrup's work there was no sign. That night, we read the seventeen lines in his *New Land* a dozen times, squeezing each phrase for some nuance that might lead us to the elusive cairn.

"Sverdrup says he collected enough stones for the cairn 'with some trouble,' so we should look where there's a scarcity of cairn-sized rocks," suggested Graeme.

I reread the passage. "When he says the cairn is three minutes north of here, did he mean three nautical miles? Or three minutes time?"

The more we examined poor Sverdrup's words at the microcellular level, the less sense they made. But after a second search of the nearby hills the following morning, we conceded failure. We hadn't missed the cairn; it wasn't there. Maybe an itchy muskox had rubbed itself against it, as muskoxen sometimes do on rocks, and collapsed it. Or maybe a military helicopter pilot had spotted it while flying this coast during the Cold War years.

That afternoon, we rounded Lands Lokk and headed northeast. This was the leg of the trip I'd been looking forward to. I rarely traveled anywhere on the island without dozens of photocopied pages from *New Land*, but Sverdrup was a little dull for my taste. He was another of those magnificent Norwegian automatons, like Amundsen, who made everything look easy and who wrote boring books. Peary, at least, was complex and troubling.

All of Ellesmere Island is wild in the extreme, and the north coast is its wildest shore: the dark side of the moon, the least seen, the most mysterious. It felt different immediately. A seaborne dampness replaced the polar desert air of Nansen Sound. Ice worms of moisture wriggled out of our hats and the backs of our gloves. All afternoon, the coastal mountains threw long shadows across our trail. In the shadows, the temperature plummeted and sent us reaching for our parkas. A mile beyond our apron of shore ice began the frozen Arctic Ocean, one of the world's worst traveling surfaces. It's been described as a giant jigsaw puzzle where none of the pieces fit.

■

So few people had traveled the northwest coast that I felt almost a part of history myself, not an explorer, perhaps, but a footnote to exploration. Peary had been the first, in 1906, but it wasn't until the early 1950s that Geoffrey Hattersley-Smith dogsledded the entire north coast in two field seasons. A glaciologist by profession but a historian by nature, he found most of Peary's cairns and remnant camps. He once sledded sixty miles with one of Peary's abandoned sleds, just as I had used one of Peary's big nails to stake down my tent in the blizzard at Payer Harbour.

Hattersley-Smith lives today near the English village of Sissinghurst, an hour and a half southwest of London. There is a castle in the neighborhood. Two ancient yew trees, among the oldest living things in Britain, spread their arthritic arms near his L-shaped home, parts of which date back to 1530. The house rests on dark beams of almost indestructible English oak. Famed travel writer Charles Doughty lived next door in the 1920s. T.E. Lawrence, a friend of Doughty's, often roared along this country lane on the Brough motorcycle that would later kill him.

We sat at Hattersley-Smith's kitchen table, beneath an ancient clock with Roman numerals, sharing some dark ale and a pork pie. He was seventy-five. He lit his pipe with a lighter engraved with the image of an arctic ship he had sailed forty years ago. The guest book I signed was a gift from Constance Conybeare, widow of one of the officers on the Nares expedition. He is one of those lucky people whose every possession has a lineage, and a look of pain crossed his face when he recalled a theft that had happened the year before.

Hyphenated British names generally indicate privilege, and "Hatt," as some of his friends called him, was educated at Winchester, a traditional boy's school whose 600-year-old motto was, "Manners maketh the man." Though informal, he was indeed a perfect host, always asking what he could serve me or do for me. The house, likewise cozy and informal, brimmed with the rare, the tasteful, and the antique.

To a boorish, unhyphenated North American, a weekend in such company was more daunting than skiing to the Pole. A pair of wooden homilies in the guest bathroom hinted at the pitfalls. Etchings of a graceful young lady and a selfish sophisticate illustrated The Perfect Guest and The Perfect Pest. Among other things, The Perfect Guest demurely accepted an invitation and disappeared in good time. The Perfect Pest announced that she was coming, stayed too long and left (to everyone's relief) only to return shortly, announcing, "I've missed the train."

Hattersley-Smith began his arctic career at age twenty, helping escort Russian convoys out of Murmansk. After the war, he went south with the British Antarctic Survey but then reversed polarity and came to Ellesmere Island. He was on the cusp of past and present, arriving in an airplane but traveling with dogs. In 1967, he made the first ascent of Ellesmere's Mount Barbeau, at 8,743 feet the highest North American peak east of the Rockies.

We talked about the Arctic in the dining room, as several distinguished figures in a large painting by Hogarth looked on. Hatt knew the descendents of the people in the painting. Presently he offered me a drink in a manner that suggested this was the hour when gentlemen did such things. Although I didn't enjoy hard liquor, I was afraid of being a Pest by declining, so I gambled on a gin and tonic. It turned out to be a wise choice: I discovered later that gin and tonic is one of those proper beverages marking an old Etonian or Winchester lad, or a savvy visitor from the colonies.

Hatt's wife was out of town, and he and I had been invited to his neighbors' for dinner. Hatt put on a jacket and tucked an ascot into his shirt. It was a short drive. Don, the man of the house, settled us in and made me a gin and tonic. He stayed in the background, only piping in an occasional, "Beastly, that," about some item in the news. Also visiting was a cousin of theirs from Argentina. He had a huge red nose and was wearing a quilted smoking jacket, which made my evening. I had actually lived to see someone wearing a smoking jacket. Because he was mildly diabetic, he restricted himself to one drink. He asked what I was having. I told him gin and tonic. He nodded approvingly.

I had never been in such a fairytale setting, and I was on my best behavior. One of the unwritten rules for The Perfect Guest is not to embarrass your host in company. Hatt was amazing, and the Arctic managed to come up two or three times in the evening. His alma mater came up once. Smoking Jacket asked him where he went to school. Hatt told him. "Winchester, hm," said the man in the same knowing tone he applied to my gin and tonic. Winchester was clearly one of the right places to have gone. Verdun High School probably a little less so, but luckily that topic did not come up where I was concerned.

This surreally civilized evening with a graceful man who fit so seamlessly into both the Arctic and the drawing room gave me an appreciation of the British arctic character for the first time. Despite their toughness, the British are famous in the polar regions largely for glorified tragedies of their own making. They are the ultimate gentlemen amateurs. It is as if they go off deliberately unprepared, in order to test their boyish mettle. No dogs, no Inuit helpers, no skis or snowshoes, only ponies, manpower, thousand-pound sleds, and naval issue clothing. No experience preferred.

This is still true today. The most bumbling expeditions to the North Pole are always British. In 1985, a Derbyshire bobby phoned an outfitter in Resolute to reserve a radio for two weeks, figuring he could walk the 450 miles in that time. "He was even so generous as to factor in two days for bad weather," said the outfitter, shaking his head. Not long ago, a Special Forces man with no aptitude but a good-looking press kit tried a similar solo, with the same spectacularly inept results. They always get injured or their radio breaks down after a few days, leading to a sudden reappearance in Resolute, bloodied but unbowed. The object of the game is not to succeed but to fail in such good form that you somehow achieve greatness.

Hattersley-Smith presented a different side of British arctic tradition: quiet and effective. But what most impressed me was how richly peopled his Ellesmere Island was. He had charming stories about names that were legends to me—bush pilot Weldy Phipps, Henry Stallworthy of the RCMP, archaeologist Eigel Knuth. His Ellesmere was alive with human texture, laced with good jokes, and well anchored in time with unforgettable characters whose generous obituaries he always wrote for polar journals. My Ellesmere had ghosts, scientific curiosities, and some interesting people, but it was mainly a wild and timeless land. His was richer.

Before I left the next morning, Hattersley-Smith gave me some of his home-grown figs and apples for the trail. "My wife does the clever work in the garden," he admitted. "I just do what I'm told."

I remembered a previous conversation we'd had about professional travelers who trump themselves up as explorers. "Exploration was already a joke when I came to Canada in 1951," he said. "Of course, it's all a matter of definition. You can explore your own asshole with the aid of a mirror." Hatt enjoyed the company of celebrity adventurers, but personally believed that "there is no limit to the good a man can do if he doesn't care who gets the credit." Now here was a gentleman amateur.

■

Graeme and I paid a quick visit to Peary's broken-down cairn at Lands Lokk, but our main objective was twenty miles northeast, at Cape Colgate. Here, Peary had left two cairns. Hattersley-Smith had removed the record and a piece of the Stars and Stripes from the lower cairn, but he had forgotten about the one atop the 2,000-foot mountain. As far as I knew, Graeme and I were the first party to walk this shore, after Peary and Hattersley-Smith, so the cairn was possibly still intact.

Cape Colgate is a major landmark in the Peary saga. It was here that he first saw, or claimed to see, new land to the northwest. He called it Crocker Land, after George Crocker, a railroad baron who had donated $50,000 to his expedition. The discovery of Crocker Land gave some sizzle to his most recent polar failure. Three days later, Peary saw Crocker Land again from northern Axel Heiberg Island. He estimated that these "snowclad summits" were a hundred and thirty miles away and he wrote in a *Harper's* magazine article after his return, "The existence of new land . . . has practically been determined."

Crocker Land doesn't exist. There is nothing north of Ellesmere and Axel Heiberg Islands except broken sea ice. In an amusing aspect of their dual hoax, Cook believed in Peary's Crocker Land and felt obliged to manufacture new land in roughly (but not quite) the same position during his fictitious North Pole trek. He called it Bradley Land, after his own chief sponsor. The existence of Crocker Land was not disproved until Donald MacMillan's 1914 expedition. MacMillan diplomatically concluded that his old boss had been taken in by a mirage.

Polar mirages are much more convincing than the desert variety. Thanks to the cooperative weather, Graeme and I had been treated to mirages daily on our 150-mile trek up Eureka and Nansen Sounds. Distant icebergs stretched into hourglass shapes. Others floated upside-down in the sky like stalactites from an invisible ceiling. Sometimes, small pieces of ice danced briefly in the air like party balloons.

Polar mirages form in calm, sunny weather. The ghostly caricatures are based on some kernel of reality that is distorted through a convex lens of air. Without icebergs or rough ice or buoys or ships or distant islands, there are no mirages. Most mirages are about fifteen miles off, although I have seen them as close as three hundred yards and some legendary ones were more than forty miles away. The Inuit called them *puikaktuq*, literally, "rising above the sea." Rather than be fooled by mirages, the Inuit used them to navigate and find food. In certain conditions, they could "see" land that was below the horizon and thus be guided home. And in summer, a sharp-eyed hunter could tell the difference between an ordinary miraged pan of ice floating in the air and the slightly smudged look of a pan with walrus lying on it.

Mirages don't occur in winter; without the sun, there is only one uniform air layer. And they rarely occur in wind because wind mixes the air layers. A polar mirage needs cold air near the ground and warm air above it. The midnight hours, ten p.m. to two a.m., seemed to be the best time for them, because the evening air near the ice cools more quickly than the air above it. The best mirages are backlit, and look much darker than real ice.

As Graeme and I approached Cape Colgate, the mirage conditions were exceptional. The thermocline was at eye level and Cape Colgate jiggled up and down with every step I took. But even more remarkable, on the Arctic Ocean to the north of us rose the unmistakable specter of land. Crocker Land! It was like one of those enchanted kingdoms in fairy tales that become visible to mortal eyes for one day every hundred years.

And yet it did not fool us and it would not have fooled Peary. It was obviously a mirage. It was changing every second, like smoke. Within a minute, it looked completely different. Twice, the mirage vanished before I could get out my camera. I took to leaving it attached to the tripod under the bungie cords of the sled. Finally, on the third attempt, I got a few frames before the mirage evaporated.

We were at sea level. On both occasions, Peary had seen his Crocker Land from 2,000-foot mountains. Mirages have occasionally been seen from high points, even from airplanes, but the atmospheric conditions necessary for that to occur are rare. The temperature gradient that creates the distortion usually ends near the ground. While it is possible to see mirages twice from that height within a few days of each other, it is not likely.

Robert Bryce, in our subsequent correspondence, was unequivocal. "Don't think for a moment that Peary made an honest mistake," he said. "He made up Crocker Land to get more money out of George Crocker." Indeed, if Peary had seen Crocker Land, why had he not mentioned it in his diary on either of the days he reportedly saw it or in the cairn notes? The *Harper's* piece, months later, was its first recorded mention.

As I watched the mirage shrink and finally disappear for good, I knew I didn't really care whether or not Peary had seen Crocker Land. We had.

■

After innumerable delays to marvel at Crocker Land, we finally hauled our sleds up beside a patch of bare ground at Cape Colgate. Then, we went to investigate the lower Peary cairn on a nearby knoll. I carried a photo that Hattersley-Smith had taken of his partner, Robert Christie, beside it, and it was much smaller now than in 1954. Graeme performed a mock bow at the cairn built by someone he made no attempt to like. We wandered back to the sleds, set up camp, and laid some clothes to air on the black gravel, which felt almost warm. It was May 10, about three a.m. The delicious warmth of an arctic spring day was quickly replacing the cool evening air. At this time of year, I often went to sleep fully co-cooned in my arctic sleeping bag and by seven or eight in the morning I would be lying on top of the bag in my underwear, as the sun turned the tent room temperature.

Graeme and I ate supper, then stuffed our daypacks with snacks, Gatorade, and spare clothing and began to hike to the top of Cape Colgate, where we could faintly see a cairn. Our hour-long climb took us over rocks and steep patches of hard, glazed snow in which we had to kick steps. The coolness of the shade in which we labored was welcome, for a change.

I was a little stronger on the flats, but could only marvel at Graeme's fitness on hills. We had earlier made a deal that I would not race ahead on the sea ice to get the first look around every corner if he would not blast up mountains to get the first view from every summit—so we reached the top together. Peary wrote that the view was "of a more truly Alpine character than any that I have seen in northern Greenland or [Ellesmere]." From someone who did not enjoy the outdoors, who merely "camped for fame," that was a ringing endorsement. Barely a breath of wind blew. It was seven a.m., about the hour Peary had stood here, and the sun was getting stronger all the time.

A handful of rocks had been removed from one side of the cairn, and my spirits fell. There would be no note. But the cairn was otherwise intact. Rather than the typical heap of rocks, a tower of closely fitting stones rose in a spiral, like a snow house. This was not surprising, since Peary's two Inuit companions had built it. A photo in *Nearest the Pole* shows one of them near the top of Cape Colgate holding the sort of long bamboo wand that Peary used for marking supply depots. Two pieces of weathered bamboo still protruded from the top of the cairn. We clustered around in awe. Regardless of how we felt about Peary, this was wonderful.

We sat on the summit for an hour, soaking up the view. Time felt pure; the seconds deposited memories as they flowed past us. It was the quiet reward for ten days of hard walking. We were five hundred miles from the North Pole, but it was almost warm enough for just an undershirt. We could, like Peary, see west to "Jesup Land." To the southeast, the austere ice cap of the Kleybolte Peninsula played the painfully beautiful but silent music that all ice caps play, and which my ears, so musically stupid in most ways, had always responded to. Fifty miles to the south, we could see the icebergs we had passed days before in Nansen Sound. Finally, to the northwest, the white polar sea, a dark zone of new ice, distant bands of water sky, but not a hint, not a trace, not a whisper of Crocker Land.

■

Frederick Cook began his arctic career at Robert Peary's side. Responding to a newspaper notice, Cook volunteered as surgeon on Peary's 1891 Greenland expedition. The collaboration worked out so well that Peary invited him on his next venture two years later. The offer was tempting: Cook was not a big-scale organizer like Peary, so for him the easiest way to travel was to sign onto ready-made expeditions. But Dr. Cook was ambitious, and Peary had refused let him publish a cultural study on Greenlanders based on their first trip. Cook shrewdly saw that there was no future for him with Peary. He declined, although the two remained friends.

Peary's need to hog the glory alienated a lot of associates over the years. The sharing of credit is a delicate issue, and many great duos— Nansen and Sverdrup, Burton and Speke, even climbers Messner and Habeler—became adversaries over it. Usually the more ambitious man seizes the lion's share, to the resentment of his quiet but sensitive partner.

To a certain extent, Peary was just being a modern professional spelling out the rules. Today's expedition organizers often have their team sign the same "feudal" contract for which Peary was criticized, which usually restricts or forbids articles, public presentations, or books on the expedition until the organizer thoroughly mines these venues first. Even personal journals are to be turned in as raw material for the official expedition book.

But Peary carried this to pathological lengths. When stepping onto new land, he had his men wait on the sea ice for several minutes, so there would be no doubt whose footsteps were first. On his last two expeditions, he even sent back all the white men, so that he would not have to share the honor of the North Pole with anyone except the native Greenlanders and his black aide, Matthew Henson, whom Peary regarded more like sled dogs than rivals. Today, thanks to black studies programs, there are more copies of Henson's North Pole book than Peary's in American libraries.

Unlike Peary, Cook admired the natives and their skills. He promptly organized two of his own trips to Greenland, but they were not in the same league as Peary's grand affairs. They were tourist excursions, the first underwritten by a wealthy professor who wanted his son to see the north, the second a paying cruise of students and professors. Cook made what he could of his experiences, and back home his popular talks about native customs, including wife-swapping, revealed his public flair. Twice he also tried to organize an expedition to Antarctica but failed to raise the money. Over the years, Cook occasionally got lucky with a rich patron but he did not have Peary's knack for mingling in financial and political upper echelons, so his expeditions remained small and informal.

In 1897, Cook was accepted at the last minute on a Belgian Antarctic expedition. Ice trapped the ship and they were forced to overwinter. During the long polar night, Cook shone. He prescribed quirky but effective remedies for the crew's illnesses. He devised little gadgets to improve life on board, including seal oil lamps and rat traps. Always interested in people, Cook closely observed the impact of their enforced captivity on the crew. He even worked hard at photography. His "unfaltering courage, unfailing hope, endless cheerfulness, and unwearied kindness" made a deep impression on another crew member, the young Roald Amundsen, who remained his friend for life.

On his return, Cook's vivid lectures, articles, and his book *Through the First Antarctic Night* expanded his reputation. His relations with Peary remained cordial, and he even returned to Greenland in 1901 as a member of Peary's relief expedition.

While Peary continued to plug away at the North Pole, Cook's varied interests and hand-to-mouth funding kept his field of operations dependent on opportunity. In 1906, he went to Alaska for the second time to attempt Mt. McKinley, North America's highest peak. He did not get very far but still came back reporting triumph. This first big hoax made the doctor hot property. Although never the establishment figure that Peary was, he was also not the loner that some writers have described. After McKinley, he was definitely "in"—the new president of the Explorers Club, a founder of the Arctic Club, a popular dinner speaker at scientific gatherings. In 1907, the patronage of millionaire hunter John Bradley gave him another chance to go north. This time his goal was the North Pole itself.

Peary considered the whole Ellesmere-Greenland area his personal duchy, and anyone who intruded provoked an aggressive territorial response. When Sverdrup showed up in 1898, a suspicious Peary assumed that the Norwegian's secret mission was a rival Pole attempt. It prompted him to make a foolish midwinter journey to Fort Conger to prevent Sverdrup from claiming it as a base. It was on that trip that Peary froze his toes.

For his 1908 polar attempt, Cook followed Sverdrup's route across Ellesmere and then north to the tip of Axel Heiberg Island. From here, he ventured out onto the pack with two native companions. To Peary, who was preparing for his own 1909 polar attempt—the 52-year-old explorer's last chance at the big prize—Cook had gone from an amiable former helper to a treacherous rival.

The world heard nothing more from the two explorers until early September, 1909. Then came the stunning news that Frederick Cook had reached the North Pole on April 21, 1908. Five days later, a cable from Robert Peary stated that he too had succeeded, on April 6, 1909.

At the time of Peary's message, Cook had just arrived back in civilization and was being feted for his accomplishment. Gracefully, Cook welcomed the news, saying that the Pole held honor enough for two. It was a sentiment not shared by Peary. When he arrived in Newfoundland, he fired off a telegram claiming that Cook's success was bogus, "a gold brick."

The public fascination with the ensuing controversy rivaled the Dreyfus affair in France or the O.J. Simpson case in our time. Peary lost the early public relations battle. While Cook continued to praise Peary's accomplishments, Peary could not contain his rage. He was like Captain Ahab, driven mad by his obsession with the white whale, and who, after a lifetime of pursuit, discovers that someone else has killed it. For the first time, the public became aware of the great explorer's unpleasant personality.

Peary's handlers eventually came to the rescue, telling him to let them take care of it. Thereafter, Peary stewed quietly while they launched what can only be described as a sophisticated smear campaign. Since Cook's claim was false, it was not hard to raise doubts. Eventually, they won. Cook was disgraced, his claim rejected. The more difficult triumph was ensuring that Peary's own claim never suffered the same scrutiny.

The no-holds-barred controversy led to a bizarre accusation that has hung on till this day. It is possible that Peary engineered the murder of Ross Marvin, Ellesmere's other homicide. Marvin, Peary's young secretary, was sledding back to land with two Greenlanders after helping his commander toward the North Pole in 1909. When the two Greenlanders reached the ship, they claimed that Marvin had fallen through thin ice and drowned. "Marvin's death . . . does not seem natural," wrote Cook perceptively when he heard the news.

In 1925, after Peary's death, one of the natives confessed that the drowning story was untrue; that, in fact, he had shot Marvin. Kudlooktoo had recently converted to Christianity and said he wanted to make a clean breast of it. Marvin had been ill-tempered all the way back and he had threatened to leave behind the second Greenlander, Inukitsoq. Out of loyalty to his partner, Kudlooktoo shot Marvin in the back and pushed him into a lead.

The murder strangely echoes Peeawahto's. Fear of abandonment, the apparent motive. Victim shot from behind with his own rifle, on the Arctic Ocean. The similarity was enough that the United States and Denmark informally agreed that the two murders canceled each other out, and neither man ever faced prosecution.

A relief to Fitzhugh Green, who was indirectly connected to the Marvin investigation. His employer at the time, the publisher George Putnam, was part of a pro-Peary group that went to Greenland to ascertain the truth about Marvin's death. They discovered little, but parts of Kudluktoo's story don't add up. Marvin was an even-tempered man who was well-liked by the Inuit. Even Donald MacMillan stated that the murderer Kudlooktoo "idolized Ross Marvin." It was Kudlooktoo and Inukitsoq who didn't get along. After the shooting, both Inuit were afraid of spirits lurking in Marvin's possessions, so they threw everything away—except a canvas pouch that sat conspicuously on the upstanders of the sled, and which happened to hold Marvin's important testimonial that Peary had reached 86°38' and was continuing north.

Kudlooktoo had a long history with the Peary family. He had been the childhood playmate of Marie, Peary's daughter. The night before Marvin turned back, Peary had had a private meeting with Kudlooktoo in his igloo. It is possible that Kudlooktoo acted as a soldier under orders.

But why? It could only be that Peary had already accepted that he wasn't going to reach the Pole, and insisted that his men join him in the hoax. Matthew Henson, who could not navigate, might not have been privy to this discussion, but the other man, the ambitious skipper Bob Bartlett, would have agreed. Perhaps Marvin didn't. He may have signed a false 86°38' affidavit under coercion, but told Peary that he would never get away with it. Perhaps Peary had it in himself to kill for the North Pole.

A lot of perhaps's. Peary's behavior after his return to the ship was more typical. He kept aloof, he had his men build a polite memorial cairn to Marvin that still stands at Floeberg Beach, and when he reached civilization, he telegraphed the bad news to Marvin's parents, collect.

Just as Peary is hard to like, Cook is hard to dislike. In a way, it's unfair, since both built their reputations by conning the public. But *c'est le ton qui fait la musique.* Peary lied for all the wrong reasons—money, power, fame—and Cook lied because, as he once wrote cheerfully, to him "right and wrong are but a point of view." Even his journals, often prescription pads or booklets with gynecological tables or ads for cure-all elixirs in the back pages, cast this sympathetic charm. I spent a rapt December afternoon among his papers in the Library of Congress just to get a whiff of the man, his handwriting, his style. In particular, I noticed how often his 1893 diary used the word "beautiful." For Cook, every day without a gale was beautiful. Studying their respective stories, I am left with an image of Peary forging doggedly ahead, teeth grit, cursing everything and everyone in his way, and Cook la-de-dahing along, whistling a happy tune, lost in his imagination.

■

For fifty-five years after Peary, the public lost interest in the North Pole. Only aircraft and nuclear submarines passed that way. Then in 1964, the modern renaissance began when Norwegian Bjorn Staib and his team struggled over the unknown surface as far as 86°31', half-way. After Ralph Plaisted's successful 1968 snowmobile expedition, periodic attempts continued to take place, but conditions on the Arctic Ocean remained a mystery. The shifting broken surface and –50°F starting temperature were unfathomable to most trekkers. Expeditions that trained by sleeping in meat lockers or skiing in Lapland usually quit after a few days, citing frostbite or the ever-handy back injury. Despite a few successes, it wasn't until the 1986 American expedition under Will Steger and Paul Schurke that the true challenges of the polar surface became widely known.

Every March, a fresh group of professionals and would-be professionals flock to Resolute to prepare for the five-hour charter flight to their starting point at Ward Hunt Island, on northern Ellesmere. In the blue light of early spring, visitors from half a dozen countries walk the frozen streets, bundled up in colorful Gore-Tex parkas festooned with sponsor labels. Enthusiastically they photograph runny-nosed Inuit kids and polar bear skins stretched on drying racks for their web sites. Although jaded locals call this the Silly Season, it injects hundreds of thousands of dollars into the local economy, mostly through airlines and hotels, which put up the support crews for the two months it takes to reach the Pole.

The hotel where I usually stay is a converted home with a large, heated garage. Here, fit Scandinavians in fleece jackets feverishly pack dried rations into Ziploc bags or tinker with sled harnesses. Silent, unilingual Japanese read paperbacks in the living room and fantasize about smoking indoors. Celebrity adventurers hold court. Newcomers study photographs on the walls from past expeditions. Competing groups work out deals to share charter costs. A foreign television crew may convert one of the larger rooms into a temporary editing studio. Always, a few ill-prepared dreamers hang outside this hubbub, looking lost.

■

Some years ago, my first wife had the unenviable task of explaining my career ambitions to her relatives in New York: "I think he wants to go to the North Pole."

"How long does he plan to stay there?"

In Resolute, the North Pole was in the air and the feeling was contagious. I had already completed two bitterly cold midwinter treks across northern Labrador and retraced Leonidas Hubbard's 1903 canoe expedition up Labrador's Susan River. The North Pole seemed like a good next step.

Although a well-defined career had eluded me, the editor of an outdoor magazine had liked an article I'd done about one of the Labrador treks enough to offer me a full-time writing job. I seemed to be there partly to give credibility to the magazine's otherwise urban staff, which meant that I could still travel for two or three months a year and even be paid for it. I also enjoyed the rest of the work.

I had done my early Labrador expeditions on pennies. Labrador is the cheapest wild place in North America to get to. Because of the Twin Otter charters, the North Pole is the most expensive. It usually takes two to three years to raise the $100,000 or so for a single, bare-bones attempt. Given the notoriously difficult surface, it was likely that I would fail once or twice before succeeding. As I became more educated, I saw that expedition professionals either had family money behind them or spent most of their lives fundraising. Three years as a businessman for three months outdoors. . . this is what being an expedition professional means. Adventurers never revealed this at their triumphant slide shows, just as none of the closet rich guys ever admitted in their inspirational lectures that the best way to follow your dreams is to have a trust fund.

The chairman of the company that owned the magazine I worked for was sympathetic to my ambitions and tried to introduce me to some of Toronto's corporate elite whom he thought might be useful. I just felt awkward. I prized endurance and understood delayed gratification. I could happily walk all day, every day, for months in forty below temperatures; but my patience for occupational boredom was low, and fundraising fell in that category. Three years for three months. I liked the excitement of a real expedition, with its formal goal, its momentum and yes, its attention, but mainly I was out there to be out there. I was, it seemed, an amateur.

■

Not all amateurs fade away like Robert Stein. For every organizer, there were twenty able-bodied seamen who did the grunt work, yet whose stories are a part of history. I remember looking through the personal scrapbook of Pelham Aldrich, the British officer who explored Ellesmere's north coast under George Nares. Aldrich is a major figure, and the cape that bears his name is the northernmost land on the continent. Yet at an honorific polar dinner, he once humbly asked the great Nansen to autograph his menu. Later, like any fan, he glued the souvenir into his scrapbook. This touching gesture made me realize that even Aldrich had been an amateur, whose daily job happened to position him in the course of history. If I wasn't cut out to be a Nares, maybe I could still be an Aldrich.

One day, my local newspaper reported that a group of Russians were in town looking for Canadians to take part in a joint expedition from Russia to Ellesmere via the North Pole. I applied and, with my future partner Graeme, was one of six accepted for consideration. Four would make the cut.

These were the optimistic days of glasnost. Communism still ruled, but the Soviet Union was beginning to open up after seventy years of being a riddle, within a mystery, inside an enigma. We were the first westerners to visit several parts of the country and we became, within the U.S.S.R., symbols of the growing détente.

The Russian polar group had been active since the 1970s. They had skied to the North Pole in 1979 from Severnaya Zemlya, an easier but more dangerous route than Ellesmere because of the open water near shore. The Russians followed this success with other extreme treks that no one in the West had heard of, including a truly frightening 450-mile ski between floating Soviet ice stations in winter darkness. They fell in the ocean; they hallucinated from the weeks of travel by starlight; they shivered all night in their skimpy sleeping bags, their toes frostbit beyond redemption. In terms of sheer misery, this ranked right up there with the winter quest for emperor penguin eggs that Apsley Cherry-Garrard described in *The Worst Journey in the World*. "Was good experiment," enthused one Russian. "It showed us how much we are able to bear."

Most of the veterans were now in their forties. One was fifty-one. The group's founder, Dmitri Shparo, was a household name in the U.S.S.R. By Western standards, he was yesterday's man, a throwback to the military-style leaders of the big Himalayan expeditions of the 1950s and 1960s. Western expeditions were now alpine-style—light, informal, among equals. But the Russian soul hungered for autocrats, and Shparo's system, with a cadre of foot soldiers who never saw the big picture, an inner politburo of trusted advisers, and himself permanently at the helm, was much like the Soviet regime itself. We knew that we were along because the Department of External Affairs in Ottawa had demanded Canadian participation before giving Shparo permission to land on northern Ellesmere. But the Canadians were an ambitious group, and few were content with our lot as foot soldiers. "We're dummies with Canadian flags on our foreheads," grumbled one.

Shparo and I did not hit it off, and it was clear that my chances of making the cut were slim. Most of the Canadians responded at least partly to his charisma. At the time Graeme was searching for a polar big brother under whom to apprentice, and found Shparo fascinating. Jacques Bouffard, a Quebecois mountaineer, had a warm, soft personality that brought out the paternal side of Shparo, who often hugged him and tenderly plucked bits of fluff from his eyebrows. Only Richard Weber and I spoke bluntly—but Weber was the strongest Canadian, a former member of the national cross-country ski team, and had already been to the Pole with a well-known American expedition, so his acceptance was considered a given. My excessive curiosity about Russia also seemed to irritate Shparo who, according to one of his inner circle, wondered whether I was a spy: "He's too curious about everything." In fact, I was simply developing a fascination for sad and screwball Russia that in time would rival my love for the Arctic.

Although Shparo was a better leader, in many ways he and Peary had a lot in common. Like Peary, Shparo moved in exalted political circles; his allies belonged to the inner circle of the Kremlin itself. Like Peary, you couldn't trust him, because in his high-stakes game, there were no truths, only half-truths, and calculated omissions. He encouraged openness, but held his own cards very close to his chest. Like Peary, he was tough and stubborn, and his political acumen was perhaps the Soviet equivalent of knowing how to raise money. "In the U.S.S.R. there is always money if necessary," one of them explained. "What is needed is permission."

It had taken Shparo eight years to get permission to ski to the North Pole. His idea to cross the Arctic Ocean was an old one too, which had had to be put off for several years because of cool international relations after the Soviet invasion of Afghanistan. They were used to waiting years and then throwing together a major expedition in a few frenetic weeks. Since official approval opened all doors instantly, the crazy pace actually worked. Their high-level connections even greased Western gears. McDonalds became an immediate sponsor, and shortly afterward received permission to open its first restaurant in Moscow.

This was exciting. It was about the Arctic, yet it was about more than the Arctic. I also had to admit that despite my distrust of this Russian Peary, he had put together a remarkable group. It was as if eight or ten of the best at anything in the United States—scientists, adventurers, musicians, software designers—were part of a single team. The moment they entered a room, the energy level jumped to a higher quantum state. The older ones were team players to the core; a few younger talents were secret individualists. When the Soviet Union broke up in 1991, so did the group. The team players retired while independents such as Fedor Konyukhov and Misha Malakhov made their own impressive North Pole treks in a freewheeling new country where no permission was necessary, as long as money was available.

Most of the Russians were arctic plodders, but that was partly due to their mode of travel. The Soviet Union lacked plastics and fiberglass, so they had always carried their loads in hundred-pound backpacks, which forces a plodding pace. Understandably, the conservative ones regarded sleds as unethical.

The least conservative of the group was Misha Malakhov, a 33-year-old thoracic surgeon from Ryazan, south of Moscow. He was also the strongest of us all, and on the training trips he had the superman's typical role of sweeper: He kept an eye on the back of the pack, and if there was a problem, he sped up to the front to alert the leaders. Malakhov had never trained but was a born endurance athlete. Unlike his compatriots, he was open to trying Western equipment and learning English. In camp, it was common to hear him practicing the new words he'd learned that day. I did my best to mislead him by offering archaic constructions as everyday jargon. He soon got wise, but not until I overheard him ask one of the others in his gravelly baritone, "Prithee, whither goest?"

My relations with Shparo remained less congenial, and rather than stealing my piece of the Pole, I walked away with the consolation prize of an enduring love of Russian travel. Three of the original group dropped out of their own accord: Graeme, because Shparo's toasts to "Victory" and "Conquering the Arctic" weren't what he wanted, and the two Quebec climbers, because they were fed up with the power struggles and because they found the Arctic dull, as mountaineers often do. Weber quickly found a couple of substitutes to fill the Canadian quota, and the expedition set off, and succeeded.

It was the first expedition to cross the Arctic Ocean in a single year, but its real legacy was the partnership that developed between Malakhov and Weber, both strong athletes in their prime, both mentally tough, both good businessmen and both with more than half a year of experience on the polar ice. By comparison, Peary had spent only forty days on that unique surface before his 1909 attempt.

Inevitably, the pair set their sights on the last great polar problem: getting to the Pole and back without air support. Since Peary and Cook had lost their credibility, the chance of becoming a part of history still existed. The first Bulgarian to the Pole, or the youngest, or the first solo, would always be a fine distinction confined to expedition literature. But to do the first unsupported round trip was to become part of a saga that dated back to Henry Hudson's farthest north in 1607, or earlier. It was to win a place, if only a footnote, in the historic quest for the North Pole.

The biggest difficulty with the North Pole has always been the tiny travel window of March to May. Before that, and bottomless night still grips the Arctic. Much after that, and the glue binding the polar jigsaw puzzle comes unstuck. The pieces drift apart, and travel becomes suitable only for amphibians. Some porridge-like ice can neither be walked over nor paddled through.

After one failure, Malakhov and Weber tried again in 1995. This time, they played a clever trump card. North Pole expeditions usually can't begin before the sun returns in early March because the pilots can't see to land at the starting point. Weber managed to convince the charter airline to land them on Ward Hunt Island in mid-February by the light of military parachute flares. They also replaced the Twin Otter's nose with a nose light from a Hawker-Siddeley 748.

The head start allowed them to ferry their loads forty-five miles out, then return to the heated shelter on Ward Hunt Island to rest and dry their sleeping bags. When they set out again in early March, they had a trail and half their gear beyond the worst of the ice. They were also the first to use a combination of backpacks and small sleds, which works best on that surface. The big sleds I use for Ellesmere travel are too heavy for a constant diet of rough ice. It's faster to make several trips with smaller loads.

Four hundred pounds per man makes for slow going, and it took them two months before they had eaten enough of their load to start putting in days of ten miles and more. Weber had found his first two North Pole expeditions relatively easy, thanks to the plodders who kept the group pace well within his comfort zone, and he spoke disparagingly of the slowpokes. But now he was paired with someone whose endurance seemed to have no limits, and a couple of times Weber was near the edge.

The expedition lasted into June, and breakup, which creeps down from the North Pole, was quickly overtaking them. The last week was a fitting conclusion to the centuries-old race for the Pole. They drove for Ward Hunt Island on little sleep as the ice disintegrated underneath them. They reached land on June 15, with no food left. The first expedition to the Pole and back succeeded through the cooperation, not the rivalry, of the two main participants.

The story briefly made the papers and networks, but it never really took off. Canadian heroes tend to be plucky cripples and ugly ducklings, not tough arctic skiers. And the starmaking U.S. media would never be that interested in a historic trek done by a Canadian and a Russian. Even *National Geographic*, which over the years had endorsed lesser North Pole successes by Norwegians, Japanese, French, and Americans, virtually ignored the story because the outspoken Weber had made no secret of his belief that Peary hadn't even come close.

By then I had abandoned the dream of my own North Pole roundtrip, but I was still a little sad at their success. Dreams don't disappear when you let them go; they stay as dreams until someone else successfully claims them. Then they die. But I remembered skiing beside Weber while training for the Russian expedition. On each stride, his skis slid about three inches further than mine. It doesn't sound like much, but on their marathon roundtrip, it would have added up to an extra hundred and fifty miles. Their margin for success had been so narrow that I would not have won the race against breakup. The North Pole without airdrops, like doing Everest solo without oxygen, demanded a higher class of athlete.

■

Six weeks after Malakhov and Weber scrambled ashore, I made my first visit to Ward Hunt Island, named after a 300-pound First Lord of the Admiralty. "It was said that he lent weight to Her Majesty's councils," said Hattersley-Smith. From the ocean side, the island actually resembles a very fat man lying on his back.

Thanks to its old military shelters, Ward Hunt Island has become the Everest Base Camp of North Pole expeditions. The accumulated garbage of dozens of broken and fulfilled dreams littered the ground, and I was helping the wardens of Ellesmere's national park with the cleanup. It was a worthwhile project, but to be here as a garbagepicker and not a dreamer embarking on a historic quest was bittersweet.

In March, when the Pole trips begin, Ward Hunt Island is a frigid, all-white world, but in summer it is dank and grey. Long sashes of fog wrap around the waists of the mountains to the south. Just off land, the Ward Hunt Ice Shelf undulates in long parallel rolls toward the polar pack. In summer, turquoise meltwater twenty feet deep fills the hollows. On his soggy 1906 trek, Peary described the ice shelf as "a gigantic potato field, with a long blue lake or a rushing stream in every furrow."

As we scooped up the cans and wrappers, Chief Park Warden Renee Wissink pointed out a tin of asparagus soup from the 1968 Plaisted expedition, the first successful surface journey. Most of the junk was vaguely comical: Hawaiian pineapple juice, root beer, Camel cigarettes, yeast, shoe polish, hot curry powder, and something called simply Brown Sauce. One Briton had prudently brought a tin of shark repellent.

It seemed a shame to burn this stuff. All Ellesmere's precious artifacts had once been garbage, and I could imagine future collectors of North Pole memorabilia bidding vigorously at Sotheby's for the asparagus soup. In the end, the only souvenir I couldn't resist was an army strongbox with the words "Explosive Bomb" redundantly stenciled on one side.

■

Mountaineers seem to be about twenty years ahead of polar travelers. Until the 1960s, climbers were often tougher mentally than physically. Legends such as Britain's Don Whillans never trained because, they said, it took away from their drinking time. Instead, they whipped their reluctant bodies into shape during the hundred-mile hike to base camp or with warm-up climbs. In the 1970s, people like Reinhold Messner and Peter Habeler brought a new level of fitness to the sport. Instead of greeting the day with a hangover and a Galoise, they ran up 5,000-foot mountains before breakfast. Their record times up classical yardsticks like the North Face of the Eiger were astonishing. When they took their abilities to the Himalayas, they accomplished in small teams what previous generations had needed armies to do.

In the early 1990s, when Messner was almost fifty and past his prime for top-level mountaineering, he discovered the polar regions. Soon he was doing remarkable treks across Greenland and Antarctica. His younger partner on the Antarctic trip, a well-known German polar traveler, could not even keep up.

Messner had discovered that even at fifty, a superb athlete can still make his mark in the Arctic because most polar travelers were like earlier generations of climbers—tough in the head but plodders, people of merely above average fitness. Some even smoked, just as Ernest Shackleton had smoked ninety years before. The successes of these plodders were sometimes remarkable, but often the failures were due, not to the nut being too thick, but to the nutcracker being too weak.

Real athletes have finally arrived in the polar regions. The Norwegian Børge Ousland skied across Antarctica at speeds of up to a hundred and forty miles a day, using a large kite to tow him in the wind. In 1998, a group that included an Olympic gold medalist in cross-country skiing tried to reach the North Pole in twenty-five days, and just missed. An unsupported crossing of the Arctic Ocean was recently accomplished; a similar trek across the entire Northwest Passage is within easy reach.

Even the psychological barriers of the North Pole have been broken. Veterans like Malakhov hire themselves out as polar consultants, so even novice crews make it occasionally. Expeditions come prepared to make only a mile a day at first, and later, to lose hard-won miles as they sleep, when southerly currents push them back toward land. The polar tread-mill can still defeat, but its powers to surprise are greatly diminished.

Exploration has given way to three types of modern expeditions: Hard Travel, Stunts, and Gimmicks. The main purpose of a Stunt is to attract attention: "Hey Ma, look at me!" It may be dangerous, such as going over Niagara Falls in a barrel, but its silliness detracts from the guts or technical inventiveness it may also require. A Japanese man who tried to ski down part of Mount Everest fell after the first few feet and now holds the record for the best-documented high-altitude slide in history. Pogo sticks are not possible on the Arctic Ocean, but the North Pole has already experienced ultralight aircraft, motorcycles, parachutes, and hot-air balloons. One motorcyclist stuffed his handlebars with jellybeans and carried an oversized sleeping bag for himself and his machine. He failed, but a later motorcyclist had better luck, or better jellybeans. "As time goes on and more and more gets accomplished, it'll get zanier and zanier," an airline manager in Resolute predicted ten years ago.

Rather than set new limits of human prowess, the professional arctic plodder now has to rely heavily on the Gimmick. In the footsteps of X, or the 150th anniversary of Y, or the first of an infinite number of increasingly meaningless distinctions—the first all-Turkish team, the first to do the North Pole, the South Pole, and Mount Everest in a single year, the first breast cancer survivor . . . anything with enough contemporary sizzle to raise the money needed to pull it off.

The Gimmick can be educational, but to my mind, Hard Travel comes closest in spirit to true exploration, which ended on Ellesmere in the late 1930s with the arrival of the airplane. In the right hands, Hard Travel can surpass even exploration. Wilfred Thesiger's crossings of the Empty Quarter or Sir Richard Burton's pilgrimage to Mecca weren't the first Western journeys, but they were the best.

Nowadays, you can cruise to the North Pole on a luxury icebreaker, or fly there on a Twin Otter, pop champagne, and whack an orange golf ball around, but for those who go under their own power, the North Pole will always be, at least partly, Hard Travel.

Chapter Five

Dance of the Sea Ice

If you're looking for hard travel, you can't go wrong choosing a place with the word "Hell" in its name. There are many hells. The United States has over six hundred of them, Canada sixty-seven. Hell Gate is Ellesmere's only official hell. Its discoverer, Otto Sverdrup, wrote of lifting sleds over boulders the size of cottages, and of ice racing through violent whirlpools. "Although it may be difficult to find a more deterring name," he said, "it is far too weak to express our impression of the place." It sounded great.

In mid-April, our chartered plane skimmed to a halt amid a shower of fine snow on Goose Fiord, near Hell Gate. Ice crystals fell out of a clear sky and transformed the sunball into a many-armed Star of Bethlehem. A two hundred and fifty mile sled journey stretched ahead of us.

Goose Fiord lies in the heart of Otto Sverdrup country. It is impossible to travel Ellesmere and not cross paths with the ghost of this phlegmatic Norwegian, whose 1898 to 1902 expedition covered 6,758 miles of Ellesmere and Axel Heiberg. His vessel, the *Fram*, spent two years frozen into Goose Fiord. Norwegian *finesko* boots had touched every hill and pass and point of land. Every place-name in the vicinity was originally Norwegian, though many have since been anglicized and at least one edited for propriety: Excrement Bay is now the polite Cross Bay.

From the air, the dark water of Hell Gate jumped out of the whiteness of the April landscape. We could see the cliffs that plunged into the narrow strait. In some wildernesses, this would indicate an impossible route; but on Ellesmere hard rock is rare, and frost-shattered sedimentary walls leave a narrow apron of rubble at the base over which a traveler can scramble. Still, our work was cut out for us.

My partner George, a forty-eight year old Toronto physicist, had spent almost every summer for the last twenty-five years on long northern canoe trips but had never sledded in the High Arctic. Canoeing hones wilderness judgment but tends to draw contemplative rather than athletic travelers. Sledding is both contemplative and athletic, and I wondered how my trail-toughened but overweight companion would take to a marathon walk.

We camped on the ice, organized our gear and set out for the polynya the next morning. Our light plastic sleds scratched along the rough, windblown ice. When I was behind, I saw that George had an uncanny knack for finding sharp nubs of ice over which to drag his fragile craft. When I was in front, George noticed that I exhibited the same clumsiness.

This was the story of our trip. The "Hell" in Hell Gate turned out not to be the terrain but each other. George was furious over my experimental sleds, which developed rips immediately. Also, like many wilderness travelers with unrelated full-time jobs, he had little sympathy for the professional aura I had tried to bring to our expedition through a few sponsors and regular photo setups. It spoiled something for him, although he too liked taking pictures.

For my part, I chafed at his pose of moral superiority. Just because he had never tried to make a living from the outdoors did not mean that he loved it more than I. Just because he had raised a family did not mean that I, childless, dwelled on a lesser plane. He gave the sort of passive-aggressive digs that I expected only from my mother-in-law, and I answered back sharply. As far as I was concerned, the moment you staked the moral high ground, you lost it, no matter how admirable your deeds. His unaccustomed role as the weaker member also increased tension.

Even among friends, it is psychologically crippling to be forever the slow one.

Our relationship had begun strangely. George was an avid collector of northern books, who pursued new outdoor friends with the same enthusiasm. An early article of mine prompted him to drop me a line, praising my work. When I moved to Toronto, we spoke again and I realized that George was more peer than fan. His house was a social center for wilderness canoeists, and although I didn't share the passion for canoeing, I liked the people. Three years later, we decided to do a trip together.

I don't remember if there were warning signs, but we were in the tent after the first hard day when the rupture occurred. I discovered that George—who had organized part of our provisions—had brought less

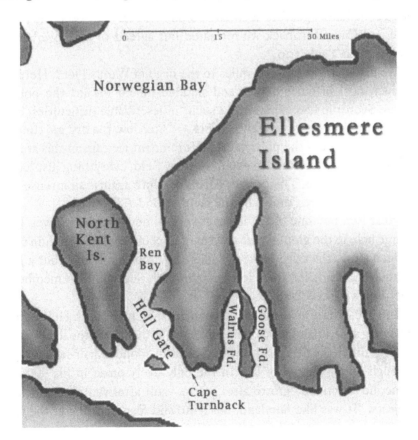

butter than we had agreed on. Husky travelers such as George often used wilderness expeditions as weight-loss programs, but I was a skinny son of a bitch who believed that if you worked like a slave, you should eat like a king. Butter added staying power to our freeze-dried dinners. "I wish you'd told me," I grumbled.

"Just fuck off!" screamed George. "You can have all my butter if you want. Now shut up. And don't tell me to calm down."

The outburst was so out of character from his usual absentminded-professor demeanor that I assumed he was stressed by the rips in his sled and would later apologize. But he never did. He seemed content to never speak again. I eventually broke the silence a day later. By now, Hell Gate had narrowed and our flimsy sleds continued to tear on the bare sea ice. George wanted to abandon Hell Gate in favor of Sverdrup's easy overland route to Norwegian Bay. I hated to give up our one bit of fierce terrain, but a conciliatory gesture seemed in order. Halfway between the Bay of Woe and Cape Turnback we retreated but agreed to hike overland to Hell Gate as a side trip.

We made an easy fifteen miles to the head of Walrus Fiord. Here, we cached most of our supplies and sledded inland toward the polynya where Sverdrup had experienced such "indescribable difficulties."

Western Ellesmere has few glaciers—it's too low, too dry, too sunny—but moisture from the polynya had left remnant ice caps in this area. In April, it was hard to tell ice cap from snow field, everything just looked indescribably pure. The perfect curves of white against an intense blue sky could have been drawn by the hand of God.

Near Ren Bay, one of the ice caps slipped down to valley level. I saw a large hole in the ground that neither of us could explain. We didn't dare get too close, the edge looked fragile, the drop formidable, but a little further on, a smaller crack led underground. Suddenly I remembered. Sverdrup's ice cave!

In 1900, Sverdrup avoided a second entanglement with Hell Gate by following an overland route similar to ours. At that time, the ice cap completely filled the Ren Valley, but Sverdrup found a hair-raising route through a long tunnel of ice. In the only lively prose in his 900-page tome, he described "grotto after grotto, vault after vault" of subglacial majesty. "It was like fairyland, beautiful and fear-inspiring at the same time," he wrote. "I dared not speak. . . . I felt mean and contemptible as I drove through all this purity."

The ice cap no longer barred the valley, but part of the tunnel remained. Leaving our sleds, we approached the crack in the ground. Drifting snow had created a ramp down which we slid ten feet into the cave. A subway tunnel of ice, carved by meltwater during the summer, led deep into the glacier. Strangely, I could see light up ahead.

Boulders of ice from the ceiling littered the floor of the tunnel. Silently we moved forward. After fifty yards, the tunnel opened into a large amphitheater. Part of the ceiling had collapsed, creating a natural skylight. Seracs leaned overhead. I felt dwarfed, yet exultant. I had often tried to imagine what it would have been like to discover Niagara Falls. A natural scene so grand that it deserved world renown, yet it was totally unknown. This was it. Humility, awe, excitement, fear.

"Sverdrup's ice cave!" I whispered to George.

"I've never seen anything like this," he whispered back.

The tunnel continued into a second amphitheater, also lit by a skylight. This skylight, now fifty feet above, was the hole in the ground we had seen. Our footprints, the first since Sverdrup's, looked out of place in the virgin snow.

Beyond this amphitheater, the tunnel narrowed. I had to stoop, then crawl. Millions of tons of blue ice pressed against my back. I was a quarter of a mile under the ice cap. Time to retreat.

I considered myself a traveler, not an explorer. Explorer was just a word that sounded good when you were trying to raise money, or when journalists needed a synonym for adventurer. Nevertheless, those two hours in the ice cave carried me back a hundred years, to an era when exploration was not just a sales pitch.

For two days after our visit to the ice cave, George and I got along, brought together by the shared emotional moment. It was still early in the trip, and I was hoping for reconciliation. George was an interesting man, and I like interesting people. When we humped our gear up a steep slope, I wondered aloud whether the heavy backpacks gave us surer footing. "Elephants are not good mountain climbers," was the physicist's wonderfully oblique response. Even if he never spoke except to utter such Confucian remarks, I would have considered him good company.

After our exploration of Hell Gate, we hurried back to Goose Fiord in a sixteen-hour push, worried that a polar bear might find our cache of food. We were lucky. A bear had recently bedded down on Goose Fiord—its belly had melted a depression in the ice—but the cache was undisturbed. We had a long sleep, cooked up a celebratory breakfast, and lounged around for hours, making repairs to the troublesome sleds.

When we began sledding, our truce quickly burst. George was still tired from the previous day and after two hours he irritably demanded to camp. The reconciliation was not going to happen. For the next two weeks, as we rounded Norwegian Bay and swung overland toward Grise Fiord, we maintained a cool civility. He obligingly posed for pictures, I took turns hauling his sled, whose bottom was now as full of homemade stitches, eighty-one of them, as the battered face of an old hockey goalie. Mine fared only slightly better. Although our sleds now pulled like bags of cement, we made our daily ten or twelve miles in increasingly short days over the good snow. Sometimes, George spoke wearily of getting old and tired. We both enthused over the landscape. Maybe we exchanged three hundred words a day.

On the twenty-fourth day, we pulled into Grise Fiord. I went off and did a second sled trip with another partner while George flew home. Once in a while, we bumped into each other socially and exchanged a few polite words, but we never really spoke again.

■

It is hard to imagine that Otto Sverdrup's well-oiled expedition suffered from such conflicts. It takes a lot of reading between the lines to get beyond the front of good chums executing their tasks with clockwork precision. Most explorers of that era washed their dirty laundry in private, but Sverdrup was obsessively reticent. "You had to take the words out of his mouth with a fork," says Kåre Berg, curator of Oslo's Fram Museum. "He was the most silent man in Norway." When he did speak, he used such a low voice that it was hard to hear him.

Photos of Sverdrup show a stocky man with an ulu-shaped beard glowering at the camera. His red beard thinned with the years, but the scowl endured. Whether in arctic wool or tropical whites, whether at age twenty-five or sixty, Sverdrup's serious, self-contained visage never cracked.

Sverdrup went to sea at seventeen, but his polar career began when he joined Fridtjof Nansen's ski trek across Greenland in 1888. Among polar explorers, Nansen was in an intellectual class by himself. By twenty-seven, he was already pioneering a Norwegian renaissance in cross-country skiing and was one of the fathers of the science of neurology. Now his restless mind turned to the polar regions. His brother knew Sverdrup and recommended him. Nansen sized him up as the ideal second-in-command—strong, intelligent but too retiring to compete for the limelight.

The success of Nansen's Greenland crossing made him famous. While the young adventurer flamboyantly strode the Norwegian capital in his wolf skins, basking in the attention, Sverdrup went back to looking for work. He applied for a post as captain of a supply ship on Lake Mjøsa, Norway's largest lake, but this man who would become the best ice navigator of his day didn't get the job because the company was unwilling to hire someone "who was unfamiliar with the difficult ice conditions on this lake."

When Nansen devised his plan to reach the North Pole in an ice-resistant ship, he offered Sverdrup the captaincy. Sverdrup's great opportunities all came to him through Nansen. Sverdrup, never forced to overextend himself by a hunger for fame, quietly accomplished every task that came his way.

Together with a ship-builder, Sverdrup and Nansen designed the *Fram*, a little ship as solid and unassuming as Sverdrup himself. In the open sea, it sailed "with the smooth aplomb of an old barrel," but its walnut-shaped hull allowed it to be squeezed upward by the pack ice, not crushed like the svelte, traditional V-hull. In 1893, they lodged the *Fram* in the moving ice off northern Russia.

For the next two years, they drifted. It became clear that their course would not take them over the North Pole, so Nansen left the *Fram* in Sverdrup's hands and set out by dogsled toward the North Pole with one companion. They fell short but achieved a new Farthest North and safely reached uninhabited Franz Josef Land. Here, they overwintered in a stone shelter, well-fed on walrus and polar bear meat. The next summer, they had the incredible fortune to bump into the only other human being in that region, the British explorer Frederick Jackson, who brought them home. With less drama but with superb skill, Sverdrup likewise managed to pilot the *Fram* safely back to Norway.

Those two years on the *Fram* must have sated Nansen with the intellectual boredom of polar expeditions, for he never went north again. He took up politics, did pioneering work in oceanography and fluid dynamics, became a diplomat and won the Nobel Peace Prize. But he remained an arctic elder statesman for the rest of his life, whom up-and-coming explorers approached for advice and endorsement. Among his lesser-known accomplishments, he popularized the pressurized trail stove that everyone uses today. Before Nansen, explorers essentially melted their drinking water over cans of Sterno.

Nansen's strength was conception; Sverdrup's was execution. Nansen was a visionary; but Sverdrup was the one you wanted on your team. During the *Fram's* drift, Nansen alienated the crew with his moodiness and haughty ways. Back in civilization, his personality could electrify a room; but that same exalted presence wore thin in the confines of a ship. Sverdrup, meanwhile, was at his best in cramped quarters. He moved about the ship so quietly that he was barely noticed, but his rock-solid competence gave everyone a sense of security.

■

I met Sverdrup's biographer, Per Egil Hegge, in Oslo's Grand Hotel, over a typical Scandinavian breakfast of cold fish strips in sauce. One of Norway's most prominent journalists, Hegge had been a member of the White House press corps during the Reagan years, and *Aftenposten's* correspondent in the Soviet Union until he was expelled for smuggling some of Alexander Solzhenitsyn's writings to the West. A short man with yellowing blond hair, impeccably dressed in a dark suit, Hegge was one of those daunting European polyglots who functioned effortlessly in Swedish, Russian, English and Spanish, as well as his native Norwegian. Though the Arctic seemed to intimidate him, he was clearly, in his own way, an extremophile.

With his most un-Norwegian dislike of cold and the outdoors, Hegge had not made a pilgrimage to Ellesmere for his research, but he did visit the town in eastern Cuba where Sverdrup later invested in a sugar plantation. "Sverdrup wanted to be a businessman," said Hegge, "but he wasn't very good at it."

Undoubtedly the laconic Sverdrup had a hard time with the charm side of business. Who would want to buy a ton of sugar from a man who glowered and fidgeted uncomfortably and said little? Hegge later showed me a pathetic book called *Commercial Cuba* that Sverdrup had read during his plantation years. Kind of an early how-to book, it revealed such salient information as, "Cubans of both sexes pride themselves in the smallness of their feet." I felt a rare pang of sympathy for Sverdrup, so trapped in his skin of awkwardness that he sought answers in this goofy volume. Over a campfire with close friends, he sometimes loosened up, but mainly the Puritan temperament ruled. On Ellesmere, his crew surprised him for his forty-fifth birthday by composing a heroic song about him. Sverdrup took the gesture impatiently but later regretted his lack of grace. In the most revealing lines in his journal, he wrote the next day, "I was stupid again. I just can't pay back properly the people who praise me. I'm so strange."

Thanks to Sverdrup's efforts, the *Fram* was preserved as a museum and today sits under a giant A-frame roof on the Bygdøy Peninsula, across from downtown Oslo. Over 250,000 people a year file through its companionways and peer into the tiny, glassed-in quarters where Sverdrup, Nansen, and Amundsen spent their vital years. Next door, the slicker, more commercial Kon-Tiki Museum celebrates Thor Heyerdahl's trans-Pacific raft journey. In my early twenties, I had loved Heyerdahl's blend of adventure and rebel science, but an unimpressed Paul Theroux writes, "In a lifetime of nutty theorizing, Heyerdahl's single success was his proof, in Kon-Tiki, that six middle-class Scandinavians could successfully crash-land their raft on a coral atoll in the middle of nowhere."

The *Fram* has no such detractors; it is indisputably the greatest of all polar ships. I spent a day at the museum, gazing at such artifacts as Amundsen's cheeky telegram to Robert Scott—"Beg to inform you *Fram* proceeding Antarctic"—and trying to guess which sled or anorak belonged to Sverdrup's voyage. A thick crystal in the ceiling of each room let in light from the outside deck.

Sverdrup's room on the *Fram* was no larger than anyone else's. It overlooked the common area, where all seventeen men ate together, Sverdrup's democratic style contrasting with the aristocratic Nansen's habit of dining apart. In the tiny galley, the alcoholic cook Lindstrøm whipped up his fish balls and muskox smorgasbord. But it was the medical chest, with the square compartments for different-sized bottles, that intrigued me most.

■

Of the three different Ellesmere harbors where Sverdrup wintered, Fram Haven is the most evocative, but few go there. The kayakers and scientists at nearby Alexandra Fiord prefer to stay in those gentle inner waters. Fram Haven lies along a storm-blasted coast. Winds at Alexandra Fiord can scream too, when katabatics flow down the Twin Glaciers, but its personality is normally sunny. Fram Haven has a raw and gloomy feel. A weathered cross overlooking the harbor adds to the dark mood.

Or maybe when last there I was just in a rotten temper. It had taken me three frustrating days to sled the eighteen miles from Alexandra Fiord to Fram Haven. I'd made some judgment errors, grappling with rough ice rather than hugging the shore. I wasted half a day battling forward at a hundred yards an hour over what resembled a large field of overturned furniture.

Using one of Sverdrup's photos for reference, I hauled into Fram Haven and set my tent on the approximate winter berth of the *Fram.* The glacier at the head of the bay had receded dramatically over the last century, but little else had changed. A rusted eye bolt, to which the ship had been moored by a long chain, protruded from the bedrock near shore. Small piles of rocks that Sverdrup's mapmaker had built as trigonometric points dotted the hills. Slinging my shotgun across my back as insurance against the polar bears whose tracks were common here, I hiked up to Johan Svendsen's cross on the knoll above Rice Strait. The writing on the wood was beginning to fade, but the doctor's name was still legible. Most prominent of all were the four elegant letters in the lower right-hand corner of the crosspiece: *Fram.*

Svendsen did not die here but about twenty-five miles away at a camp called Fort Juliana. The outline of a tentsite plus a few small items, most notably a rusted jackknife, remained on the gravel bench. Fort Juliana was much more cheerful than claustrophobic Fram Haven. A stream ran past. Snowbirds flittered and twittered, and glaucous gulls and guillemots wheeled about, uttering sharp cries. Svendsen had been alone here looking after the dogs while the others were away hunting. They were within sight of Fort Juliana on their return when they saw the doctor pacing nervously back and forth outside the tent. Then to their horror, he put a rifle to his head. The noise of the gunshot was lost in the wind, but they saw him crumple to the ground.

Svendsen, thirty-three, had been a popular physician in Norway's remote Lofoten Islands. The expedition group photo shows a man with big melancholy eyes and a handlebar moustache, looking as far away from the camera as possible. Those evasive eyes guarded a dark secret. Svendsen had been a morphine addict who had gone north hoping to cure himself. He had not succeeded. All winter, he dipped into the expedition's morphine, perhaps from the same medical chest that sits today in his old quarters at the Fram Museum. Now, as the Arctic pulsed briefly with life, he gave in to his despair.

In his understated way, Otto Sverdrup was devastated. "That scoundrel of a doctor, why should he go out and kill himself?" he lamented in his journal. No one had had any idea of Svendsen's demons until they read the dead man's diary. Gloomily, they trudged back to Fram Haven with the body. After a ceremony, they committed it to an open part of Rice Strait and erected the memorial cross which looks out from Fram Haven toward the cliffs of sinister Pim Island.

Sverdrup never revealed the cause of his physician's death. Until recently, it was thought that he had died of a heart attack. In *New Land*, Sverdrup merely states that Svendsen "had overrated his strength. The

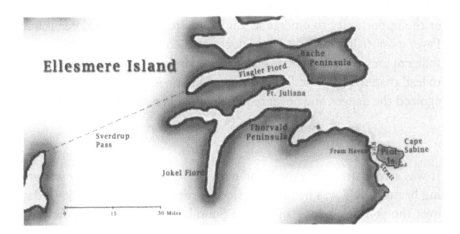

great mistake had been that, whereas all the other members of the expedition had undergone strict medical examination, the doctor had never been examined."

Remarkably, Sverdrup never mentions in his journal that the doctor on the first *Fram* expedition, Henrik Blessing, had also been a morphine addict. During their trans-polar drift, Blessing had injected himself with morphine for six weeks, supposedly to test a theory that laxatives reduced withdrawal symptoms. The daily injections of morphine soon replaced scientific curiosity about withdrawal symptoms, and Blessing was noticeably fuddled on several occasions. Sverdrup was aware of this and even tried to lock the morphine away, yet after Svendsen's death at Fort Juliana, nowhere did Sverdrup write down what must have passed through his mind: "Oh no, not another Blessing."

Sverdrup's two morphine addicts weren't the only medical troublemakers in the annals of polar exploration. Doctors often had stormy relationships with their leaders that went beyond professional differences of opinion. Adolphus Greely's physician despised him and tried to incite mutiny, and Greely had longed to execute him for insubordination. Three of Peary's four doctors understandably fell out with their meanspirited commander. Dr. Harrison Hunt disliked the clay-footed hero MacMillan. And Dr. Bessels probably put the arsenic in the coffee that poisoned Charles Francis Hall.

Sometimes this conflict was the individualist rebelling against military rule. Sometimes the doctors were the only ones perceptive enough to see that their emperor had no clothes. Others nursed secret ambitions and volunteered their medical skills in exchange for an arctic apprenticeship or the opportunity to emerge as the real hero. Austrian explorer Julius Payer essentially warned against doctors when he wrote that, "The intelligent crew, by reason of its greater independence, is one more difficult to lead than the ignorant." It was the pragmatic Amundsen who first recognized the danger, and never brought a doctor on any of his expeditions.

■

It was a year after the expedition with George, and everything was going beautifully. I was hauling my sled twenty-five to thirty miles a day over the styrofoam snow of Eureka Sound, on my way from Eureka to

Grise Fiord. There was little time to do anything but walk, but I didn't mind. It made existence so simple. For once, the meaning of life was clear. Mileage was everything. At the end of every twelve-hour march, I ate a freeze-dried supper in my little mountain tent and gazed proudly at the huge gulps of map I had consumed that day. That first spoonful of supper was bliss. The chores were over, I could relax. I could sleep as long as I wanted. Only a full bladder eventually drove me out of the bag, and that was the signal for the next stage to begin.

The hundred-and-thirty-pound sled bounced easily behind on the sastrugi. I stopped briefly every hour to swig from my water bottles and to grab some food to nibble as I went. My feet flew in their sealskin boots, a hundred and twenty steps a minute. Even hard snow has better and worse patches, requiring nimble judgment calls that made each step a kind of dance. I called it the Dance of the Sea Ice. "I could have danced all night, I could have pranced all night," I sang aloud. Occasionally I shouted nonsense words like "Yolt!" and "Galaboof!" at the top of my lungs. Days passed in the joy of perpetual motion.

I was putting in such long hours that it took about four days to work my way around the clock. Twelve hours on the trail makes each day roughly thirty hours long. That is why High Arctic travelers refer not to days but to sleeps. If I woke up shortly after midnight, my journal might register two May 7s but no May 8. I enjoyed having breakfast at ten p.m. and manhauling all night in broad daylight. It was like being on another planet with twin suns. At this time of year, the snow was also firmer at night and on calm, clear days, of which there were many, the daytime sun kept the tent almost room temperature as I slept.

These long days were hard, but the purity of the white world around me and my dedication to the task at hand made my mood light and happy. I was a walking machine. I was born to walk, programmed to keep walking. Around hour ten, when my body began to feel the strain, I knelt down in the snow and bowed my head repeatedly as if dipping to Mecca in a series of grand stretches that revitalized me for another hour.

The good travel continued, and I covered the three hundred miles to Grise Fiord in eleven days, the fastest sledding pace ever recorded in the Arctic. I learned little about the country, yet that little walk had the purity that travelers seek in travel. You can only sled that close to perfection once.

■

The following year I picked another canoeist as a sledding partner. I enjoyed solo trips—and very hard, personal projects should perhaps all be done solo—but I preferred good company. Sledding partners were hard to find in Toronto. The people best suited, marathon runners and triathletes, considered arctic travel as crazy as everyone else did. Mountaineers, kindred spirits in many ways, viewed it as an unrewarding slog. They were high-adrenaline sprinters, who pushed for three days on little food, water or sleep, often in near-constant terror for their lives, then returned to base camp, shook hands and went home. Only three people in North America sledded regularly, and the capital investment in arctic equipment was too steep for the casually committed. A complete Ellesmere rig costs about four thousand dollars.

Larry was forty, older than I was but still in prime years for a long-distance traveler. We had a lot in common. He was an outdoor writer, had a wife, no kids, lots of energy, a sense of humor. He had turned his full-time job with a state park in the Midwest into a plum position that gave him plenty of time to write and travel. His output was impressive. He had been to Alaska a dozen times. He was an enthusiastic photographer. If there was a gap in Larry's extensive outdoor background, it was that at his relatively late age, he had never done a hard expedition. One hard trip toughens you in a way that a thousand easy ones do not. Nevertheless, he had always dreamed of undertaking an extreme arctic journey, in the spirit of the old explorers.

When we first met, Larry told me a story that made me like him immensely. He was just old enough to have been drafted for Vietnam, but he escaped by giving a performance which convinced even the cynical draft board doctors that he was psychotic. This medical record made it impossible for him to work as a federal employee, but he eventually landed what sounded like a state government sinecure. Or maybe he was just well-organized, with great work habits. Either way, we began to plan a two-month, six hundred mile trip around Axel Heiberg Island.

We lived a thousand miles apart but kept in close touch throughout the preparations. Larry trained by backpacking enormous loads through the woods. I did my usual extra running and walking, less for fitness than to toughen up against repetitive stress injuries. Finally, in early

April, we boarded the jet for the Far North with our small mountain of luggage.

"Jesus," muttered Larry, his eyes wide, as the plane approached Resolute. For hours, we'd flown over nothing but white. White sea, white land, white everything. This was no Alaska, tempered by trees, roads, ferries. The High Arctic was as far north of Alaska as Alaska was north of California. You could fit five Alaskas into the High Arctic. An Ellesmere weatherman had once spoken to me of his plans to retire "somewhere south, somewhere like Alaska." The High Arctic is so extreme that it made normal extremes seem, well, normal.

We settled into the inn, unpacked our gear and loaded it on the sleds. We hoped to charter out the following morning, but when we woke up, a twenty-five-knot wind was whistling through the wires around town. No one was going anywhere. I champed to get started, like a horse in the gate, while Larry patiently read in our room.

The bad weather persisted for days, and a change came over Larry. He seemed worried. He began calculating and recalculating our mileages. We had nothing to worry about but I felt like a doctor trying to reassure a hypochondriac. Larry had ears only for the bad. We spoke to a geologist who had just returned from an ice island camp off western Axel Heiberg. One point along our planned route, called Bad Weather Cape, had the same wicked allure for me as Hell Gate, and this researcher had briefly stopped there for seismic readings. He spoke bitterly of eighty-knot winds: "It was the worst weather I've ever seen. The worst weather I ever want to see. It was hell."

Every wilderness traveler meets these types. They think you're crazy, they think you're going to die, they want to bring you to your senses. You learn to listen politely and ignore them. But Larry had misplaced his positive core and brooded continually about the scientist's dire warnings. "Desolate Resolute" seemed to have cast an evil spell on him. I tried unsuccessfully to reassure him. In an article he later wrote about the experience, Larry presented me with a mixture of horror and fascination which was not exactly unflattering but made it clear that he dismissed my optimism as the ravings of a committed lunatic. He felt he was being swept up in my enthusiasm, as in a dangerous rapid, with no control. Unsure what to do, we agreed to shorten the trip. This put an end to the fretting arithmetic but did nothing to rekindle his spirit for the adventure.

The weather eventually cleared and we flew to Eureka, our new starting point. I hoped that once we started sledding, the monkey would get off his back. It was mid-April and although the air temperature was –15°F, the blazing sun allowed us to haul in just our undershirts. Larry sweated heavily, and frost turned his damp hair white. The moist air from his eyes also frosted up his glasses. You can scrape it but it just keeps re-forming. "I'm legally blind," he wailed. "Polar explorers never mentioned this in their books." Everyone has to wear sunglasses to prevent snow-blindness, but fogging is only an issue for those who sweat a lot. You partly get used to it but mainly you just tough it out. Larry knew this, but he was in a state where every pea was a bed of nails.

I had assured Larry that sled hauling was easy compared to carrying a backpack, but he did not find it so. He felt like an ox in the yoke. He foresaw weeks of monotony. We camped early that evening. A memorable night ensued. Long ago, during our preparations, I had confessed to Larry that I snored and he had warned me that he was hypersensitive to snoring. To save weight, we didn't have separate tents, so Larry armed himself with a combination of earplugs, headphones, an oversized toque and a parka hood before turning in. They did no good. About twenty-five times during the night, or so it seemed, I received a wake-up jab from Larry's elbow. Women tend to be good-humored about snoring, eventually training their partners to roll over on command, like hounds, and European men get used to it during their military service. But some North American men have a fragile relationship with sleep, and a snore will shatter it every time.

In the morning, when Larry said he wanted to quit, I wasn't surprised. I was more surprised when, half an hour later, he asked if I'd agree to fly to an empty science camp on western Axel Heiberg, where we could do a series of short trips focusing on photography. Our planned circumnavigation was already dead, so I had no objections. Western Axel was beautiful, and I was sure Larry would enjoy it once he escaped this funk. We hurried back to the weather station to catch our pilot before he left for Resolute.

Larry sat in the lounge while I persuaded the pilot to fly us to the camp. When I rejoined Larry, his head was in his hands, covering his eyes. "I must be going crazy," he said.

"Oh no, Larry, you're not . . . ?"

He nodded glumly. "I've got to go home."

A Twin Otter happened to be leaving for Resolute and it had space for Larry. Within an hour, he was gone.

Thoroughly discouraged, I pondered my options. It was not too late to sled around Axel, but I didn't have the heart to do such a long journey alone. Solos take mental preparation: In the weeks leading up to one, for example, I try to oversocialize, so I can digest the company on the trail. In the end, I decided to fly to the science camp with the pilot. From there, I would do half the island—a four hundred mile trip that should take only a month.

Axel Heiberg is the third largest uninhabited island in the world, after nearby Devon Island and Alexander Island in Antarctica. It is similar to Ellesmere but more mysterious. In April, Axel Heiberg is a magnificent whiteness. It is as pure as white gets, as white as land can possibly be. From the air, long silent glaciers slip down between hundreds of nameless peaks. "They don't need names," a companion once said. "They're bigger than names."

The science outpost, at the head of the Expedition River, has the island's only permanent structures. Every spring since the early 1960s, glaciologists have come here as part of an ongoing study of two glaciers. The Thompson Glacier is a mighty Mississippi River of ice, broad and flat, while the little White Glacier tumbles down from the peaks like a mountain stream. The forty continuous years of data make these the best-studied arctic glaciers in the world.

The scientists were not due for another month, and I had permission to use the camp, which consisted of a kitchen hut and a lab-cum-bunkhouse. I spent two days skiing and reorganizing my supplies for the shorter trek. Sulphur-colored bands gave a painted desert look to the mountains, despite the mantle of snow. I noted the bad ice in a corner of the river fed by mineral springs. I watched a fox kill an arctic hare by biting it on the nose.

No wind blew in this protected nook, and wind is the hauler's friend. The soft snow alarmed me. It was knee deep. I hoped to slog beyond it to the outer fiord in three or four days, but I'd forgotten how bad hauling in powder could be. I broke trail with half the supplies on my back, then ferried the sled and the rest of the stuff forward. Even with this divided load, every fifty steps was a victory. I had to fight the temptation to catch my breath at forty-two steps, or thirty-five. The loudest sound on Axel Heiberg Island was my heart thumping. After six hours I was exhausted and had covered just three miles. I skied ahead to scout the next day's route. More of the same, as far as the eye could see. It would take a week to clear this, and I had no stomach for it. The next morning, I returned to the science camp.

I sat there for a few days, depressed and lazy, reading paperback novels and five-year-old issues of *Sports Illustrated*. I made one more try to escape the clutches of the snow but I couldn't commit to the task. When you want to do something, nothing is a hardship; when you don't want to do something, everything is a hardship. Finally, paring my equipment to the bone, I left to ski the hundred miles back to Eureka.

Given the original plan, it was a pitiful distance, but at least the route had the mystique I sought. It followed a natural chink in the armor of the Axel Heiberg ice cap. I knew of only one other person who had walked Strand Fiord Pass, a geologist named Jack Souther in 1957. Coincidentally, his daughter had been one of the guides on my first trip to Ellesmere.

The light sled allowed me to make six miles a day despite the snow. When I reached Strand Fiord, the powder decreased. Under a thick grey sky, I hauled and stumbled up the pass. The clouds acted like a photographer's reflector, filling in all shadows. Flat light is common on overcast arctic days, but it is rarely this dramatic. I tripped over invisible bumps in the ground. I only knew when I was going uphill by how hard the pulling became. Once I fell off a six-foot ledge, rolling frantically out of the way before the sled impaled me. A little later, a warning voice made me stop in my tracks. Ahead was some faintly darker snow. I lobbed a snowball ahead of me. I didn't see it hit bottom. Nope, not that way. In this queer light I could easily have skied off the cliff without noticing it was there.

The crux of Strand Fiord Pass was a six-mile section of glacier. The air photo I carried showed no crevasses, but just the same I inched forward, probing every step. Around me, the purity of the ice cap contrasted with my dark mood.

Near the coast, local geography had created a solar trap which had already sublimated the snow. A fifty-knot headwind blasted me with flying sand. I felt as if I were in some frigid Sahara. I had to haul over bare mud. I'd done this before and had even enjoyed it, the fierce commitment to the task, the slow glacial persistence that eventually wore down the obstacles. Not now. I was going forward but I wasn't getting anywhere. I had done six hard sled trips in a row, and they were becoming repetitive, blurring one into another. Same old dragons slain. Same bridges crossed.

I hauled with my nose almost to the ground. The sled inched forward as the tireless wind shrieked. "I hate this place!" I shouted, shaking my ski poles at the wind.

I camped at the far end of Buchanan Lake, known for its char fishing and Paleoeskimo sites. I was forty-four miles from Eureka, and polar bears were on my mind. I didn't want to risk an encounter so near the end of this bad-luck trip, so the following day I walked to Eureka in a sixteen-hour marathon. Forty-four miles was the farthest anyone had ever manhauled in a day, but I didn't care. I just wanted it to end.

When I opened the foot-thick doors and stepped into the weather station, I wasn't expecting a flourish of trumpets—maybe a cup of tea. After nearly a month alone, I was surprised when two off-duty workers glanced up briefly from the sofa, then went back to watching a video. I had just increased the population of Eureka by ten percent, but they looked right through me.

After this trip, I fell in love with another part of the world and didn't return to Ellesmere Island for three years.

Chapter Six

Life in the Freezer

Backs to the wind, the herd of arctic hare grazed on the purple saxifrage on the slope near Eureka. Despite the midnight sun that blazed from the north, this was the coldest time of day. The forty hare, all aligned in the same direction, had assumed a posture that exposed as little surface area as possible to the breeze. From the rear, they looked like snowballs.

Of Ellesmere's mammals, wolves and polar bears are the most exciting but they are rarely seen. Watching muskoxen and caribou is like watching paint dry. But arctic hare can fascinate for hours, especially if they're in herds. One hare usually just eats dwarf willow in a businesslike manner, but forty hares are a troupe of entertainers.

Only on Greenland and Ellesmere, at the extreme limit of their range, do hares gather in numbers. Thirty is common. I have seen up to two hundred. One October, an invading army of hares thousands strong advanced on Eureka in the blue twilight. On the Hazen Plateau one summer, a pilot noticed a snow-covered hill—a common sight on Ellesmere, except it was July and none of the neighboring hills had snow. Also, the snow was moving.

No one is sure why this High Arctic subspecies herds, but safety in numbers has something to do with it. When startled, the herds condense into a flurry of hares in perpetual motion. They weave in and out of the collective so swiftly and erratically that it is difficult for a predator, such as a wolf, to target an individual. I've tried to keep track of one but it's like following a single snowflake in a blizzard.

In photographing hares, I found that many have a flight distance of twenty to thirty yards. Breach that invisible barrier, and you also reach their trust. They won't let you approach even that close again.

In herds, however, the animals appear more skittish but also more forgiving. That was the case with this group. They scurried upslope in a long line when I was still a hundred yards off. I wondered if the all-terrain vehicle that I'd borrowed for the evening disturbed them, but biologists have noted that loud machines don't bother arctic wildlife. There is no innate blueprint to help them interpret this unnatural sound, so they regard it as neutral. It was the object moving toward them, not the noise, that made them retreat.

This hill had so much saxifrage that the hares seemed reluctant to abandon it. I parked the ATV, put on my longest lens and shot them from a distance. Since I couldn't get close, I looked for patterns, when their random movements briefly impersonated order. After an hour, I was able to use a slightly shorter lens. Whenever a close approach made them nervous, they bunched together and briefly went crazy, zipping around, boxing with each other and leaping into the air and lashing out with their back legs like rodeo bulls.

I spent all night with the hares. After about five hours, something wonderful happened. Half the group came up to the dirt road where I was standing and seemed to become obsessed with man-made objects. They clustered around a post in the road, they nuzzled a stick and pulled at a piece of red ribbon. They acted stoned. In their general fascination, they even approached me, coming with unhare-like cockiness within three feet of my tripod.

I replaced the telephoto with a 28mm wide-angle lens, left the tripod and walked among them. Their noses twitched, but they continued to nibble the purple saxifrage. I sat down and was soon surrounded by arctic hares. I felt like Adam before the Fall.

■

Of the seven subspecies of arctic hare, Ellesmere's is the largest. Large enough, in fact, to earn the Latin qualifier *monstrabilis*. Twelve pounds is common. One explorer shot a fourteen-pounder.

Ellesmere has more than big hares, it has lots of them. "In twenty hours of flying on northern Ellesmere, I saw more hares than I've seen in twenty-six years elsewhere," says biologist Frank Miller. In 1971, a loose convention of 25,000 hares congregated in five square miles of the Fosheim Peninsula, just north of Eureka, a density equivalent to eighteen per football field. The following year, they were gone. No one knows whether the population crashes, as snowshoe hares do every ten years, or whether they just scatter.

Watching arctic hare, you have to wonder how closely related they are to felines. Even if you've never seen an arctic hare, you can accurately picture their yawns and stretches by thinking of a large, lazy cat rising after a nap. They lick their huge forepaws like cats, then rub them over their faces or smooth down their long ears. When they wet their hind feet leaping across a stream, they kick off the water in that dainty feline manner. In a wind, with their ears folded over their backs, their sitting position is sphinx-like.

Alas, the uncanny echo is just coincidence, "part of the general mammalian repertoire" reinforced by their common size and shape, says paleobiologist Richard Harington of the Canadian Museum of Nature in Ottawa. The last common ancestor of hares and cats was *Eutheria*, a primitive marsupial that lived with the dinosaurs back in the Mesozoic era.

Often the first thing anyone notices about arctic hares is their habit of fleeing on their hind legs. Explorers' accounts are tinged with wonder. It is as if they have just seen, not arctic hare, but the March Hare. One man couldn't believe his eyes until he saw just the hind prints in the snow. Their six- to ten-foot leaps cover more than thirty miles an hour. After bounding off, the hares drop to all fours, then stand up on their tiptoes again for a better view of what they've just run from.

■

David Gray is an Ontario biologist who has studied arctic hares and muskoxen on Ellesmere and Bathurst Islands. First as a student and then as an ecologist with the Canadian Museum of Nature, Gray was a perennial figure in High Arctic science for almost thirty years. After the museum shut its vertebrate ecology department in 1994, Gray's northern visits became more sporadic and dependent on contract work. When I met him, he was doing a small, upbeat book for the military about Alert. Anything to get north. Eclectic and multi-talented, he also collects antique dolls and raises horses with his wife on their small farm outside Ottawa. His sketch of muskoxen decorates the Ellesmere Park mug.

Camping out for two summers with arctic hare, Gray made the remarkable discovery that the young hares, or leverets, nurse every 18 hours and 35 minutes. You can almost set your watch by it. Few people have ever observed young hares nursing, because the meal only lasts about 90 seconds. The rest of the day, they forage like adults.

Park headquarters at Tanquary Fiord had a resident hare family, and one August I spent time photographing the whitish mother and her greyer but almost full-sized leverets. Only fifty-some hikers come to the park every year but the wardens remain all summer, and the hares are used to people. I could lie on my belly inches away and count their long eyelashes.

Hares have a good life at Tanquary. The buildings deter wolves and snowy owls. The white-phase gyrfalcon that nests on a nearby cliff every year keeps its distance. Willows grow on the gravel around camp. Fuel drums by the airstrip serve as windbreaks.

It was ten p.m., and I'd just finished breakfast. I preferred to sleep during the day, because of the better weather and light for photography at night. Long, Modigliani-like shadows stretched across the tundra. These were the last days of the year that the night sun cleared the mountains to the north. The five leverets sprawled on their sides near the plastic pink flamingos with which then-warden Renee Wissink had decorated his gravel "lawn."

Suddenly the leverets all snapped awake. Their mother was slowly hopping this way from a creek drainage. When she arrived, they converged on her in a scrum. Crawling over each other, and almost bowling her over in their exuberance, they fought for a free nipple. I could see the successful ones tugging desperately. In seconds it was over. She tore herself free and ambled back to the meadow. But the mood of the leverets had changed completely. They sprang into the air or stood on their hind legs and playfully flailed at each other with their soft forepaws. "They get all silly after feeding," said Wissink. "It's as if they're supercharged."

I had only managed some distant shots during the nursing bout, but thanks to their predictable timetable, all I had to do was return just before the next feeding. This time, I had the right lens, a fresh roll of film, and the camera preset for the hares' light fur and quick movements.

The ritual was the same: The leverets lazed around, snuggling against each other—something the adults don't do, even in herds. Then the mother came. The brief feeding frenzy took place at the same spot and was followed by half an hour of high spirits. This time, I got the photo.

Tanquary's daily spectacle did not last much longer that year. The next day I flew to another part of the island. When I returned a week later, I could never pick up their schedule, although I had made a chart of their feeding times. But it was now mid-August, and they may have weaned during my absence. David Gray was lucky enough to have witnessed this one year at Sverdrup Pass.

"The young hares and I waited ten hours for her, but she never showed, " he recalled. "Yet I could see her feeding half a mile away through my spotting scope."

Persistently, Gray and two of the leverets came back to the feeding place for three days in a row. The leverets even rushed up to a strange adult hare, but it rebuffed them. On the fourth day, they didn't show.

Newly weaned hares soon face another trauma. Winter comes quickly to Ellesmere. By the third week of August, a dusting of snow had settled on the mountaintops around Tanquary, and it was moving lower down the slopes every day. Constant winds whipped summer's lovely fiord into a dark turmoil. The wardens packed up for the season, pink flamingos and all, and I headed out with them.

■

Just as people are conspicuously absent from Ellesmere, wildlife is conspicuously present. There are no trees, bushes or concealing folds of darkness. Prey and predator have abandoned stealth and their lives are as open as the land itself. Even fear of man is absent.

David Haig-Thomas, a minor explorer of the 1930s, nailed the experience: "We sat in the open in front of our tent and, without moving, we could see a polar bear walking across the fiord, two wolves sleeping on the ice and a herd of some twenty muskoxen. What could be more wonderful than this . . . !"

I was reluctant to take up photography because I was afraid it would ruin such moments. I finally bought a camera because I wanted to write about extreme journeys, and magazines need photos. Taking pictures was inconvenient, especially since the best situations coincided with the times I least wanted to shoot, mostly during danger and hardship. But I discovered that photography was something that I could do every minute. When I was not taking pictures, I could think about pictures to take. It filled every waking minute with purpose. Unfortunately, I only felt this way when I traveled. The rest of the time, the camera sat in the closet.

Although some of my first photos were published, they weren't very good; they just showed hard travel. There was a paradox: Hard trips made these ordinary photos mildly interesting, but they also made it hard to take anything but ordinary photos. The harder and purer the travel, the less time for photography. Yet I only knew hard travel, and the thought of an easy trip was so alien that I never considered doing one. Life was easy; trips were hard. That's how the world worked.

My first trip to Ellesmere happened to be my first commercial tour. Tours, even hard tours, were not made for travelers who craved exhaustion and difficulty. To divert the energy somewhere, I took pictures. To my surprise, I loved the trip, and I actually came back with one or two good photos—my first. I also discovered that I was able to do two types of trips: hard ones and easy photographic ones.

But I remained a bad photographer. I loved my own shots too much. Good photographers were good critics of their own work. This was a difficult gulf to cross.

Working for a magazine, however, exposed me to professional photos in their raw state. Peering through a loupe at these slides every day, I gradually began to understand what sharpness was, although accepting the difference between a slightly blurry and a razor-sharp image took years. Technique was my weakness; I could never figure out anything on my own. But I had a photographer friend who was a technical wizard and who shared his hard-won information with me. Once I had the mechanics and some critical sense, all I had to do was travel and let the passion for photography take over. When the hard trips began to pall, photography gave me a reason to return to Ellesmere. It was also an excuse to spend time with the animals. I would never be a wildlife photographer, because I became so excited behind the viewfinder that even domestic cows fled from my body language. Shooting them eventually forced me to relax, to dawdle, and in dawdling I was able to share some of their intimate moments.

■

Most mammals live in relative obscurity but a few species—larger, cuter or more dangerous—become media stars. Professional wildlife photographers and environmental groups even rank the box-office appeal of celebrity animals. Penguins, for example, are the world's most popular bird. Puffins are number two. Other reliable money-earners include pandas (cuteness), tigers (danger), and whales (size).

In this four-footed Hollywood, wolves have always been the bad boys, combining magnetism with a dark reputation. At the outdoor magazine where I worked, we loved wolf stories because they generated the most mail. Some readers hated wolves—I had never seen real hate before. Others were passionate defenders. No one, it seemed, was neutral. A wolf on the cover invariably caused a spike in newsstand sales. Every year or two, we put a wolf on the cover.

Few people ever see timber wolves. The same is not true with Ellesmere's white wolves, which have never learned to fear man. If you travel Ellesmere, you will see them eventually, sometimes very close. Up close they have the same mystique as the wolves you never see.

Notoriety came to Ellesmere's wolves in 1987, when a well-known scientist and a well-known photographer combined for one of *National Geographic's* most popular articles, which was followed by films and books, on a wolf pack that lived near Eureka. It was the first time that wild wolves had been observed intimately, raising pups, killing prey and interacting with observers. Before this, wolf science was mainly the old analyze-their-scat and track their movements with a radio collar. The Ellesmere work replaced this arm's-length relationship with stunning photos and observations of life in a wild pack.

Over the years, I've bumped into both Jim Brandenburg, the photographer, and David Mech, the wolf biologist. Both Minnesotans, both originally friends, they no longer speak to one another. Ostensibly, the rift was over how to divide the royalties of their planned joint book. It probably had more to do with two alpha males competing for top billing on this, the biggest story of their lives. Mech's photos were poor, but his knowledge of wolves was second to none; Brandenburg's photos were superb, but it was Mech's rigorous observations that elevated the story beyond the coffee-table book. Eventually they published separate accounts.

One May, my sledding partner and I arrived in Eureka after two hard months on the trail. We were in the dining room eating the muffins, turnovers, blueberry squares, lemon meringue pie, cookies and Devil's food cake that Frank, the weather station's big-hearted, half-crazy cook, had offered us in between throwing meat cleavers at people who irritated him. Jim Brandenburg, soft-spoken with thinning blond hair, introduced himself when we came up for air. He was here to finish his documentary film on the white wolves. Although Brandenburg was not strictly a wildlife photographer, his images of animals against artistic landscapes—Namibian dunes, blurred prairie marshes, Ellesmere icebergs—were brilliant. Top wildlife shooters felt his wolf work raised the bar to a new level.

Unlike Brandenburg, David Mech continued to return to Eureka every year to further his wolf studies. I didn't run into him until 1996, but the Ellesmere grapevine kept me informed about the cute blonde girlfriend he once showed up with, for example, or how Mech had not discovered the Eureka wolf den; a Canadian researcher had published a paper on it ten years earlier. As part of my general Ellesmere education, I wanted to spend a day at the den with the world's premier wolf biologist. Mech, antennas twitching when he discovered that I was aware of a recent attack on him in a Minnesota paper, warily agreed.

The girlfriend had long been replaced by more politically correct assistants, in this case a fellow researcher at Mech's International Wolf Center. I remembered what a friend of Mech's had told me: "Wolves and opera are his life now." Although I was a struggling nobody rather than a renowned expert, my so-called adventurous lifestyle also came with a high personal cost that became higher as I got older. I could sympathize with a guy with graying hair who crawled into an empty bed every night, put on Puccini, and fell asleep thinking about his obsessions. Besides, the attack in the Minnesota paper had been cheap and petty.

I arranged to meet Mech near the den site. His instructions were like an old-fashioned treasure map: Walk forty-five minutes up a creek to a large rock, then follow the left fork to a cliff, et cetera. It was early July and the newborn pups were in the den, so we would have to watch from a respectful distance.

The den was a two-hour walk from the weather station, in an outcropping of broken rocks. I found Mech and his colleague glassing it from a hilltop four hundred yards away. The adults were away hunting, but a herd of eleven muskoxen had grazed their way in front of the den. The young wolves must have been staring with big puppy eyes at the milling hooves inches from their hiding place. As for the muskoxen, all the wolf scent made them antsy. To discharge the tension, some of them butted heads. It was not a relaxed meal.

This was one of those off-days when Mech would normally have read a book—"I do most of my year's reading up here"—while keeping one eye open for wildlife. Some researchers are so bogged down in the scientific method that it is impossible to discuss their work with them in English, but Mech was a communicator. He made the people around the weather station feel that he was just a guy who liked to watch wolves. He was always acutely interested in their wolf sightings. When he took his pad out of his shirt pocket and made a note of one of my own observations, I felt as if I were contributing to Science.

"The pack," explained Mech, "exists not as a killing machine but as a strategy for raising offspring." Two wolves are often all that's needed to take down a muskox. David Gray once even witnessed a one-wolf kill, in which the wolf bit out one eye of the muskox with a lucky lunge, then waged a war of attrition until the muskox collapsed from loss of blood. When timber wolves chase moose, the wolves usually pursue in a long line, so the trailers are useless. They are likely there just to profit from the hunt, says Mech. If the parents had to bring their offspring to a kill site, scavengers would have time to strip the carcass.

The number of wolves in the Eureka pack fluctuated from year to year. From a high of seven adults and six pups in 1986, it was now down to one old male, a female and an adolescent male. The ups and downs of wolves, hares, muskoxen, and caribou are one of Ellesmere's great unsolved mysteries. The island is so big, so sparsely inhabited, so rarely visited and so expensive to research that major booms or crashes simply go unnoticed.

During Mech's twelve seasons on the island, the Eureka wolves had used five dens, ranging from this palatial outcropping to a mere depression in the ground. The palatial den was similar to the other two Ellesmere wolf dens I had seen. In all three, broken rocks partway up a hill overlapped to form small caves for pupping. Grassy terraces overlooked the open country below. The wolves could sunbathe at the foot of warm boulder faces. All dens were near water; Mech believed that lactating females needed to drink frequently. Finally, the dens overlooked traditional muskox routes. It was as if the wolves lived right beside their supermarket. The nitrogen from old muskox skulls and bones nourished carpets of moss. Carbon-dating of these bones has shown that some dens have been used intermittently for 3,500 years.

Despite the drizzle, it was a fine way to spend an afternoon, sitting on a hilltop on Ellesmere Island and discussing wolves with the expert. Mech gave me his version of the quarrel with Brandenburg (royalties) and explained how a disgruntled former employee of his lay behind the Minnesota paper's attack. It sounded reasonable, but it also sounded practiced. Like all public personalities, Mech knew how to reveal little while seeming to be very forthcoming.

More interesting, anyway, were the wolf tidbits: how wolves saw reds and yellows (blood and urine?), how a wolf could see a camouflaged leveret at 1,200 feet and hear a willow leaf crinkle at 75 feet. How he once saw a wolf sniff a hare upwind: "He picked up the scent on some eddy, went over and caught the hare."

That we saw no wolves that afternoon wasn't important. In fact, it emphasized the oriental nature of Ellesmere learning. To paraphrase Peter Matthiessen: Have I seen Ellesmere's famous wolves at their den? No! Isn't that great!

■

The pups at Eureka did not survive that winter, and neither did the female. After she died, the others ate her. By 1998, the old male was gone too. Although wolves still occasionally pass through Eureka, drawn by the muskoxen of the Fosheim Peninsula, the dens will lie empty till another pack finds one and moves in.

All the wolves of Ellesmere seem to have withdrawn into a dark phase. The park dens have been empty for three years. The island's fourth known pack, the wolves with the dirty fur that used to hang around Alert and once gave birth among cardboard boxes, disappeared after the dump was cleaned up. Grise Fiord Inuit shoot several wolves a year for parka trim, and summer hikers in the park continue to glimpse wolves passing in ones and twos, but where they've come from and where they're going is a mystery, as wolves should be in some ways.

In his forgotten 1946 classic, *The Natural History of Nonsense*, Bergen Evans exposed some of the fallacies then prevalent about wolves, especially their ungovernable lust for human flesh. Evans pointed out that between January and March, 1929, according to *The New York Times*, wolves devoured "five Poles, sixteen Austrians, an aged Bulgarian priest, and many Czechoslovakians." They also besieged villages in Moldavia, Bosnia, and Yugoslavia, threatened Italy, and menaced Istanbul, a city of more than a million.

Following Evans' lead, I looked further into that golden age of wolf treachery and turned up many other fine reports—the man driven insane from spending all night in a tree tormented by howling wolves below, for example, or the hunger-maddened pack that tried to devour a bronze statue of Venus in a garden. One 1911 report from Russia claimed that wolves had killed all 130 members of a wedding party.

Not long after Evans' book came out, personnel in the newly established Ellesmere weather stations were shooting wolves on sight. Then in the 1960s, wolves underwent a public reappraisal, partly thanks to Farley Mowat's impassioned novel, *Never Cry Wolf*, and partly thanks to the early work of Mech and others, who showed that predators lived in balance with prey populations. Eventually, wolves became minor celebrities at Eureka and Alert and behaved around people like pigeons in a city park. At times, a disrespect for the wolves' wildness replaced the earlier fear and loathing. One dimwit at Alert smeared her face with peanut butter and lay on the ground so that the wolves could lick it off. They did.

In 1995, a rabid wolf bit three people at Alert, only the second recorded case of rabies on the island. In a strange 1977 encounter, six wolves came within fifteen feet of a group of paleontologists working on a hillside. One of the wolves leapt at the chief researcher and "grazed her cheek, leaving it wet with saliva," before retreating.

"It was probably just curious," says Mech. "The wolves could have killed them all."

Finally, in the 1950s, geologist Ray Thorsteinsson was alone in Borup Fiord, sixty miles north of Eureka, when a single wolf bounded toward him at full throttle. At twenty feet, the wolf showed no sign of slowing down, so Thorsteinsson fired his Luger, wounding it in the leg. It retreated.

Inuit oral history sometimes mentions attacks by *kajjait*, or famished wolves, but details are lacking. Overseas wolves that became used to feeding on the corpses of European battlefields have on rare occasions attacked people. However, North American researchers, perhaps fearful of rekindling old fears, are reluctant to classify incidents such as Thorsteinsson's as actual attacks. "Wolves and humans can communicate, so there is plenty of room for misinterpretation," says David Gray.

Until recently, I wondered what he meant about communication. I had seen many wolves over the years, usually trotting past my camp, giving it one or two curious looks but not lingering. All business. Then one July on northern Ellesmere I spotted a single wolf lying on a small knoll about three hundred yards away, watching me with idle interest. I dearly wanted a photograph of that wolf, but a direct approach would have been futile.

Then I remembered an old magazine story about a possible wolf attack in northern Ontario. The body of a native woman had been found in the woods, half-eaten by wolves. But she had been epileptic, and it was impossible to determine whether the wolves had killed her, or much more likely, scavenged the body after she died of exposure or attacked her while she was having a convulsion. A human on the ground, especially behaving in such a strange way, would give off the signals of a sick animal without the usual inhibitory human cues. "The two-legged posture is very intimidating to most animals," a biologist told me. "At ground level, things seem to change." Wildlife photographers sometimes wear a long poncho to hide their legs and make it easier to approach the animals.

I set my tripod at knee height, attached a long lens, and as with the nursing hares, I preset the camera for the wolf's white fur. Then I did my best to feign an epileptic seizure, reeling around, then collapsing to the ground and twitching melodramatically.

The wolf's response was electric. It got up from its knoll and trotted straight in my direction. When it was thirty yards away, it swung downwind to catch my scent. Then it continued upwind toward me, in an unnervingly direct fashion.

Half-intimidated and half-concerned that the wolf would come too close for my long lens, I sat up and started shooting. The wolf hit the brakes. It was confused for a few seconds, but then it abruptly made up its mind: Whatever I was, I was no longer of interest. It began to trot away, just as directly.

I fell to the ground again, thrashing and moaning loudly, but the wolf just flashed me a disgusted backward look. It reached its knoll and sat down.

Perhaps I was no better than the idiot with the peanut butter on her face, but I wanted the wolf to continue to acknowledge me. I howled.

The wolf threw back its head and opened its mouth. At first nothing came out. Then a thin whine, followed by a deep, protracted howl filled the air.

I was elated. It may have been miffed by the deception, but at least we were still on speaking terms.

■

"Ungulates are not geniuses, no matter how you look at it," said the ungulate researcher. Muskoxen, in particular, have been known to ignore a group of scientists playing baseball fifty yards away, yet stampede in terror when a handful of snow geese waddle in their direction.

Ellesmere explorers loved muskoxen because they were easy to shoot, and their meat made a refreshing change from the diet of salt beef. When surrounded by wolves, their natural enemy, muskoxen place their young in the center of a defensive ring, or if threatened from only one side, behind a serried line, guarded by the horns of the adults. But against explorers armed with rifles, this circling of the wagons is suicide. Between 1875 and 1917, at least 1,252 muskoxen were killed to fuel the men and dogs of various Ellesmere expeditions.

In spring, it's common to see muskoxen foraging on windswept slopes and ridgetops. From a distance, they look like slow-moving boulders. The herds are hard to approach because of the newborn calves. The frisky calves dance and leap and blow off steam in a most un-muskox-like way. It is as if they believe they are gazelles. They do not realize that they will grow up to be stolid creatures that chew their cud and do not dance. Watching muskox calves at play is a sad sight because it symbolizes how youthful dreams often fail not because they are impossibly ambitious, but because time turns us into muskoxen, not gazelles.

Judging from published papers, muskox science tends to be, like muskoxen, a little on the stolid side. *Muskox Dung: Its Turnover Rate and Possible Role on Truelove Lowland,* is a typical title. As you may expect, it is not a page-turner. But to see a muskox itself, standing on the wild tundra with the wind rippling its outer fur, the longest of any mammal, is to step back in time ten thousand years and witness prehistoric cave paintings in the flesh.

The first reported sighting of muskoxen was in 1689, a hundred miles north of Churchill, Manitoba. Explorer Henry Kelsey described "two Buffillo" in his journal: "Ill-shaped beasts, their Body being bigger than an ox, head and foot like ye same . . . their Horns not growing like other Beast but joyn together upon their forehead. . . ."

Trappers soon discovered that the muskox's light inner fur, or qiviut, was a golden fleece, eight times warmer than wool and finer than cashmere (but not quite as warm as goose down). A muskox sheds about ten pounds of it a year. In summer, streamers of qiviut flutter from boulders like tundra flags. A garment of spun qiviut has always been an extravagance. Qiviut sells for $300 a pound, and some government personnel around muskox-rich Eureka make a lucrative hobby of gathering it in their spare time. If their ragged summer appearance is any indication, the muskoxen of Ellesmere grow a much thicker coat of qiviut than the sleek herds of the subarctic. A handful of qiviut in each pocket is the Arctic's best handwarmer.

With the demise of the plains buffalo, fur markets in the south turned to muskox pelts. Early in the twentieth century, the wealthy in Toronto and Montreal wore thick muskox robes on their horse-drawn sleighs. Between 1864 and 1916, over 15,000 hides were shipped from northern Canada. But the muskoxen couldn't handle such popularity, and by 1917 only five hundred remained on the mainland and a few thousand more on the arctic islands. That year, the Canadian government gave the muskox complete protection. Slowly, the population recovered. There are now about 4,000 muskoxen on Ellesmere, 1,000 on Axel Heiberg, and 130,000 more across northern Canada and Alaska.

During winter and spring, the energy a muskox expends getting food is greater than the energy it gets from the food. To eat the willows that sustain it, the muskox has to paw through the snow, sometimes first breaking the hard crust with its chin. A biologist graphed the number of pawings against the number of chewings and concluded that the effort surpasses the reward.

So why do muskox eat at all during that time? Wouldn't it make more sense to conserve energy and live on accumulated fat? "Pawing through the snow keeps them warm," explains biologist Frank Miller.

The greatest danger for muskoxen and caribou is freezing rain. Twice in the last thirty years, during the winters of 1973-74 and 1995-96, the better-studied muskoxen and Peary caribou of Bathurst Island, near Resolute, were almost wiped out when autumn rain coated all the vegetation with an impenetrable glaze. In 1996, Miller found the bodies of dozens of muskoxen, leaning against one another like statues. "It was as if they just gave up," says Miller. The area's muskox population had fallen from fifteen hundred to under one hundred.

It isn't known whether such rainstorms occur on Ellesmere, which is drier. But a hard winter still kills many, and sometimes no calves survive for years. When food is scarce, the muskoxen don't exactly starve, they die of malnutrition. To help with digestion, they have to keep their rumen full with something, anything, so the bellies of the carcasses are often found full of dead grass and other junk food. "It's like trying to survive only on celery," says Miller.

In summer, the muskoxen leave the windblown ridgetops for the meadows. By August, the rut has begun and the bulls become testy. They send out a musky odor, noticeable at a third of a mile, according to the sensitive nostrils of one explorer, and are apt to threaten hikers with snorts, baleful glares, and much rubbing of their heads onto a foreleg. (They are transferring scent onto their fur from a gland near the eyes.) These fine nasty signals are lost on our crude olfactory organs, but the approach of a 500-pound, twin-horned locomotive prompts anyone with half a brain to back off.

"No one has ever been killed by a muskox, but I know some people who should have been," says biologist Anne Gunn. Some qiviut collectors with a death wish, for example, tried to rake it off live muskoxen. A German tourist on Ellesmere approached one animal too closely and was struck from behind as he bent over to take film from his bag. He wasn't seriously hurt, but the vibrations from the impact knocked all the fillings out of his teeth. A charging bull hooked a horn under the boot of a flee-ing biologist and flipped him twenty feet in the air with a toss of its head. He did a double somersault and crashed unhurt—right in front of the muskox. It glared at him, then walked away.

Muskoxen often move in small herds. Otto Sverdrup, a sharp observer of wildlife, once noted, "As a rule, each herd consists of 11 animals. The number 11 seems to play an enigmatic part in the herding of the muskox. I have on various occasions counted larger herds numbering 22, 33, 44, 55 and 66 animals, and usually I have found the total to be divisible by 11."

Biologists dismiss Sverdrup's odd observation, but looking over my journals through the years, I am surprised by how many 11-muskox herds I have seen.

■

On Ellesmere, eleven Peary caribou is a major herd. Only about twenty-five hundred survive, including five hundred on Ellesmere and Axel Heiberg.

This small, whitish subspecies first appeared about 120,000 years ago. They may have remained in the High Arctic through the ice ages in non-glaciated oases called refugia, but more likely, they moved in right af-terward. An 8,000-year-old caribou antler found on northern Ellesmere dates almost to the day the glaciers retreated.

Peary caribou were first described in 1787 from a skin. "The Indians . . . said it came from a place where there was little or no day." When Robert Peary brought back a specimen in 1902, it was classed as a species, but was later made a subspecies of the woodland caribou. A sub-species is an animal that has begun to evolve into a separate species but is not quite there.

The seesawing populations of caribou and muskox on Banks Island in the western Arctic, which were once ruled by caribou, and are now dom-inated by muskoxen, suggest that the two may compete in a way that is not clearly understood. In summer, however, the two lead separate lives. Muskoxen hunker down in wet sedge meadows and work like thorough, four-legged lawnmowers, while the caribou nibble and move, nibble and move. Muskoxen have twice the rumen capacity, so are able to process worse food. In early summer, the pickier caribou feed on purple saxifrage;

sometimes their muzzles are purple from the feast. Later, they follow the yellow poppies. By late July, the poppies are found up around 2,000 feet or on the cold north end of the island.

To photograph an endangered animal in the wild is a supreme experience. The next roll of film may capture the best Peary caribou shot that will ever be taken. Another freezing rain or two, and the door could close on Peary caribou and images of them forever. Or like the cheetah, the Peary caribou may recover from its brush with extinction.

Ellesmere has only seven land mammals: muskox, caribou, wolf, hare, fox, ermine, and lemming. (A polar bear spends most of its life on the sea ice and is considered marine.) The wild, psychotic eyes of an arctic fox, the fearful little butterball lemming and the hyperactive ermine, with its twenty-espresso-a-day personality, burn themselves on the brain. Ellesmere's birds paddle or beach-walk quietly in the background, except the shy arctic loon, with its electrifying mating tango, and the chubby little guillemots which orbit a kayaker like moons around Saturn. Sometimes, the incongruous buzz of a huge bumblebee breaks the silence. Little else. You turn over a rock, and nothing is there, no "untold slithering millions." It's too cold: even insects must live in the open. Ellesmere life is like shakuhachi music, a few notes piercing infinite emptiness.

Only the sea teems with life. The endlessly curious whaler William Scoresby examined a drop of arctic sea water under a microscope and found "about 26,450 animalcules." It takes about ten million pounds of this algae to support a single thousand-pound polar bear.

Seals, the preferred diet of bears, appear as dark coneheads popping up quizzically near shore in summer or as distant turd-like blobs on the ice in spring. But the walrus is more approachable, if one dares. It is the Arctic's most dangerous animal. Bears and walrus maintain an uneasy truce. Polar bears may prey on young walrus but the adults are too tough-skinned and thick-skulled; and one explorer even found a bear that had been killed by a walrus.

On Ellesmere, a walrus chased one man thirty yards across an ice floe (which, luckily, was larger than thirty yards). Others have ripped open kayaks. One tried to crush the bow of a kayak in its flippers, like some walrus kill seals. Rogue walrus are solitary bulls with yellow tusks—"like chain smokers," says Renee Wissink—from eating seal fat. Abraham Piyamini of Grise Fiord had such a walrus puncture his wooden skiff with its tusks. His passengers had to step on the holes with their boots while Piyamini gunned the motor for shore.

Since walrus do not float, they sometimes rest by hooking their tusks on an ice floe, or the cockpit of a kayak. "Just lift the tusks and remove them gently," a marine biologist advised us in Resolute before our first kayak trip. Inside his house on the edge of town, a mounted muskox head smoking a pipe gazed down serenely from one wall. The scientist held forth on walrus biology while we stood around, eyeballs popping at his anecdotes, scarcely knowing what to believe. To make a point about the walrus's vibrissae, or whiskers, he suddenly disappeared and raced back dragging a large garbage bag, which we helped lift onto the table. Out rolled a huge frozen walrus head, inexpressibly ugly. "In uncouthness of form, [the walrus] surpasses even the ungainly hippopotamus," *The World's Wonders*, a nineteenth century nature book, tells us.

Yet a Stanford biologist, who has raised walrus by hand, claims that they are among the most affectionate of sea mammals. Thomas Poulter bottle-fed young walrus with three quarts of whipping cream and a pound of clam meat a day. They gained up to twelve pounds a week on this diet.

This mothering earned Poulter the dubious affection of his subjects. "The walrus is not satisfied unless it can climb all over you, even after it gets up to fifteen hundred pounds or more," he writes. "One may be so pinned down as to require help to get up, particularly if there is more than one walrus."

The walrus carry this desire for mutual contact into adulthood, and in summer it is not usual to spot an ice floe with a heap of walrus stacked one on top of the other. Sverdrup, ever practical, called this configuration a meatberg.

Walrus were part of the traditional Polar Inuit diet, harpooned from kayaks by men with balls of steel. Often the meat was left to ripen a considerable time. Explorers uniformly despised the taste, to the amusement of their Inuit hosts, who considered it a delicacy. Geoffrey Hattersley-Smith once turned the tables by offering his guides blue cheese, which they declined in disgust, thinking it had gone bad.

Sometimes, I let the kayak drift toward one of the meatbergs, nose pointing at them to minimize my profile, before quietly backpaddling away. To photograph them, I edged up to a nearby floe and laid my bunched-up jacket on it as a beanbag to steady the long lens. As a walker, kayaking was unnatural for me—my legs cried for action from their dark prison—but in small doses the experience sparkled. Now and then, the dark backs of narwhal broke the surface a few feet away. Terns, guillemots, and ivory gulls investigated me. Once, a walrus surfaced silently beside my hips, and I found myself looking into the bloodshot eyes of the cousin of the head in Resolute. I noticed with some relief that it was not a chain smoker, and presently the uncouth form melted away into the black water.

Wildlife photography was, like well-ripened walrus meat, a delicacy. But day to day, it was the landscape that drove my passion for images. White and simple in spring, grand and sprawling in summer. Some photographers would not like it: for much of the traveling season, there is only one f-stop difference between noon and midnight. But in March and August, six hours of warm light a day bathe the face of the earth. And the face itself is magnificent. Al McDonald, one of the High Arctic's great bush pilots, was flying over Otto Fiord one March when he first felt its spell. The pink sky glowed off his wing tip, and a final few rays of light speared the massive face of the Otto Glacier. The frigid landscape below suddenly became warm and inviting.

"I was listening to my Walkman, and the words of the song were saying, 'Put your receiver on,'" recalled McDonald. "Everything seemed just right, then."

Chapter Seven

Inanimate Things

"Behold, how good and how pleasant it is for brethren to dwell together in unity."

—Psalm 133, often recited by Greely

On a sunny July evening, I wrestled my loaded kayak over the ice foot that ringed the shore of Pim Island like an Elizabethan collar. An easy job at high tide, beaching the kayak was hell at low water with the icy overhang eight feet above, dripping and dangerous. As I squeezed my craft through a gap in the barrier, a nearby piece of ice the size of a refrigerator broke off and crashed into the sea. I sped up. I was in search of ghosts, but I did not want to become one myself.

If I did join the spirit world, I would not be lonely. This was Camp Clay, sometimes known as Starvation Camp. In 1884, American explorer Adolphus Greely and his twenty-four men had wintered here under an overturned boat, trying to stretch forty days of food over eight months. Only six of them, including Greely, survived.

To get here had taken me two ten-hour days of paddling and dragging my kayak on a little komatik over deteriorating ice in the inner fiords. I wasn't sure what I'd find. I knew something remained of the low stone walls on which the stricken crew had rested their boat, but it might be too faint and impersonal to evoke the actual men who lived there.

Ashore, I weighed down the bow and stern lines with chunks of the red granite that composed Pim Island, mindful of the sudden gales that rip through this exposed spot. Though the evening was deceptively gentle and schizophrenic Kane Basin was in its mirror-calm mood, some larger boulders still had jagged ice beards on their leeward side from a recent squall.

I walked among barrel hoops, shreds of sail canvas—one piece twisted like a man in agony—and rusted cans whose meagre contents had been apportioned so carefully. But the place spooked me, and after a quick look around I hurried back to sheltered Buchanan Bay. A day later, I regretted my hasty departure.

■

After that first visit, I became obsessed with the Greely tragedy. I'd already been traveling the island for years, but Camp Clay opened up the history to me, which I'd long ignored. I had an aversion to the subject that dated back to my dutiful memorization of too many boring facts in school. But the presence of so many physical reminders, in a place where the events of a single day a hundred years ago could still be reconstructed like a fresh crime scene, was impossible to resist. "This climate deals gently with inanimate things," one of Greely's men had written with chilling irony, and the inanimate things brought back to life those whom the climate did not treat so gently.

Several books and scholarly articles, drawing on survivors' accounts and expedition members' journals, had already painted a detailed picture of the Lady Franklin Bay Expedition, especially its dramatic unraveling at Camp Clay. None of the historians, however, had actually been to Ellesmere. I was just a fledgling scholar but I hoped I could give a fresh interpretation of the events through the eyes of an experienced traveler. In particular, I wanted to understand how much the fault lay with Greely himself and how much with those down south who had bungled the relief attempts.

The United States had considered establishing a scientific outpost on northern Ellesmere for some time, and Lady Franklin Bay was the natural choice. It had two advantages: a sheltered harbor and a nearby coal vein, discovered by a previous expedition. It was not, however, easy to reach by ship. Even in late summer, thick floes choke much of the narrow channel between Greenland and Ellesmere. "Ye unmercifull yce" had crushed many arctic ships. Greely was relieved when their chartered vessel, the *Proteus*, safely reached Lady Franklin Bay in August, 1881. Working double days, Greely's men built the station, called Fort Conger, within two weeks.

Fort Conger is still not easy to reach today. Most of the annual thirty or so visitors arrive via charter aircraft from Resolute Bay, five hours away. They poke about the ruins for an hour or two, while the Twin Otter waits at a rough gravel strip nearby. To be left here and picked up a week or two later costs as much as Greely paid to charter the *Proteus*, $19,000. Luckily, it's a little easier to share a flight to nearby Lake Hazen, one of Quttinirpaaq National Park's two "visitor nodes." From there, it's a straightforward seventy-mile hike to Fort Conger.

At first glance, Fort Conger resembles a small garbage dump from the pre-plastic era. To walk the ground is to step over cans, bones, pieces of wood, frost-shattered kettles, chimney parts, broken crockery, square-ended nails, barrel hoops, shards of glass, sled runners, thermometer fragments and many pieces of metal whose original function is hard to

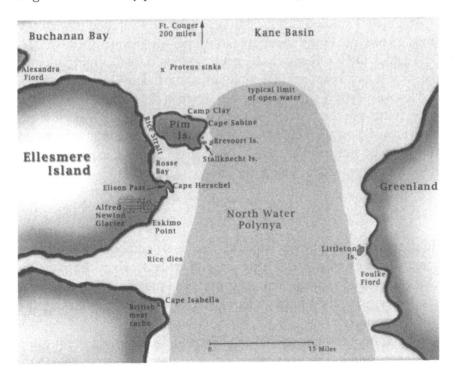

figure out. It is also a National Historic Site, giving it the same lofty status as the Parliament Buildings in Ottawa.

Relations between Greely and his second-in-command, Lieutenant Kislingbury, soured even before the station was complete. Greely was insecure about his authority and reacted to any perceived threat in the worst possible way, by pulling rank. He and Kislingbury fell out over some silly matter, and Greely relieved him of his duties. The two antagonists never mended their differences, and for almost three years Kislingbury had no official role. He was reinstated during the last weeks at Camp Clay, where he died singing, "Praise God, from whom all blessings flow. . . ."

Greely remained an unpopular fussbudget throughout their time at Fort Conger. One of his trip journals, written in obsessively small script, shows his overattention to detail: "4:08 pm. Connell's knee gives out . . . 4:29 pm rested 5 minutes . . . 4:59 pm rested 2 minutes . . . 6:25 pm rested 2 minutes . . . 6:46 rested 2 minutes. . . ." Each time it must have taken him almost two minutes to take out his journal to record that he was resting for two minutes.

The more I studied this expedition, the more I recalled how all the leaders I had met in the contemporary Arctic—airline managers, wilderness guides, OICs (officers in charge) at weather stations, chief park wardens, coast guard captains, even military commanders—were easy-going and low-key. Type A personalities may thrive in the corporate shark cage down south, but they do not lead well at isolated stations. They just get on everyone's nerves. One of Greely's more perceptive men recognized this when he wrote in his journal, "To manage an arctic expedition as if it were a body of troops before the enemy seems absurd."

■

To deepen the connection with the Greely expedition, I'd longed for some time to find my own little trove of artifacts. Over the years archaeologists and geologists in helicopters had preempted all the major spots. Revisiting their finds on foot just wasn't the same as making the discovery oneself.

Not far from the station, the expedition had established a tent camp for sledge parties to gather before striking east for Greenland or north up the coast. Later explorers had passed by, but no modern party had visited this spot. It was marked on Greely's maps as Depot A, a little plum waiting to be picked.

It was three hours to Watercourse Bay, the overland shortcut to Depot A. Dozens of trickles from the thawing permafrost sparkled in the sunshine and nourished broad pastures. These back meadows had been a meat market for the men and dogs of nineteenth-century exploration machines. Later travelers found nothing but empty hills but now the animals were repopulating the place. I kept running into small groups of muskoxen and skittish hares that zigzagged off on my approach.

I set up camp by a stream, ate supper and gazed at Greenland which, because I had never been there, seemed like a beautiful stranger crooking her finger at me. Polaris Bay was lost in heat haze. There, explorer Charles Francis Hall was buried. I could see tiny Joe Island to the south, in front of a big paw-shaped glacier that slides down from the Greenland ice sheet. Hall had affectionately named this island after Joe Ebierbing, one of his Inuit companions whose food and igloos he shared. While expeditions such as Greely's struggled, Hall had discovered that "Esquimaux-izing" yourself, as he put it, was the only sensible way to travel.

I reached Depot A around three in the morning. It lay on a sloping meadow above the high tide line. Little remained: the outline of a tent, sun-whitened tentpoles, a ridgepole, a few cans, a section of stovepipe. I found a saw blade and two pickaxes. Had Depot A been further south, visitors from Greenland would have appropriated these tools decades ago, but this was well beyond the range of hunting parties. A few steps away was something I'd read about and hoped to find: the remains of the one-and-a-half tons of coal that Greely's men had transported here from the vein at Watercourse Creek.

It wasn't much of a find, but I was buoyant. I spent an extra hour on the hike back to camp taking photo after photo of grounded floebergs, just as Greely's photographer, George Rice, often did at Watercourse Bay when he was feeling ambitious.

■

Of the nineteen who failed to return from Starvation Camp, George Rice's silence speaks the loudest. Before his death on April 7, 1884, he was the most popular man on the expedition. One of the survivors later spoke of him as "the life of the Greely party, full of hope, buoyancy and energy."

Rice was born in Cape Breton, Nova Scotia in 1855. He was not a soldier. The only Canadian in the party, he had enlisted in the U.S. army as a formality to be able to join the expedition as photographer. His lack of military background gave him a common-sense outlook about the conflicts.

Rice's official journal surfaced only recently when an anonymous vendor put it up for auction at Sotheby's. Purchased for $8,000, it is now part of an impressive collection of polar books and manuscripts at Dartmouth College, an elegant old school in wooded western New Hampshire. The journal is about the size of a thick bookkeeping ledger. Its dry leather binding flakes if not delicately handled. At the back Rice had glued a woodcut of an Arab girl bringing water from a well. She is wearing a loose, clinging outfit, one breast partly exposed. In the Arctic it helped him remember, perhaps, that humanity consisted of more than smelly, bearded fellow males.

His early entries, in a flamboyant script full of curlicues and sprawling letters, show a mixture of regret and expectation. "I see very clearly I have made a great mistake in leaving civilization," he wrote after ten months. "Nothing can recompense me for the time lost."

Although the Arctic never got inside him, Rice cheerfully kept up their murderous sledding pace without complaint. They marched for twelve hours on two crackers. Like expeditions before them, they were always thirsty; neither Thermos bottles nor trail stoves for quickly melting snow had been invented yet. There is nothing wrong with twelve-hour days, but to do them on two crackers and no water is like trying to drive a car two hundred miles on a cup of gas: The engine soon shuts down, and you have to push the rest of the way. You can do it, but it's very slow and inefficient.

Despite his endurance, Rice was accident prone. If he was not slicing his finger open on a pemmican can, he was breaking his collarbone in a fall or spraining an ankle just fooling around. In one bizarre incident, he fell out of bed and hit his face on the floor. In two years, he had seven injuries.

Today, raised earth still marks the perimeter of their house at Fort Conger. Ceramic piping from the chimney occupies the ground where Rice's alcove had been. A section of floor, iron bedsteads, and even a human jaw that Greely plundered from an old Inuit grave also litter the interior, but nothing suggests George Rice. I kept coming back here, but Rice never liked this corner and his ghost, wherever it may be, does not haunt this place.

Despite tensions, the first year at Fort Conger was a success. Data on meteorology, astronomy, tidal and magnetic variations were meticulously collected. In spring, 1882, Greely's new second-in-command, Lieutenant James Lockwood, reached a Farthest North that stood for fourteen years. Greely himself made two important journeys that year and discovered Lake Hazen, the largest High Arctic lake in the world.

I'd followed bits of Greely's routes on past trips and came to respect his accuracy. It is often impossible to reconstruct exactly where an explorer has been from his writings. You go to the general area and read the passage that supposedly describes where you are, but either he screwed up the mileages and you're in the wrong place or he made the entry a couple of days later, by which time he'd half-forgotten how the hills lined up or how a bay was shaped. Even the great Otto Sverdrup made a mess describing his route up western Axel Heiberg Island. But Greely's caches and cairns were always easy to find. That was the flip side of his irritating, "4:26pm . . . rested two minutes."

■

"The mark of a successful adventurer," writes Chris Bonington, the modern British mountaineer, "is a romantic streak tempered by an analytical mind." Actually, the romantic streak is a feature of our time: Most explorers were pragmatically driven. The need for an analytical mind, however, spans all the ages and Greely had it. He knew that the Grand Idea was built on a million tedious details. Unfortunately, he had no control over one crucial aspect of the Lady Franklin Bay Expedition: the ride home. That was in the hands of people in Washington. The men at Fort Conger had needed a Greely down south to bring them home safely; instead, they got men who failed to think through all the possibilities.

The 1882 resupply mission had been a half-hearted affair. The relief ship *Neptune* reached Littleton Island, just off the Greenland coast, where it ran into pack ice and gales. Its attempts to push north were unsuccessful. Eventually, the crew established small caches here and on Pim Island, then returned home with most of the supplies.

Since Fort Conger was equipped for three years, the supply ship's failure was not crucial. But for the station's morale, it was a disaster. Isolation paranoia now began to spread, especially among the high-strung. "The worst," wrote Rice, "is that the failure of the ship to come this year has shaken the confidence of many in her coming next year."

If the relief ship did not show up by August, 1883, Greely's orders were to head south in small boats in order to meet the ship somewhere between Fort Conger and Pim Island. But everyone except Greely believed that this plan was crazy, and likely fatal. Even for sailors, which they were not, early autumn is the worst time for a two hundred and fifty mile boat journey. With new ice forming, it's too late for boats and not early enough for sleds. Nor could they hike overland, because packs can't hold enough supplies. Years later, Robert Peary took ten days to sled in spring the route Greely needed fifty-one days to boat in the fall.

All the murmuring made Greely feel under siege, and he reacted by further tightening the screws of discipline. In early October, someone spotted polar bear tracks and three men took off in pursuit, without informing him. Piqued, he sent a party after the hunters, with orders to relieve them of their weapons. One of the three resented having his hunt ruined and made a snappy remark. Greely instantly demoted him to private and declared that he would be tried by court martial down south. Greely read this decision aloud to the men. "He rather surprised us by speaking of it as a mutiny!!" wrote Rice, using his only two exclamation points in four hundred pages.

Greely was not finished. Using the old authoritarian tactic of penalizing everyone for the misdeed of one, he ruled that henceforth no enlisted man could walk more than five hundred yards from the station. This put a stop to the two- or three-mile walks that everyone took to relieve the monotony. "These little circumstances," Rice concluded gloomily, "promise us a pleasant arctic winter."

Thanks partly to the determined lobbying of Greely's wife, Henrietta, the 1883 relief expedition was better organized. It should have succeeded but for bad luck, more vague orders and mediocre personnel.

Its two ships included the sturdy *Proteus*, which had first brought Greely to Fort Conger, and the *Yantic*, a fragile backup vessel with instructions not to risk itself in the pack ice. The mission was under the command of Lieutenant Ernest Garlington. His orders were to reach Fort Conger without delay; failing this, to set up winter quarters near Littleton Island, then cross to Cape Sabine and continue as far north as necessary to meet the Greely party. Everyone would winter together near Littleton Island.

Logical enough, if all went well. But what if the *Proteus* went down with all its supplies? What if both ships did? What if the *Proteus* sank far to the south, in notorious Melville Bay, and the *Yantic* couldn't proceed within reach of Greely? What if neither ship managed to clear Melville Bay? There was not just one calamitous scenario, there were several.

On July 22, ten miles north of Cape Sabine, ice closed in around the *Proteus*. It was alone; the slower *Yantic* was still struggling northward. The pressure exerted by pack ice can be tremendous. Floes grinding against each other produce mountains of ice along the edges, just as the grinding of continental plates produces mountains of land. When a piece of wood is squeezed between these plates, it splinters, even if the piece of wood is a 467-ton ship. Its crew escaped in lifeboats, but within a few hours, the *Proteus* lay 1,200 feet down at the bottom of Kane Basin. It remains there today, ignored for a hundred and fifteen years, despite the fact that it is North America's northernmost shipwreck.

■

On my last evening at Fort Conger, I walked south along the mossy shoreline to Dutch Island, a speck of land so small that its name has been left off modern maps. When I reached it, the tide was running out, and the tongues of gravel on Dutch Island and the mainland were drawing closer. A couple of quick hops through ankle-deep water put me on the island.

Dutch Island is just a mile and a half from the station. A popular destination for the walkers and ice-skaters of the Greely expedition, it is a little turtleback of tilted shale some thirty yards across. From here, they set out on their terrible boat journey southward on August 9, 1883. On this day, the boredom of Fort Conger ended and the tragedy of Pim Island began.

A ten-foot length of timber remained from that day over a hundred years ago. Was it repair material, or a spare mast discarded minutes before their hurried departure? Although a soft midnight sun warmed

Discovery Harbour, progress beyond Dutch Island looked nightmarish. Bobbing ice floes choked the water. On another journey I had tried to cross such a surface with my kayak, but the ever-shifting channels were too narrow and winding. Dragging the kayak over the unstable floes was so slow and perilous that two hundred yards took the afternoon. Manhandling heavy boats for miles through that stuff was fighting the Arctic rather than adapting to it.

Had Greely's men remained at Lady Franklin Bay, everyone would have survived to head south in the spring. But despite all the vague orders, this one was unambiguous, and Greely had no reason to override it. It was likely that after a little discomfort, they would run into the relief ship and be home that year. Nevertheless, it was this Washington-based order to abandon Fort Conger that stands as the opening of Pandora's box. From the moment they left the station, their lives depended on meeting a ship somewhere down the coast.

With four boats and just eighty days food per man, they struggled southward. All the latent resentment toward Greely surfaced during these difficult days. Greely himself faltered in near-hysteria, screaming, insulting, threatening, as he endeavored to keep command of his crew. Meanwhile, Rice stood on the foredeck of the lead boat and guided the bickering party through the ice, cracking jokes whenever a sudden bump tumbled him into the frigid sea. "If there is any problem with Rice," said an admiring Kislingbury, "it is that he works too hard."

The unwieldy caravan progressed until August 26, when the ice stopped them. By morning they were frozen in place about forty-five miles from both Cape Sabine and the Greenland coast.

Throughout the retreat, Greely had wavered on their ultimate destination. At first they had to stick to the Ellesmere side because that is where they expected to meet the relief ship. If the two failed to connect, Greely's original plan had been to make a last-minute crossing to Littleton Island, where the 1882 ship had presumably unloaded all its supplies, and where the 1883 rescuers were supposed to overwinter. But when the going to Pim Island looked good, Greely changed his mind. A few days later he changed it back to Greenland. Eventually he settled on Ellesmere.

Wilderness travelers have to constantly adjust their expectations to changing weather and terrain, but Greely seemed to regard Ellesmere and Greenland as equal choices. They were not. When the ship failed to materialize, there was only one possible destination: Greenland. Littleton Island would have disappointed them at first. Neither supplies nor rescuers were there, but muskoxen grazed all winter on the rich slopes of Foulke Fiord. In late winter, grunts of walrus echoed from the cliffs of nearby Cape Alexander. By May, the air twinkled with dovekies. In June, eider eggs were so plentiful that a later expedition gathered six thousand of them from Littleton Island alone. And Greenland hunters would likely have stumbled across the party long before this.

By contrast, the Ellesmere coast around Cape Sabine is an asteroid. Ice caps lurk just behind the austere coastal peaks. Cold north winds make the little unglaciated land raw and sterile. It is Ellesmere's most savage face. The meadows around Fort Conger were a Vermont pasture by comparison. Littleton Island versus Cape Sabine was hardly a toss-up.

In mid-September, still trapped in the ice, Greely again toyed with dashing to Greenland, but he abandoned the idea. This was sailor thinking, and even an intense month at sea could not turn these landlubbers into old salts. Yet Greely's men could certainly have managed the forty-five mile crossing, just as the *Proteus* crew did in their lifeboats. All Greely's justifications for not taking that course, typically beginning, "The uninformed may wonder why . . ." sound hollow.

And so they continued to drift, like ants on a piece of styrofoam, first south, then north, then south again, then east, then west. A month after their besetment, a gale drove them south past Cape Sabine and almost into Baffin Bay. But they came within four miles of shore, and after hours of hard work, they stepped onto dry land at Eskimo Point. It was September 29, 1883.

■

When I wrestled my sled over the vertical plates of ice guarding Eskimo Point, it was spring, not fall. The High Arctic has two springs, marked by the Return of Light in mid-February and the Return of Warmth in late April. This was still the Return of Light phase, and my sled hauled poorly over the cold snow. It would be another week before the sun rose high enough to soften those steely granules.

Greely had named the site Eskimo Point because of its stone rings, old Thule encampments. A few hundred yards to the north, the Alfred

Newton Glacier slipped into the sea. When the North Water washed right against the snout, native travelers had to risk the three-mile glacier crossing. Eskimo Point was a good place to stop before the long trek to Cape Isabella.

Around 1980, the Alfred Newton Glacier surged, and a crossing today is much more dangerous than it used to be. The terminus is a mess of seracs, and hidden crevasses thickly mine the upper reaches. I had no intention of hanging around Eskimo Point long enough for a gale or spring tides to tear away the sea ice, my safe road to Pim Island.

Spring is a poor time to visit historic sites such as Eskimo Point because snow hides all the treasures. Even the remains of their ice-boat, the *Beaumont*, was buried somewhere. Only the stone foundations of the three unfinished huts poked above the knee-deep snow. On this sunny evening, the stone walls cast long blue shadows over the snowscape. From this angle, the Alfred Newton Glacier looked benign. Greenland must have been a cheering sight, because Littleton Island and even the warm brown cliffs of Foulke Fiord, sure salvation, were within view. Nevertheless, I couldn't get over how sterile Eskimo Point was. They really knew how to pick them. No muskox or caribou would find its way here in a thousand years. Only polar bears and foxes occasionally pass by. The summer walrus would have already left for Greenland. Littleton Island and all its riches may have looked next door, but the Greely expedition was on the wrong side of a life-or-death gap.

Greely planned to winter at Eskimo Point and instructed his men to start building winter huts. Meanwhile, Rice and Jens, one of two native Greenlanders accompanying the expedition, set out to search Cape Sabine for news of the *Proteus*. The sea ice was not yet solid, so the two crossed the Alfred Newton Glacier and edged their way north through an unknown strait, which Greely later named after Rice. Circumnavigating Pim Island, they squeaked past ever-nightmarish Cape Sabine to Stallknecht and Brevoort Islands. Here they found a small food cache and Garlington's note about the fate of the *Proteus*.

They returned to Eskimo Point with the news. Their prospects could hardly have been worse. The *Proteus* was at the bottom of Kane Basin. They had food for another forty days at most. Garlington's note that he would do "everything within the power of man" to rescue them promised nothing concrete, but Greely's men devoured the encouraging words as they now devoured their rations, without criticism. Even Greely believed that Garlington was at Littleton Island and would come for them when the light returned in February. To the south lay open water, but Greely remained unwilling to stake their lives on a boat crossing. He ordered the party to move to Cape Sabine on Pim Island, the probable landfall of the rescuers. Meanwhile, the energetic Rice left on another volunteer mission to locate an old British food cache at Cape Isabella, twenty miles south.

The message at Cape Sabine did not tell the whole story. It couldn't give the crucial news that after picking up the *Proteus* crew in Greenland waters, the *Yantic* had set a course for home. Most of the food had gone down with the *Proteus;* Garlington's crew had taken much of the remainder for themselves, leaving only the one small depot. Greely's men were on their own.

For all its vagueness, the message struck a hopeful note. After reading it, Greely felt warmly enough toward Garlington to name Pim Island after him. When he later heard the details of the botched rescue, Greely withdrew the honor. Given the nature of the place, leaving it as Garlington Island might have been a fitter insult.

■

Although it is the fate of the Greely expedition that gives Pim Island its haunted-house creepiness, even the earlier British seemed uneasy about it. "This place is sterile and barren to the last degree," wrote George Nares, "and for the future I shall keep as far from Red Granite Rock formations as possible."

In 1972, geologist Fritz Mueller considered Cape Sabine as a scientific base but rejected it more on emotional than rational grounds: "Although an ideal site to study the North Water, it is the most inhospitable place I have ever seen in the Arctic and I could not bring myself to establish a station here."

Today scientists still occasionally visit Pim Island. Some geologists believe that in the last ice age it was a pivotal place where the Greenland and Ellesmere ice sheets collided. A few years ago, archaeologists studying an old Thule camp were treated to some memorable Pim weather. "A wind came up suddenly, and I noticed all these scraps of blue nylon blowing past," recalled Karen McCullough. "My first thought was, 'Now who left that garbage lying around?' Then I realized it was the remains of my tent."

Recalling such stories, I felt uneasy when, around midnight, the sky south of Eskimo Point turned bruise purple. I'd never seen Ellesmere clouds look that weird before. The perpetual anxiety of the solo traveler pursued me into the sleeping bag that night, and after five restless hours I broke camp and hurried north to put the Alfred Newton Glacier behind me. In Herschel Bay, the ground winds became so strong that the taut sled traces hummed like a mouth harp. To keep from being blown backwards over the bare ice, I had to slip a pair of studded soles over my sealskin kamiks. Even then progress was difficult, as the sled behind me slewed crazily whenever a crosswind caught it.

Soon the ice became rougher. Sea ice conditions vary unpredictably from year to year. Every summer, the ice breaks up but doesn't completely disappear. Pieces of ice about four feet thick drift to and fro with the tides, winds and currents. A bay that is completely open one day may be choked with loose blocks the next. In September, freeze-up catches the blocks where they happen to lie and for the next ten months that's where they remain. These irregular blocks can make the going, as explorer Isaac Hayes put it, "like traveling from one end of New York City to the other over the house-tops."

By putting in a long day, I finally made Stallknecht Island, at the southeast tip of Pim. While wrestling the wind to set up the tent, a sudden gust snapped two poles. It took forty-five minutes and several hundred pounds of rocks to secure the damaged shelter with guy lines.

Greely's arrival at Pim Island was no more auspicious. It was, on the contrary, "the worst night of our lives," according to Brainard. But the blizzard eased up by morning, and on October 15, 1883, they reached Camp Clay. Over the next four days they hurriedly built a three-foot high wall. Then they laid their whaleboat over it as a roof and covered everything with a white canvas tarpaulin, scraps of which still lie everywhere about the site. Finally, they banked the outer walls with snow and built a pantry of snow blocks beside the entrance. They moved in just as the sun disappeared for the winter. "I wonder," reflected Brainard, "how many of us will ever look on his glorious face again?"

Rice, meanwhile, had located the old British cache at Cape Isabella but he needed help to retrieve it. He sped back north and reached Camp Clay on the same day as the rest of the party.

For the next two weeks, Rice was too busy to return for the cache. He and the others had to transport to Camp Clay the other supplies left by Garlington and the earlier relief ship. They also left notes on their whereabouts for rescuers and brought back two barrels of moldy dog biscuit that Nares had stored on Stallknecht Island eight years earlier.

During a lull in the storm that pinned me down for the next three days, I looked for signs of this activity. All I found were a one-foot pile of rocks on Stallknecht Island and the scattered remains of Nares's cairn on the rounded summit of Brevoort Island. Consisting of about three hundred rocks, it must have been gigantic in its time. The cairn was gone now, dismantled by recent visitors in search of goodies, perhaps the Hydrographic Survey mapmakers whose yellow nylon X's and metal frames sully the tops of many otherwise virgin hills.

■

On November 1, 1883, with the active work complete, winter rationing began. It consisted of six ounces of bread, four ounces of meat and trace amounts of lard, rice, soup, canned vegetables and dog biscuit. It added up to one pound a day per man—about half the necessary amount.

Although Greely occasionally gave small supplements to those who, like Rice, exerted themselves for the good of all, it was otherwise an equal split. In the unwritten etiquette of survival, this division goes unchallenged even today, yet it raises a lot of questions. Should a thin man get the same as a heavy man with plenty of reserves to live on? Should a hundred-pound woman get the same as a hundred-and-seventy-pound man? Should a twenty-year-old get the same as a fifty-year-old, whose body no longer needs as much food? Most of us fantasize about how we'd fare in emergencies relevant to our lives, and questions about the fair division of food in such a situation had always haunted me, because as a slender male with a high metabolism, I knew that I'd always be among the first to die of starvation. Sometimes even-steven is not fair, and I wondered how I could have accepted that arrangement at Camp Clay.

Untroubled by such thoughts of self-preservation, Rice finally left on November 2 for the meat cache at Cape Isabella, accompanied by three of the tougher men, Elison, Lynn and Julius Frederick, whose five-foot-two stature earned him the nickname Shorty.

Dragging a small sled, they reached Cape Isabella on the third day, excellent traveling by hungry men in what was now perpetual darkness or twilight. In fact, it was too torrid a pace for Elison, who began to drop behind on the way back. When Elison slowed, hypothermia set in. His nose, feet and fingers froze. Soon he could no longer move, and they had to ferry him a short distance on the sled, then leave him on the ice while they returned for the meat.

The waiting during these shuttles worsened Elison's condition. To save his life, they finally had to abandon the meat. Marking it with a rifle stuck upright in the snow, they hurried to Eskimo Point. In the half-finished stone hut, they placed Elison between them in the four-man buffalo-hide sleeping bag. As his limbs thawed, the nerves around the damaged tissue also revived. "No person can imagine how that poor man suffered," wrote Frederick later. They had traveled forty miles in fourteen hours, an excellent pace under any conditions, on a cup of tea and no food.

By morning, the wind had not let up. They continued into the gale and soon Elison's limbs were frozen again. At the head of Herschel Bay, they didn't even have the strength to drag him up a gentle ridge to what is now called Elison Pass. So Lynn and Frederick lay down on the ice foot and sandwiched Elison between them in the frozen bag while Rice—the mind boggles—continued another eighteen miles by moonlight to Camp Clay.

Shortly after the exhausted Rice reeled into camp, rescue parties hurried out. They found Elison, Lynn, and Frederick locked helplessly in their frozen sleeping bag. The wind was still whistling through that gunsight pass. Elison begged for death, but the rescuers dragged him on the sled back to Camp Clay. He survived, but some weeks later, his gangrenous hands and feet dropped off.

Their shared suffering, the emerging heroism of people like Rice, Brainard, and Frederick, and the moral frailty of some of the other men, created an emotionally naked atmosphere at Camp Clay. One of the biggest surprises was Greely himself. Since his hysteria on the drift south from Fort Conger, Greely had pulled himself together. As things got tougher, his spirit grew rather than diminished. Occasionally he secretly gave a portion of his own food to one of the weaker men, or resolved squabbles over some unpleasant chore by doing it himself. He was evidently a wartime commander who became human under stress but struggled in peacetime, a typical Ellesmere extremophile. It was too late to win everyone's respect, but more than one person noticed the change that had come over him. "Lt. G. has shown himself in every way greater than I believed him to be," Biederbick wrote in his journal. "I am very sorry not to have sooner found out his full worth. While at Conger and on the retreat, I so often did him injustice in my thoughts. Now I think it better that he and our records be saved than all of us together."

■

Rainbow-colored lenticular clouds hung over the Ellesmere icecap, and Greenland remained uncharacteristically black and evil-looking, but otherwise the storm had passed, so I set off again. Near Cape Sabine, the ice worsened. To coax the sled over the ice blocks, I had to get down on all fours like a dog.

One of the "northern pillars of Hercules," Cape Sabine had always been a prominent landmark for ships. Explorers also aimed for it when dogsledding to Ellesmere from their Greenland bases. The only danger is that the young ice can break off and drift into open Baffin Bay. In the most marvellous rescue in arctic history, an 1872 party floated south for 2,500 miles before being accidentally spotted eight months later by a whaler off the coast of Newfoundland.

At Cape Sabine, the ice foot, usually a popular sidewalk for explorers and polar bears alike, was an ice cliff some thirty feet high, formed by high tides and pounding waves. At the bottom of the cliff, a narrow moat of slush separated the pan I was on from the shore. It was easy to see how the ice could break away, since it was not really attached. Although solid enough, this ice was so new that the sled runners left moist dark tracks behind me.

It was April 16, and the sun still set, although not by much. The three hours around midnight performed a joint sunset/sunrise ritual in which the sky never quite turned fiery red and the land never quite turned twilight blue. By the time the sun appeared again, it was over Greenland and I was in my tent, chipping frozen pieces of cheese into a potato gruel.

■

"Nov. 16, 1883. Memorandum: tripe, eggs, Boston baked beans and brown bread at Godfrey's.
Nov. 23. Chewed up a foot of a fox this evening raw."

—from Lockwood's Camp Clay journal

Their winter at Camp Clay was a living nightmare: twenty-five men drifting in and out of sleep, lost in fantasies about home and food. Thanks to the insulating snow walls outside and the cram of bodies inside, the temperature of the hut was bearable. Even when it was –33°F outside, for example, it was 32° inside.

The listing of exotic dishes to enjoy back home became their chief pastime. For Lockwood in particular, reveries about food became an obsession. His journal hops from grim reality ("Elison does not know about the loss of his feet yet") to incessant "memorandums" about lemon butter, Charlotte of apples, stuffed eggs à la Paris, chives with scrambled eggs, chicken croquettes and even "Mrs. O'Shea's figs." Once, after torturing himself endlessly this way, he wrote with unconscious humor: "My two dog biscuits today were slightly moldy, but they tasted better than the most delicious morsel in civilization." Then the list began again: "Omelettes at the Vienna Café, cranberry pie. . . ."

The Inuit have lived off the land in the Arctic for over four thousand years, and even white explorers have managed it on occasion. For nine months in 1895-6, Fridtjof Nansen and Hjalmar Johansen overwintered in a shelter similar to Greely's on an island off the Russian coast, and grew pudgy on a diet of polar bear and walrus meat. "We are as well off as if we were at home," boasted Nansen. In the early twentieth century, Vilhjalmur Stefansson, touting the Arctic as a place overflowing with game, survived for four years by hunting. However, the fact that eleven people perished on one of his exploits showed that his "friendly Arctic" concept had its limitations. For one thing, twenty-five white men in one spot is too much for the High Arctic to sustain.

But survival was possible, even on seemingly dead Pim Island. Muskox country lay just around the corner in Buchanan Bay. Two of Greely's men made a brief trip to Alexandra Fiord, but the muskoxen are a little further north, and the hunters came back empty-handed. Since an earlier British expedition had also seen no game, Greely dismissed the inner bay as sterile. It is anything but. There were so many muskoxen that in 1899 Otto Sverdrup established his hunting camp at Fort Juliana, a two-day walk from Camp Clay. Had Rice devoted his energies to probing Buchanan Bay rather than continue to chase after the small Nares cache, almost everyone would have survived.

■

The summer I first visited Camp Clay, I was based near the abandoned RCMP post in Alexandra Fiord, which as usual was being used by some botanists. Most Ellesmere scientists practice northern hospitality, but these particular graduate students never even offered me a cup of tea. It was a relief when a planeload of Inuit elders from Pond Inlet and Grise Fiord camped on the beach for a few days. They were former RCMP special constables or their children who had wintered here in the 1950s or early 1960s, when the post was open.

I already knew Abraham Piyamini from past trips to Grise Fiord. At sixty-nine, Piyamini was the oldest person in the hamlet, and was one of the few of his generation to bridge both worlds. He was a respected carver and polar bear hunter who for years had made an annual pilgrimage to Las Vegas to play the slots. He had even been to India once with a friend. "Me not like India food. Very pepper," Piyamini recalled. He had guided tourists on snowmobile trips, and adventurers passing through Grise Fiord always found their way to his doorstep for advice.

In winter, seal breathing holes are covered with snow, but in early July the sea ice was bare, and in my walks on Buchanan Bay I kept noticing all the holes.

"How was the hunting in winter?" I asked Piyamini, over a cup of tea in his tent.

"Many seal," he said.

At Fort Conger, Greely's men had some half-hearted success hunting seal in springtime, but that's a different art. The seal sunbathe on the ice and the trick is to sneak close enough for a head shot. (A merely wounded seal slithers back into the hole and is lost.) But in winter, you first need to find one of their concealed holes—an acquired skill—then patiently wait with a harpoon or a gun. This can take minutes or hours, because a seal has many breathing holes. When you hear the seal exhale, you thrust the harpoon at the sound, or fire and quickly thrust a mittened hand through the snow to grab the animal. A polar bear hunts essentially the same way, only its job is easier, because it can smell the holes.

Greely's men had no idea that seal could be hunted in winter. Even Jens and Fred, their two Inuit hunters, did not know because they were from the wrong part of Greenland. Of the three native Greenlandic cultures, only the Polar Inuit have the skills to hunt seals at their hidden breathing holes. Jens and Fred were from Proven, near Upernavik, a part of the island kissed by the warm North Greenland Current. Its long open water season gave it a fishing economy and a history of contact with Europeans. White explorers didn't know the difference between the cultures, but the Polar Inuit would have considered Jens and Fred almost as foreign as white men.

So, sitting on a barren rock but surrounded by plenty, the Greely expedition passively waited out the winter. Now and then someone shot a passing fox, but four pounds of meat does not go far among twenty-five men.

On January 18, William Cross became the first to die. He was an alcoholic who had drunk bottles of specimen preservative at Fort Conger and continued to steal rum at Camp Clay. His body was placed three hundred yards east of the hut, on a gravel saddle that became known as Cemetery Ridge. "One cannot conceive of anything more unearthly," wrote Brainard, "than this ghostly procession of emaciated men moving slowly and silently . . . in the arctic night, having in their midst a dead comrade."

In early February they made their one attempt at self-rescue. After gaining strength on a week of extra rations, Rice and Jens set out for Littleton Island in the hope of meeting rescuers. If no one was there, they were to seek help from nearby Greenlanders.

Littleton Island is thirty miles southeast of Pim Island, so Rice and Jens innocently headed in that direction. Some years this direct route works. In 1914 Donald MacMillan crossed in six hours with dogs. Other years, the open water arcs far north into Kane Basin, and a detour of several days is necessary. In 1909, Frederick Cook claimed he had to travel sixty miles north of Pim Island before hitting solid ice. Cook's numbers are rarely reliable, but a thirty-mile detour is common.

Four days after they left, Rice and Jens returned to Camp Clay, defeated. They had run into open water two miles east of Brevoort Island, so they followed the ice edge south, but found no bridge to Greenland. Their makeshift trail stove broke down, and they'd had almost nothing to drink for two days. They barely made it back.

By mid-February the open water had almost reached their camp, but they were now so weak that they couldn't move their big whaleboat from the roof to launch it. One depressing day they began to break it up for fuel. All around them was salvation, the muskoxen and seal of Buchanan Bay, the ice bridge further north, but all they heard were the "waves and whitecaps . . . rolling in against the edge of the fast ice with a dismal roar which sounded like the knell of our impending doom."

In March, an important new chore diverted Rice's substantial energy. With their supplies almost gone but the Return of Light season upon them, they desperately pursued new sources of food, such as the chunky little guillemots that flitted around the open water. The resourceful Brainard invented a net for catching what they called shrimps, tiny crustaceans one-eighth to half an inch long, and Rice made several trips a day to a bay beyond Cemetery Ridge. At first Rice had limited success, but soon his fishery was rolling. One day he caught thirty-two pounds of them.

As time went on, these crustaceans became a larger and larger part of their diet. By April 2, their daily ration was three ounces of guillemots, two ounces of bacon, two-and-a-half ounces of bread and twelve to fifteen ounces of crustaceans. By May 13 they were eating almost entirely crustaceans. The men didn't like them much, and the chitin in the shells caused digestive upsets, but by now everything from ptarmigan droppings to candle wax was fair game. "The shrimps are of very little benefit," wrote Brainard. "They possess little or no nutriment, and in fact they serve only to fill the stomach."

■

Fritz Mueller, the scientist who rejected Cape Sabine as the site for his research station, eventually built it near Elison Pass in 1972. It has seen intermittent use over the years. In 1998, scientists from different nations were based there to study various aspects of the North Water, including the wildlife and why the sea in this area should remain open when several feet of ice covered everything to the north and south of it.

That year, I was visiting some nearby Greely sites and I stopped in to say hello to the only other humans on the island within two hundred miles. The primitive camp sat on a plateau overlooking Rosse Bay and consisted of one small permanent building and three portable tube shelters called parcolls. The scientists included two Japanese, an American from the National Ice Center in Washington who made it clear that he didn't like the cold and found the accommodations too spartan, the soft-spoken Canadian camp leader and three grizzled Polish marine biologists who had just arrived and were busy setting up their parcoll. They seemed happy working outside for hours in this region's near-constant winds. They belonged to that breed for whom work is an excuse to have a hell of a good time. One of them, Wojtek Moskal, had skied to the North Pole with a companion in 1995, on a shoestring-budget adventure they had dubbed Poles to the Pole. The trio's head researcher, Jan-Marcin Weslawski, had studied arctic marine life everywhere from Spitsbergen to Antarctica. His specialty was crustaceans, and his hobby was the Greely expedition.

"Crustacean specialists all know about it because it's the one famous case where crustaceans saved lives," said Weslawski. Rather than possessing "little or no nutriment," they are high in lipids. Although two-thirds of their weight is shell, the remainder is packed with calories. When I did the arithmetic, I estimated that each man received four hundred to four hundred and fifty calories a day for two months from these crustaceans. There was no doubt that the survivors owed their lives to these "miserable shrimps."

As we strolled over to some old wooden crosses near the station, memorials to three of Fritz Mueller's sled dogs, Weslawski explained the natural history of the crustaceans. In summer, they eat mostly dying plankton falling from the sea surface. But when the ice forms in the fall, blocking the sunlight, this "rain of cadavers" stops for eight months or so. The crustaceans lie quietly on the bottom conserving energy until their sensitive chemoreceptors detect carrion. Then they shoot up in packs of thousands and snip away chunks of meat with their strong jaws. "They're known as the hyenas of the ocean floor," said Weslawski. Two internal sacs along their sides store excess meat and allow them to go up to ten months without eating. It is ironic that Greely's men were saved by creatures even better at enduring starvation than they were.

From where we stood, the rough ice below looked like frozen white-caps. Our parka sleeves flapped in the tireless wind. In the midst of this primeval scene, Weslawski and I exchanged e-mail addresses and I gave him the satellite coordinates of Camp Clay from my GPS.

■

"They were all of them brave men. . . . But I think if any distinction should be made, Rice should have the palm."

—Maurice Connell

"I hope Long gets a seal today; it will be our salvation."

—April 5, 1884, last entry in Rice's journal

In early April, Rice convinced Greely that despite a recent illness, he was strong enough to go after the meat cache he had abandoned on the ice the previous fall. By now things were desperate at Camp Clay. Several were dying. Supplies were almost gone. Soon there would be nothing but the crustaceans, which some simply could not hold down. There was no sign of Garlington's rescuers. Reluctantly Greely agreed.

Although he struck a vigorous pose while arguing his case to Greely, in his journal Rice was realistic. "I am pretty well used up," he admitted, before leaving on the mission with Shorty Frederick. "[My] face and hands are freshly frozen. Eskimo Fred died this morning. Lynn, I fear, will soon follow, and Jewell and Lt. Lockwood are also failing again."

That night, in fact, Lynn died, and Rice had to share the sleeping bag with a corpse.

Four men dragged a sled and sleeping bag to the top of Pim Island to give Rice and Frederick a head start. The 1,200-foot climb took them over four hours, a measure of how weak they were by this time. It's an hour at a reasonable pace.

Stepping feebly from rock to rock, Rice and Frederick nursed the sled over the grim plateau and down a gully to Rosse Bay. A gale rose. Arctic gales usually hit from one direction, but in this turbulent region, they can come from almost anywhere. The two struggled on but eventually they had to take shelter in the sleeping bag. They had no tent. In the wind they couldn't light their lamp to melt water, so they gnawed on a piece of frozen pemmican as the snow swirled over them. Even Camp Clay must have seemed like home compared to this.

When they set out again twenty-two hours later, they had to walk for an hour before they were warm enough to make tea, their first drink in a day and a half. After another windy day and night, they reached Eskimo Point. Here they stashed their sleeping bag and plodded seven miles further south to where the cache had been. It wasn't there. Either a polar bear or open water had claimed it. They searched for hours until Frederick noticed Rice failing. As a vicious wind blew, they took shelter behind an iceberg. Rice protested that he was just a little tired and kept up the "cheerful jocoseness" with which he had dismissed all his past mishaps until his mind began to drift. He rambled on about family and food until he lost consciousness and died in Frederick's arms in the grey light of an April storm.

By now Frederick was himself half-frozen. To survive, he had to reach the sleeping bag at Eskimo Point. "I stooped and kissed the remains of my dead companion and left them there for the wild winds of the Arctic to sweep over," he wrote. It took him seven hours to cover the seven miles to Eskimo Point. Here he managed to force his way into the bag, which was frozen as stiff as two pieces of plywood.

In the morning Frederick did something truly astonishing. In an act of respect, he trudged the seven miles back to Rice's body and spent several hours chopping pieces of ice to cover it in a makeshift burial. Only then did he return to Camp Clay. Clearly elevated by the memory of his friend's unselfishness, he brought back all Rice's unused food to be shared. These were probably the finest acts of Frederick's life, and looking back in later years, his eyes must have watered many times when he recalled the heights to which he had briefly risen.

Although they had already become hardened to death—two more had died in the meantime—the news about Rice caused an unprecedented outburst of emotion. One man wailed loudly. Several paid high tribute to him in their journals that evening. Brainard called him "as brave and noble as any that the world has ever known." Yet Rice was essentially an ordinary man who under ordinary conditions would not have shone, except to his family and friends. Some desire to be heroes and work all their lives to be regarded that way; Rice had heroism thrust on him by the extremes of Ellesmere Island.

For the next five weeks death took a holiday, thanks to the crustaceans and to a small polar bear which the two hunters, Long and Jens, shot on April 11. The only casualty during that period was Jens himself, who drowned when a piece of ice punctured his skin kayak during a seal hunt. The forty-one year old Greenlander's father had likewise died in a kayak accident.

Like a loaves and fishes miracle, their forty days of supplies from the previous October had persisted well into the spring, but it finally ran out on May 14. Five days later, a fresh spate of deaths began with one man who had been unable to eat the crustaceans. By the end of the week, three more bodies lay on Cemetery Ridge. Almost everyone felt the dark wing of death over them. In their last days of lucidity, they seemed able to sense its approach, and after an outburst or two of despair, became reconciled to it. A mental wandering mercifully preceded the end itself. "At the first wanderings we looked at each other, conscious that still another was about to pass away," Greely later recalled.

By now, suffering had exposed and simplified the character of the survivors. There were the Good, the Bad, and the Ugly. The Ugly were the weak who begged piteously for extra rations or who tried to evade their share of duties in a vain attempt to conserve strength. The Bad applied mainly to Octave Pavy and Charles Henry, whose unpleasant characteristics at Fort Conger consumed them utterly at Camp Clay. Some of the Good, such as Greely, Brainard, and Frederick, had actually become better through this trial by fire. One of the benefits of hard wilderness travel is that it simplifies your own character, so that if you are basically good, the effort can make you purer and better than everyday life usually allows.

This would have been incomprehensible to Pavy and Henry, who practiced survival at any cost. Pavy had had one desire: to win acclaim by reaching the Farthest North. He had even hatched a scheme to steal the best dog team from Lieutenant Lockwood, his chief travel competitor. "[Pavy is] a tricky, double-faced man," confided Greely in an unsent letter to his wife. Though Greely was myopic about his own behavior, he saw others 20-20.

Charles Buck Henry's motives for going north were cloudier. He had journalistic pretensions, and possibly he wanted to be the Arctic version of Henry Stanley, the famed African explorer-correspondent who had tracked down Dr. Livingstone. Or maybe he was just escaping from his shady past. His real name was Charles Henry Buck, and he had been dishonorably discharged from the cavalry for passing forged checks. A strong man, he later killed someone in a bar fight. Before heading north, Henry cut a deal to write stories on the north for a Chicago newspaper. He was twenty-seven.

Henry was the biggest eater at Fort Conger and had put on twenty-five pounds in two years. In other ways, his performance was less exceptional. He did not like hard work and feigned crippling joint pain in order to be sent back from one sledging trip. His companions later discovered how quickly the supposed invalid made it back to the station. "So much for huge men for arctic service," commented Brainard witheringly.

Henry's shirking and dishonesty would have been forgotten had they not presaged a darker development at Camp Clay. Throughout the ordeal on Pim Island, numerous thefts of food outraged the starving party. Henry was not the only perpetrator, but as time went on he became the most conspicuous.

When Henry's stealing became blatant in early June, the resort of execution, with which Greely had threatened others in moments of anger, finally seemed justified. Still, Greely tried to reason with him and gave him a last warning. But Henry did not seem to consider the weakened survivors a threat. When he stole again the following day, Greely secretly issued the execution order to Brainard, Long, and Frederick. It is written on a small, unlined page torn from a notebook and is smudged and crinkled around the edges. Considering that Greely was now almost too weak to stand, it shows a remarkably firm hand and a clear mind, the only stridency being the unnecessarily underlined words in the last sentence—"This order is *imperative* and *absolutely necessary* for *any chance* of life"—as if he already saw himself defending this action at a court of inquiry in Washington.

Later that day, Brainard, Long, and Frederick drew lots to decide who would carry out the order with their one good rifle. They made a vow of lifetime secrecy over the result. Then they asked Henry to help carry some wood to their tent just below Cemetery Ridge, where they were now living to escape the flooded lower ground. When they read the order to him, he lunged for an ax to fight them off but was shot twice, once in the chest and once in the head.

Later that day, two more died, including Pavy, who took some poison out of despair or dementia. The unlikely frontrunner for last survivor, a thought which must have been on their minds, even though they never wrote about it, was now Elison. Although he had lost both hands and feet to frostbite, his extra rations all winter had left him in apparently fine shape. In a macabre acknowledgment of this, one man tied a spoon to the stump of Elison's arm, so that when the rest of them died, he could still feed himself on whatever crumbs remained.

■

"I want Brainard commissioned [and] my daughters raised as analytical chemists."

—Greely, listing his last requests

By the third week of June, there was almost no food. Hunting was unsuccessful. The plankton had bloomed again after two months of open water, so that even the tiny crustaceans were now hard to get. In mid-April the haul had been so great, up to forty-two pounds a day, that the men could eat all they wanted. By May 26, the daily catch was down to eight pounds; by June 2, two pounds. When I tried to net them even later in the season using a pound of hamburger meat, far better bait than their sealskin scraps and guillemot legs, I caught just two specimens in twenty-four hours.

With only pieces of skin clothing and boiled lichen left to eat, the seven survivors—Greely, Brainard, Frederick, Long, Biederbick, Elison and Connell—hunkered down for the last vigil. They were, by now, almost the "brethren dwelling together in unity" that Greely had encouraged during his lectures. Only Maurice Connell kept apart. A few days earlier Connell, who was feeling strong, horrified the group by suggesting that it should now be every man for himself. But then he took a sharp turn downhill. His sore gums and swollen limbs suggested scurvy—the first appearance of the disease since Cross back in January. Connell was suddenly the next in line to die. With what he thought were his last words, he wrote bitterly to a friend, "It is the blunders of the heads of this expedition . . . who are to blame for our misfortune. . . . I hold Lieut. Greely personally responsible . . . it is well that he should not be made

The six survivors. Other key figures include Rice (seated, far right),
Henry (standing between Biederbick and Long) and Pavy (standing, third from right).

a martyr of and if ever he returns to the U.S. he ought to be tried and hung for murder."

June 22 was a typical summer day on Pim Island: a raging gale. Around midnight, Greely thought he heard a ship's horn. It might have been the wind fluting through a cavity in the rocks, but natural and artificial sounds have a different feel which an experienced ear comes to recognize, so he sent Brainard and Long to investigate. They climbed the ridge of broken rocks that separated their tent from the ocean but saw nothing except dark water breaking against the ice foot. Brainard returned disconsolately to the tent while Long climbed a little higher on the ridge to put up their signal flag—a shred of white flannel undershirt and one leg of long underwear tacked to an oar. Long's feelings at that moment do not seem to have been recorded, but his frail body must have felt a dizzying excitement when he saw a boatful of men near shore, especially since they had also seen him and were waving.

Long picked up the flag and waved it back feebly, then hobbled down to the ice foot, where the boat was mooring. "Who all are left?" shouted one of the rescuers.

"Seven left," Long managed to say. From somewhere far away, the already awakening voice of civilization called out faintly to Long. He removed his glove and shook his rescuer's hand.

Long was left in the care of one man while the others hurried to the half-collapsed tent. After gaining strength on judicious amounts of milk and beef tea, the survivors were transported on stretchers to the boats. Frederick melodramatically preferred to stagger to the waiting launch, propped up by a sailor on either side. Meanwhile, the bodies on Cemetery Ridge and near shore were also brought aboard. The outlines of at least two shallow graves remain on the ridge today, but so much windborne gravel flies around up there that most of the others have disappeared.

On rescue, Greely weighed 120 pounds, surprisingly robust, considering that he and the others were days from death. He had lost forty-eight pounds since Fort Conger. Such a loss, though severe, is not considered a verge-of-death weight for a man of his build. Many concentration-camp survivors of World War II were under a hundred pounds. And in that other famous tale of starvation in the Canadian north, Dillon Wallace dropped from a hundred and seventy pounds to ninety pounds during the tragic Hubbard expedition in Labrador and survived. It is likely that most of Greely's men perished not from starvation but from a deficiency disease such as beriberi.

■

"Greely is lionized as much as he will allow himself to be, but he is so modest, so reticent, that it is a bold person who will trench on his reserve. He is very tall. . . . He has superb eyes, black, lustrous and soft. . . . It is needless to add he is a great favorite with women."

—Chicago Tribune, January 1885

In studying the aftermath of the Greely expedition, what surprised me was how similar their era sounds to ours. The same media circus, even in 1884. No sooner did Greely land in St. John's than a lecture-circuit impresario cabled him, twice, with offers of an extended tour. Teenage girls wrote him the poetic equivalent of screeching chalk on a blackboard: "Wreathe the chaplet, twine the laurel, for our Heroes safe returned. . . ."

For days, the story dominated the front pages of newspapers across the nation. It began as a tale of tragedy and heroism, although sometimes the reporters let their descriptive skills run away with them. One vigorous passage recounted how the weakened survivors collected lichens by "rolling over and over away from the tent, and rolling back again," a style of travel that might be possible on a fairway but difficult on the boulder field that is Pim Island.

Editorial pages did the predictable. "With the rescue of the survivors of the Greely party there should come a surcease of the monstrous and murderous folly of so-called arctic exploration," fulminated the *Philadelphia Inquirer,* just as newspapers did a hundred years later about the space program after the *Challenger* shuttle disaster.

The coverage became particularly juicy when word got out that six of the bodies showed evidence of cannibalism. In those days *The New York Times* was not America's sober newspaper of record but an ambitious upstart that wasn't above presenting rumor as reportage: "There was scarcely anything left [in Henry's coffin] but a pile of glistening bones," it wrote breathlessly. "The head was missing, and a block of wood was made to do duty in its place." In Rochester, New York, Kislingbury's family had the body exhumed. An autopsy revealed missing slices of flesh from the trunk and thigh; there were also traces of human remains in his digestive tract.

The prospect that starving American soldiers had indulged in cannibalism was touted as "the shame of the nation." Greely himself seemed genuinely surprised by the revelations. It's likely that he hadn't known. Because of the clinical elegance of the cuts, the doctor was considered one of the chief suspects, shades of Jack the Ripper, four years later. But Pavy could not have been the only one, since he died on the same day as Henry, and Henry's body was one of the six cannibalized. Besides, by that time all the men had had two years' experience cutting up animals and were deft with a knife.

Decades later, in his foreword to *Abandoned*, Alden Todd's fine book about the Greely expedition, Vilhjalmur Stefansson speculated that all the cannibals died of "rabbit starvation," a debilitating ailment of those who eat only lean meat, with no fat in their diets. But from what we now know about the lipid content of the crustaceans, this would not have been the case.

Cannibalism stories make readers goggle-eyed, but the eventual verdict always seems to be that eating the dead bodies of your comrades is justified in a survival situation. Even the Vatican gave its blessing to the act after the famous 1972 plane crash of a rugby team in the Andes, when some Catholic passengers died rather than eat human flesh because they were afraid that it went against their religion. The public ordeal of Greely and the other survivors soon ended.

Thanks to Greely's efforts, Brainard was commissioned and eventually rose to Brigadier-General. Brainard's fair and honest handling of the supplies at Camp Clay had made him a symbol for the perfect chief commissary and he eventually became head of the army's Quartermaster Corps. My second-hand copy of *Six Came Back*, the published version of his journals, has Brainard's autograph on the flyleaf. The writing is hasty but remains as clear as the hundred and ten pages of menus and day-to-day horrors he carefully penciled into his long vertical notebook at Camp Clay.

Just as thwarted ambition seems to have pushed Pavy and Henry into the heart of darkness, Greely's success transformed him into a magnanimous figure, scarcely recognizable as the peevish little martinet of Fort Conger. He emerged as a national celebrity, America's greatest living polar hero. He too became a Brigadier-General. He helped found the American Geographical Society and the Explorers Club, directed relief after the San Francisco earthquake and during his long, energetic career, was involved in many other high-profile endeavors. Every year on June 22, the anniversary of their rescue, he and Brainard got together to eat one of the dream menus that Lockwood and the others had drawn up at Camp Clay.

When Greely died in 1935 at age 91, Brainard became the last survivor of the expedition. In his youth at Camp Clay, that might have been a matter of some pride. But now he was almost eighty years old, "and to be the last man," he admitted, "is a lonesome job."

■

Three years after my first brief visit to Camp Clay, I kayaked there again. This time, I was determined to linger. The stone walls of Greely's winter hut, eighteen by twenty-four feet, stood right by the shore. Twelve men had squeezed along one wall, thirteen along the other, giving only two feet of shoulder room per person. Barrel hoops remained, but no staves. Four staves a day had mildly warmed the pathetic rations of Greely's men.

I was hungry but too excited to make supper. Besides, there was something wrong with exploring Starvation Camp on a full stomach. Instead, I slipped a few precious squares of chocolate as an offering in the rocks at one corner of the hut.

Along the southwest wall, where the pantry of snowblocks and canvas had stood, dozens of rusted cans lay strewn among the rocks, as if the men hadn't had the energy to carry their garbage very far. Beside the entrance, a length of hemp rope and a square of tin with a hole through which a stovepipe had gone. A little further, a real find: dozens of the matches they'd used to light their stove. Inside the hut, sodden rags of green woolen clothing, one of them with a button still attached. On the site of Henry's execution, I found a single shell casing, green with rust. Paranoid about it being lost to souvenir hunters, I hid it in some nearby rocks.

I spent the next seven hours at this informal inventory. Tragedy had invested each item of century-old junk with an intense poignancy. Under a midnight sun you can choose to live what Frederick Cook called a "double day," in which magic moments are never prematurely shortened by night and you just keep going as long as you have the energy. Around eight a.m., however, I began to wilt, so I set up camp nearby and, feeling a little guilty, ate a good supper. As I drifted off to sleep, the west wind rose, and it sounded like voices.

Chapter Eight

The Ken Dryden Factor

Hard travel gave purity to my Ellesmere trips and photography gave them an artistic purpose. But history's role was more elusive. That I should become so immersed in it was strange, for I spent high school history classes cracking *sotto voce* jokes or memorizing chessmaster games and *pi* to sixty decimal places—nerd escapism. Anything but history. My eyes still glaze over at most of it; even the explorers of the central Arctic have a dull patina. But after Pim Island, Ellesmere's past came alive. I realized that I could keep returning to the island forever in search of ghosts. And as I trekked the obscure polar archives, I discovered tales as great and moving as the Greely saga, yet virtually unknown.

October 12, 1892. For young Swedish explorer Johan Alfred Björling and the four other members of his expedition, the situation was desperate. The trouble had started two months earlier in mid-August, when their ship, the *Ripple*, a 37-ton fore-and-after, had been wrecked off the shore of a small island between Greenland and Ellesmere. Björling and his party were able to salvage their supplies, but were faced with a grim prospect: spending the arctic winter on this barren island. But this in itself was not disastrous. They had enough food to last till the following

June. A whaling ship would likely come eventually to look for them. So they built a camp in a small ravine on the south side of the island and settled in for the wait.

The last days of summer ticked away. By now there was evening frost, despite the midnight sun, and days hovered around freezing. Even the dovekies and murres were flying south to their wintering grounds on the Grand Banks.

Experienced arctic travelers know not only when to move but also when to sit still. But Björling was not good at sitting. Though the forced overwintering would have been an impressive feat in itself, Björling was apparently determined to salvage something of his original expedition. On August 27, the five castaways set out in the *Ripple's* rowboat to push a hundred and twenty miles further north to an area where earlier expeditions had overwintered. It was their first big mistake.

Loaded to the gunwales with all their supplies, they rowed north across stormy Baffin Bay. Their first day out, a ship carrying American explorer Robert Peary home from northern Greenland passed within a few miles, but they did not see it. Rough seas threatened to swamp the rowboat, forcing them to dump most of their food to lighten the load. Against all odds, they managed to reach Northumberland Island, not quite halfway to their goal. Here, for what Björling called "various reasons," they decided to retreat to the Carey Islands.

They made it back to their original base in late September. Björling's last message, on October 12, omits much but still gives a clear picture of their situation. They now had enough food only until January 1. And they had other problems, too. The cryptic last line of his entry reads, "We are now five men, one of whom is dying."

By the time that message was found, Björling and his crew had vanished without a trace.

■

The island where Björling's ship came to grief now bears his name. It's one of the Carey Islands, six small outcroppings in the High Arctic and one of the most isolated places on earth. These wind-blasted, treeless specks of rock sit in the throat of Baffin Bay, between northern Greenland and Ellesmere Island, some 2,000 miles due north of Quebec City.

Björling is the easternmost island of the Carey group, measuring barely a half-mile across by one mile long. Only a handful of people have ever stood on what one early explorer called "this bleak and desolate island, which a wealth of bright sunshine could not relieve of its aspect of dreariness."

Getting to the Carey Islands these days may be easier than it was a hundred years ago, but it's still no simple matter. Last August, I flew north on a Canadian C-130 Hercules cargo plane to Thule, the U.S. air base on the west coast of Greenland. The Thule area has been occupied more or less continuously since the twelfth century, an important fact not known in Björling's day, and has yielded more ruins than anywhere else in the High Arctic. Thule was home to an Inuit settlement in 1952 when the U.S. Air Force picked the site for a strategic base. Its peak Cold War population of 10,000 has now shrunk to 1,000 people, mostly Danish support staff.

In Thule, a hired Greenlandair helicopter was ready to make the trip to Björling Island, about a half hour flight away. From the helicopter, a wind-whipped sea spray made the Carey Islands ghostly and insubstantial, but we could make Björling Island out immediately, a long dark line with a distinctive bump on the north end.

I wasn't sure what I was looking for. I only knew that I wanted to look.

■

Johan Alfred Björling came from an old, intellectual, but not wealthy, Stockholm family. His father died in 1871, a week after Björling was born, and he was raised by his mother. Johan was one of those kids who seem always to have been miniature versions of their adult selves. At two years old, Björling had the same chunky face, outsized head and blonde brush cut as when he put to sea at twenty-one. Behind the childish proportions, his gaze already looked mature. Björling reminded me of the kid brother of one of my emigré European friends back in high school, who when eight years old seemed decades older than I was. The only hint that he was also a normal kid was the poster of hockey goalie Ken Dryden in his bedroom, just above a bust of Mozart.

By twenty-one, Björling had had only limited experience in the Arctic. Yet his goal was ambitious: to sail up the eastern side of Ellesmere, to cross to the unexplored west coast (the size of the island was not yet known), and to then retrace his route back south before the polar winter set in.

The other members of Björling's expedition were even less experienced than he was. His partner, Evald Kallstenius, was 24 and had never been to the Arctic. Their ship's captain, a baby-faced Dane named Karl Kann whom they enlisted in St. John's, Newfoundland, was Björling's age. Never before had such a young group attempted so much in the Arctic. Those who preceded Björling, and those who followed, were all much older. Robert Peary was 35 when he commanded his first expedition; George Nares was 44; Adolphus Greely, 37; Otto Sverdrup, 40. Polar exploration was a game for the middle-aged, yet Björling had launched a children's crusade. What's more, most of the expeditions of the time were large, well-financed and well-equipped. But Björling set out with a ragtag crew of only four others.

Few have ever heard of Björling, though if he had reached western Ellesmere, he would undoubtedly be ranked as one of the great polar explorers. (Seven years later, Sverdrup would accomplish Björling's dream of crossing Ellesmere and with the discovery of Axel Heiberg Island, step into the front ranks of arctic explorers.) While other disastrous expeditions have gone on to receive a twenty-one gun salute in the Encyclopedia Britannica, Björling earned little more than a brief obituary in a Swedish polar journal.

I'd stumbled upon occasional references to Björling in my reading and eventually turned to Swedish sources for more information. I was fascinated not only by his disappearance and obscurity, but because any twenty-one-year-old's death by misadventure hits close to home. Rare is the adventurer who has not done stupid things in his youth. In Banff, Alberta, where I live, the throb of a low-flying park rescue helicopter often signals that yet another twenty-one-year-old dishwasher has fallen off a mountain. My most reckless summer came when I was a year younger. I was knocking about Europe, and in a three-week span I rappelled off a cliff on a clothesline, got stuck ropeless two-thirds of the way up a hundred-foot cliff in France and kamikazed down a mountain highway near Gruyère, Switzerland, on a one-speed bike with no brakes. I wasn't suicidal, just overconfident and giddy with the freedom of my first big trip away from home. Of course, I was also lucky. Björling wasn't.

■

Björling's obsession with the north began in 1889 when, as a seventeen-year-old student from Stockholm, he went to northern Sweden with two schoolmates to make what they believed was the first ascent of Kebnekaise, the highest peak in the country. (Unknown to them, a French climber had topped out six years earlier.) By today's standards, the 6,965-foot peak presents no great challenge. Guidebooks describe the route as "safe, toilsome, and rather unexciting," and the summit register includes seven-year-olds and families of five. But in 1889, the seventy-mile trek in, plus a glacier that has since shrunk back, taxed the young adventurers. An unroped Björling even fell into a crevasse but landed on a ledge of ice. Fuelled on the twenty-three-hour push by just a little chocolate and coffee—a shortage of food and sleep would mark all Björling's trips—they reached the summit.

For his two friends, it was the trip of a lifetime, but for Björling, it was just the beginning. He was already, in the words of a companion, "afflicted with the most absolute polar craziness, 'bitten by a mad Eskimo,' as they say in Copenhagen."

Later that year, in search of a mentor, Björling approached Sweden's most famous polar explorer, Baron A. E. Nordenskiold, who was impressed by the intense young botany student. The following summer, Nordenskiold managed to place Björling on a landmark four-month expedition to Spitsbergen, a wild Scandinavian island of fiords and ice caps and sawtooth peaks. A zoologist on the expedition was surprised when the teenager showed up at the dock. "In our eyes [he was] little better than a schoolboy," the zoologist wrote, "a fat and flourishing sixth-former, beaming with well-being, and with round innocent eyes."

On a Spitsbergen glacier, Björling had a close call even more serious than his fall into the crevasse on Kebnekaise. Ill-equipped as usual, he was the only one of the skiers without climbing skins. Wet snow balled up under his wooden slats, and eventually Björling removed the skis and tried to keep up with the others by postholing through the snow. The trek went on longer than anticipated; fog added to the confusion. Eventually, Björling could go no further. The team had almost run out of food. In desperation, they left Björling in a tent with their remaining supplies and hurried back to the ship.

Before they could return for him, a storm swept over the glacier. When it lifted a day later, Björling tried to reach the ship himself, but headed in the wrong direction. The relief party caught up to him by following his tracks. They found him confused, possibly hypothermic. He tried to hide from them behind a rock.

Rather than deter him, Björling's early misadventures seemed to galvanize his will to explore ever deeper into the North. Within a year, he had set his eyes toward the northernmost inhabited corner of the globe, the mythic place the ancients called Thule. Greenland.

■

As the nineteenth century was drawing to a close, the pace of arctic exploration was accelerating, but only a daring few had penetrated the waters of far northwest Greenland. In 1891, Björling set out for that terra incognita. His plans were modest—to explore part of the west coast—but this was still a place where explorers could lose themselves forever.

After a Danish trade ship deposited Björling at Upernavik, halfway up western Greenland, he and four hired native oarsmen embarked on a furious journey northward. His time was extremely limited, as he had to return to Upernavik in time to catch the ship home. The hyperactive Björling pushed the hired crew and himself mercilessly, all the while collecting plants and taking a series of ocean temperatures that provided the first evidence of warm upwellings. Within six days, despite contrary winds and ice, they had maneuvered a hundred and fifty miles north. No one ate or slept much; Björling took only brief catnaps. His men were so exhausted that they fell asleep while rowing in a snowstorm. The bad weather persisted but Björling, tenaciously botanizing till the end, managed to return to Upernavik in time for his rendezvous with the ship. He had covered an impressive three hundred miles in just over two weeks.

In 1892, Björling was ready to attempt the expedition that he hoped would make his name: a crossing of Ellesmere Island. One source I've read claimed that Björling's real goal was to scoop the North Pole, but that's unlikely. Björling's long-range ambitions may have involved the Pole—what young explorer of that era wouldn't have had lurking designs on the ultimate polar prize?—but his expeditions show a mature progression toward acquiring ever more experience.

Björling's correspondence reveals how markedly different he was from such well-known young modern romantics as Everett Ruess and Chris McCandless, who also perished in the wilderness. The twenty-year-old Ruess was an artist who disappeared in 1934 near Escalante, Utah, murdered, some say, and who has been the subject of numerous recent articles and short films. McCandless was the twenty-four-year-old who died of starvation in Alaska in 1992 and became the subject of Jon Krakauer's bestseller, *Into the Wild*. Both these young men were mystics of the Thoreau school, who rhapsodized about nature as they groped for an artistic voice. Björling's voice was much more business-like; he sounds a lot older.

On this expedition, Björling planned to travel to St. John's, Newfoundland, and buy a ship to enable him to stick to his own timetable.

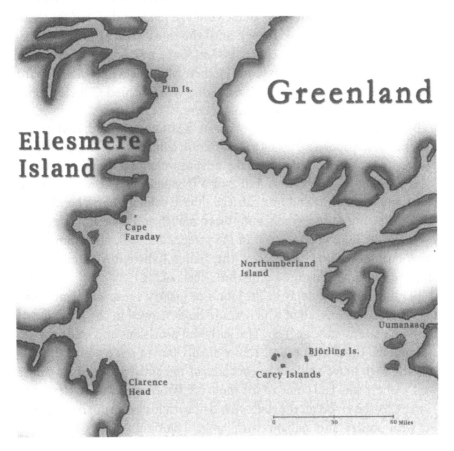

Impressively practical, he raised money from private sponsors and scientific societies. He also sought out a zoologist to complement his botany work. A professor he knew recommended Evald Kallstenius.

Björling and Kallstenius left Sweden and made their way to Liverpool, living in fleabag hotels and traveling third class. They crossed the Atlantic on a tramp steamer and arrived in St. John's on June 1. Both spoke English well, and letters of introduction from the influential Nordenskiold gave the students a certain profile in town, despite their hardscrabble budget. They dined with the governor of Newfoundland and Labrador and met with the Swedish consul, Robert Prowse, who offered to sell them his boat. When the students purchased a cheaper one, Prowse became their secret enemy. He spread word around town that their little schooner, *Ripple*, was a floating coffin.

The arctic summer is brief, and Björling and Kallstenius had counted on a quick start. But Prowse's quiet sabotage made it difficult for them to find a captain and crew. It took until the third week of June for Björling to enlist three local knockabouts. Karl Kann, a Dane, was twenty-one but had been at sea for seven years. Herbert McDonald of Prince Edward Island joined as cook, while a "wandering waif" named Gilbert Dunn, originally from England, signed on as crew.

Björling's three weeks in St. John's are well-documented, thanks to a series of newspaper articles by a local fixture named Reverend Dr. Moses Harvey, who befriended the young adventurers. "Björling," he wrote, "was a young Norse giant, 6 feet 2 or 3 inches in height, with a broad chest, muscular arms and fine carriage. I have seldom seen a handsomer face—fair complexion, finely sculptured mouth and nose and large blue eyes. People here used to stop in the streets and look after him in admiration." According to Harvey, the frailer Kallstenius "almost worshipped Björling," despite being three years older.

Björling used the delay in St. John's to make a series of inland treks for plant specimens, all of which would be destroyed in the great fire of St. John's later that year. They also gathered provisions and made the social rounds. Björling and Kallstenius finally put to sea on June 22, dismissing with brave smiles the concerns of the small group of St. John's well-wishers who had come to see them off. Wrote the effusive Reverend Harvey, "As he stood on the deck that day, with his beautiful face lighted up with smiles and radiant with hope, [Björling waved] his cap in farewell as the vessel glided from the wharf. I had but a faint hope that I should ever see them again."

From here, the story of the expedition relies mostly on letters home and sketchy notes left in rock cairns. Although Björling's minimalist style leaves many questions unanswered, we can reconstruct the main events of the 1892 expedition. Herbert McDonald, the cook, was drunk when he came aboard and apparently went insane after a week at sea. Although he partly recovered later, he seems to have remained dead weight, because Kallstenius writes how they all did their own cooking on a small camp stove.

For three weeks, the *Ripple* groped northward in a fog without seeing land. Fighting ice and gales, it took them nearly five weeks to reach Godhavn (now Qeqertarsuaq), the largest town in Greenland. It was already late July and they were still in central Greenland, drastically behind schedule. The arctic summer was now almost over. August has good ice conditions for sailing, but winter can set in any time after mid-month.

Björling and Kallstenius spent five days in Godhavn provisioning themselves for a possible overwintering. They didn't have enough money to buy everything they needed, so they planned on supplementing their stores from the food cache that George Nares had left on the Carey Islands in 1875. Thanks to the arctic deep-freeze, most of the food would still be edible.

Despite the floating-coffin rumors spread by the Swedish consul in St. John's, the little *Ripple* proved perfectly seaworthy. The *Ripple* even crossed treacherous Melville Bay, an ice-choked gauntlet that had sunk many a stout whaling ship, in one day. Nevertheless, Greenland is the largest island in the world, and they didn't reach the easternmost Carey Island, site of the Nares depot, until August 16.

Björling had originally hoped to begin his Ellesmere crossing two months earlier, but either he did not realize how late in the season it was or the idea of failure was alien to him. He still hoped to follow a condensed version of his plan, and he was no doubt pushing himself and his crew with the same relentless energy he had successfully used on his rowing marathon the previous year. He'd been in tough spots before, and his determination had carried him through.

Probably working day and night, he and the others used their rowboat to shuttle Nares's 3,600 rations onto the *Ripple*. They had just shifted the

Ripple to the south end of the island when a storm came up. Maybe they were exhausted and were sleeping on shore. Maybe there was nothing they could have done. But during the night, waves drove the *Ripple* onto the shallows, wrecking it.

■

The helicopter's blades thumped loudly as the aircraft slowed, flared and landed on the rocky hide of Björling Island. It was seven p.m. on a lovely bright but windy August evening. Dazzling white icebergs drifted south with the Greenland current, like an armada of tall ships. The sun blazed out of a cloudless sky as it angled northwest. It would not set for another month, but just circle the horizon endlessly, dipping a little lower at midnight, rising a little higher at noon. Crashing surf ringed the entire island like a reef. There were no harbors and many cliffs, but sailors would have been able to beach a rowboat on one of several rocky aprons. The pilot set the helicopter down on the west side, next to the only freshwater pond on the island.

Glaucous gulls cawed over our heads, constantly fine-tuning their wing angles to hold place in the roaring wind. The meadow around the pond, an ideal campsite, yielded little but the remains of a silk tent probably left by geologists who came here thirty years ago.

I was using a topo map plus a reference sketch drawn by a Swedish zoologist who had visited the island two years after Björling. But the island was much bigger and more rugged than the poorly detailed charts suggested. Ravines and small cliffs made progress more an Eco-Challenge than a hike. The terrain seemed to be mocking my desire to sniff out any traces of Björling.

After a fruitless search of the area, we piled back into the helicopter and did a slow, low tour of the island. I panned for artifacts while trying to make sense of the increasingly frustrating sketch. Finally, we spotted a scattering of wood and put down. It was not all old, but some ancient timbers, bully beef cans and a wooden barreltop suggested that this was the spot on the east side where Nares had left his cache.

The *Ripple* had foundered on the south side of the island, and the crew had camped nearby in what Björling called a "cut." Sure enough, flying south, a series of finger gullies replaced the cliffs and aprons of the east side. The rocky fingers reached a long way into the shallow sea. It would have been easy for a storm-tossed ship to sink on these petrified reefs.

One of the gullies looked full of junk. The big Bell 212 banked and jockeyed in the wind like the gulls, as it settled down nearby. Unlike the compromised Nares site, which had left me wondering whether that truly was his depot, this gully was undoubtedly where Björling and his four companions had huddled after the sinking of the *Ripple*. Hand-blown bottles, hemp ropes, broken crockery and the remains of a linen shirt with pearly buttons lay amid the lichen-coated rocks. Two of Björling's botanical specimen bottles were intact. Even after the loss of his ship, Björling had carefully preserved the tools of his trade, by which he expected to make his reputation.

As hoped, I found the cairn in which Björling had left his four curt notes, written in English, still standing at the highest point of the island, five hundred feet above the sea. The cairn has changed little since George Nares built it for his own notes back in 1875. The original canister for messages has disappeared, but Nares's broken flagpole still protrudes from the top.

■

By the time Björling left his last note on October 12, 1892, the expedition had collapsed. Their ship was a wreck. They had lost half their supplies on the unnecessary journey to Northumberland Island. They had been stormbound on the island for some time, and by now, the snow lay knee-deep. In another week, the sun would disappear for the winter. And one of them was dying.

Björling does not mention who this was or why he was dying, but two years later, in 1894, searchers found a skeleton, "mistreated by gulls," somewhere on the island. From stains on the teeth, they concluded that the victim had been a pipe-smoker who held his pipe in the left side of his mouth. Kallstenius did not smoke; it is unlikely that Kann, their fresh-faced captain, had been smoking long enough to discolor his teeth. It had to have been either the wandering waif or the crazy cook.

According to his last message, Björling decided to head to Ellesmere Island. "I now set out to the Eskimos at Clarence Head or Cape Faraday," he wrote, addressing some whaler who might find the message the following summer. "I would be most obliged to you, if you would go to Clarence Head (50 statute miles from here), where I will leave a message in a cairn on the easternmost cape concerning our life during the winter."

Björling wouldn't have known it, but Clarence Head is the most austere part of Ellesmere; in most spots here, the ice cap meets the sea. Though the history of the Inuit in the High Arctic dates back over 4,000 years, no one has ever lived at Clarence Head. It would be like living on the Antarctic plateau. Except for an occasional passing polar bear, the region is wholly barren.

Cape Faraday has good whale, seal and bear hunting but these are difficult prey for inexperienced explorers. While the Inuit have migrated through the area on occasion, no one usually lived on Ellesmere's southeast coast. Björling and his reduced party might have survived at Cape Faraday despite the loss of most of their rations, but it would have been hard.

Nonetheless, the lack of bodies and boat on Björling Island suggests that Björling did set out for the distant shore. But no further trace was ever found of the young explorer or his party.

■

Since Björling went north prepared to overwinter, his disappearance did not raise immediate concern. But the following summer, in 1893, a Scottish whaler found his cairn notes and the wreck of the *Ripple*. It was clear that the young Swede's expedition had come to grief.

The public obsession with the disappearance of Sir John Franklin thirty-five years earlier had financed many search expeditions, but Björling's fate did not get the same response. Only two search parties made brief stops at the Carey Islands in 1894, on their way to fry bigger fish. One of the expeditions also quickly checked Clarence Head on Ellesmere Island for signs of Björling, but found none. Subsequent visitors to Clarence Head and Cape Faraday have never reported any signs of white explorers.

In 1916, Peter Freuchen, a writer who began his career managing a trading post at Thule, made a thorough inventory of the expedition's artifacts on Björling Island, removing a few for museums. After that, the world forgot about Johan Alfred Björling.

On her death bed, Björling's mother claimed she could feel that her son was still alive. But while the absence of bodies always leaves open far-fetched possibilities, there is only one conclusion: Somewhere between the Carey Islands and Clarence Head, their boat swamped and they died in the icy waters of Baffin Bay. Fifty miles to Clarence Head, Björling had said in his last note. At the pace he had managed the year before, that was a day and a half. A quick run, in good weather. But in fact, it's almost ninety miles from Björling Island to Clarence Head, and over a hundred miles to Cape Faraday. A hundred miles over one of the stormiest seas on earth. Ernest Shackleton overcame worse in the Antarctic, but he was an experienced sailor, with a veteran crew. Björling still made a practice of surviving everything by the skin of his teeth. Despite his European old-soul maturity, he was vulnerable.

As I stood on the island, looking across the water at the brown cliffs of Greenland thirty miles away, I found it hard to understand why Björling so persistently ignored the haven of Greenland. The Thule area might have been occupied. If not there, one of several small communities north of it. At Northumberland Island, during their September push, they were a mere thirty miles from Peary's Greenland base, where supplies and local people might still be gathered. Even if they hadn't known about these settlements, a beeline to Greenland was the obvious choice. It looked so close, while even from our helicopter, the high ice caps of Ellesmere were too far away to see.

Still, they'd had luck on their side and dodged the final bullet several times. Salvation may have been close, but Björling knew only one direction: forward. The loss of his ship, the death of a man, and the disappearance of the summer could not suppress his optimism.

As it turned out, one of his companions on his earlier trip to Spitsbergen had him dead to rights: "When it came to his all-absorbing interest, [Björling] proved able to manifest an utterly unbelievable will-power, an iron energy capable of overcoming any obstacle. Except death."

Chapter Nine

Inside the Arctic Triangle

Beyond our camp on western Axel Heiberg Island, a mirage of mountain peaks floated in the air, while nearby Amund Ringnes Island had vanished entirely in a creeping sea fog. These were common conditions in the arctic summer, but they emphasized the sleight-of-hand nature of this place. If islands could be conjured out of nothing and real islands could vanish, how likely were we to find the remains of Dr. Hans Krüger, who disappeared in this region seventy years ago?

Only a few sketchy references to this German explorer existed before 1993, when William Barr, now a researcher at the Arctic Institute of North America in Calgary, published a summary of Krüger's life and death in the *Polar Record*, a scholarly journal out of Cambridge, England. Barr is a rangy man with a mane of white hair, a talent for languages and a consuming interest in arctic history. He is known as the Professor of Lost Causes, because of his fascination with quixotic ventures. He has investigated everyone from the Russian count who disappeared looking for an imaginary land to the man who tried to walk to the North Pole from Winnipeg.

I had already tried twice to search for Krüger, so I hungrily latched onto the details that Barr had ferreted out. Inspired by the story, I flew to Good Friday Bay on southwestern Axel Heiberg Island, the prime search area, to look for his last camp. In this nearly rot-free environment, bones, clothing, tents, possibly even journals, would be intact.

Similar mysteries had been solved decades later. In 1930, the year Krüger disappeared, the last camp of an 1897 Swedish ballooning expedition to the North Pole was accidentally discovered on an island in Svalbard. Likewise, the expedition that found the body of British mountaineer George Mallory, lying upon Mount Everest's wind-raked upper slopes for seventy-five years. I knew that finding Krüger was a needle in a haystack, but Axel Heiberg was a beautiful haystack in which to spend three weeks. And I'd become obsessed with the needle.

■

Hans Krüger was born in Posen, Prussia in 1886, and later settled near Darmstadt, Germany. He took up science late in life, at age thirty-eight. Before that, he had led an adventurous, knockabout life in southern Africa. He tended a game reserve and managed a vanadium mine. During World War I, he fought with the Boers against the British, was captured, sentenced to death, escaped, was recaptured and finally pardoned. Two earlier arctic expeditions in which he'd tried to participate never materialized. Finally in 1924, he began planning his own major expedition to the Canadian Arctic.

His inspiration seems to have been Vilhjalmur Stefansson, the Manitoba-born explorer whose 1921 book, *The Friendly Arctic*, painted the north as overflowing with game. Stefansson's style of living off the land, à la the Inuit, fired the imaginations of a lot of dreamers. It offered a cheap alternative to big, government-backed expeditions or Peary-style extravaganzas requiring millionaire sponsors.

It took Krüger five years to bring his grand scheme to life. In between, he published a spate of scientific papers and became engaged to a woman sixteen years his junior. Twenty-six-year-old Hilda Schad von Mittelbiberach was completely smitten by the handsome scientist-explorer, whom she affectionately called "Jack" or "Daddy."

"So strange is life, that someone comes out of the wilds of Africa and becomes your destiny," she wrote him. "I will never be free of you in my life again."

In June, 1929, Krüger finally sailed for Greenland. Accompanying him was a Danish assistant named Åge Rose Bjare, who had spent five years in West Greenland. Fellow passengers formed contrasting opinions of Krüger. Inspector A. H. Joy, the greatest of all Mounted Police travelers, was impressed by the German's knowledge and quiet confidence while Frederica de Laguna, a young woman who later became an arctic anthropologist, found him overbearing and sensed tension between him and Bjare. "One never sees them together, and there does not seem to be any spirit and enthusiasm in their expedition," she wrote.

In early August, Krüger and Bjare settled in for the winter at Neqe, Greenland, within view of Ellesmere. In early March, the two Europeans set out with four hired Greenlanders across frozen Kane Basin to the RCMP post on Ellesmere's Bache Peninsula.

Bache Post was established in 1926 as part of a growing awareness of Canada's fragile claim on the arctic islands. No one was sure whether any new, undiscovered islands still existed, so expeditions such as Krüger's were viewed as potential land grabs. Partly in response to Krüger's early inquiries, the government introduced the Scientists' and Explorers' License to control foreign access. Krüger had to write several reassuring letters to Canadian officials insisting that his interest was science, not sovereignty, before he was granted the necessary papers.

The post looks south toward a high ice cap discharging elegant little glaciers. It is an oasis of sunshine and gentle winds. Thanks to a small nearby polynya, marine life is abundant, and even in early summer the basso grunting of walrus echoes from the cliffs.

Hans Krüger arrived at Bache on March 12, 1930. He and Bjare did not look ready to embark on an ambitious journey. Their dogs were scrawny, and Krüger was suffering from one of the serious bouts of cramps and vomiting that had plagued him and Bjare all winter, possibly trichinosis from the raw dog meat they had eaten during a disastrous shakedown trip the previous fall. At the invitation of the presiding RCMP constable, they rested at Bache for a week.

On March 19, Krüger's party struck out west across Ellesmere Island, with a "punk outfit and a badly overloaded sledge," one unimpressed Mountie reported. Near the present-day weather station of Eureka, their two support sledges turned back, leaving only Krüger, Bjare, a highly experienced Greenlander named Akqioq, one sledge and seventeen dogs.

Bjare, the return party reported, had frozen toes. Krüger was spitting blood. Their sled was so heavy that Krüger had to walk in front to spur the dogs on, while Bjare and Akqioq pushed from behind. This unpromising vignette is the last of Krüger or his companions that anyone would ever see.

■

But this was not the last word from Krüger. Over the years, three of his notes have been found in old cairns. The notes are both revealing and maddeningly inconclusive. All say essentially, "Everything okay. Continuing on to Such-and-Such Island." And then silence.

In 1997, while retracing part of Krüger's route around Axel Heiberg, I visited two of these cairns. Both were originally built in 1906 by Robert Peary. Explorers built cairns and left messages in them to show they had visited a spot and to inform other parties about their travel plans. It was customary for later explorers to replace the cairn note with a faithful copy of it, along with a message of their own. Krüger, who clearly viewed his journey as a historic one, went out of his way to visit the cairns of his famous predecessors.

The first cairn lies near Lands Lokk, Ellesmere's northwestern tip, on the stony shore of the Arctic Ocean. The pile of rocks that Peary's Greenland assistants carefully assembled now lies in lumpy disarray. In modern times, it was first visited in 1954 by Geoffrey Hattersley-Smith and Robert Christie. In an empty film can wrapped in sealskin and walrus hide, Hattersley-Smith found a note from Krüger, written in German and stating that they had arrived here on April 22, 1930, that they were proceeding to Axel Heiberg Island and that all were in good condition.

Manhauling from Lands Lokk, my partner and I reached Axel Heiberg that same day. A two-hour climb brought us to the flat dome above Cape Thomas Hubbard. Here stood Peary's second cairn, a massive six-foot construction, its north side plastered with wind-driven snow. Krüger's second note was found here by RCMP Corporal Henry Stallworthy during his magnificent 1932 circumnavigation of the island in search of the missing expedition. The German's brief message declared that they were continuing on to Meighen Island.

While my companion wandered off to explore the dome, I rummaged hopefully at the base of the cairn. I was about to give up when I spotted something dark green among the rocks. Scraping away the hard snow with my Swiss army knife, I drew out a broken bottle with a frozen note scrolled up inside it.

That night in the tent, I thawed the note over our stove and carefully unrolled it. In faded pencil was the date June 16, 1957, and a brief message from Ray Thorsteinsson, another great geologist-traveler of that decade. I knew Ray, as I knew Hattersley-Smith. We had met once or twice, corresponded, spoken on the phone. They were legends and I was in awe of them. Ray alone had found approximately a hundred cairns in his career. But that was not the most exciting part of retrieving his note forty years later. I was now, in a tiny way, part of the chain that led to Krüger, and even further, back to Peary. MacMillan had found Peary's note. Krüger, coming from Lands Lokk, had found MacMillan's. Stallworthy had found Krüger's. Ray had found Stallworthy's. And now I had found Ray's.

Stallworthy could not follow Krüger's trail to Meighen Island because of bad ice, but conditions were better for Thorsteinsson. His geological survey brought him to the cairn that Stefansson and his party had built

in 1917 to commemorate their discovery of Meighen Island. Beneath the squat pile of brown rocks lay a note from Krüger, dated May 6, 1930. It stated that they were on their way to Cape Sverre, the northern tip of Amund Ringnes Island. In average conditions, that seventy-five mile trek across the sea ice takes about four days by dogteam.

Krüger's three notes cast doubt on the sorry picture of an overloaded, sick expedition brought back by the support team. It took Krüger one day to travel the twenty miles from Lands Lokk to Cape Thomas Hubbard, a good pace. Cape Thomas Hubbard to Meighen Island required eleven days; Ray Thorsteinsson, traveling with good dogs and moderately loaded sledges, did it in nine days. No difference.

It is true that after first separating from the support party, Krüger took about three weeks to sled the two hundred miles from Depot Point to Lands Lokk, a route I walked in ten days. Dogteams should be about fifty percent faster than manhaulers, not slower. But snow and ice conditions vary. They also may have taken some time to eat through their supplies, or to collect rock samples in Nansen Sound. In any case, by the time he reached Meighen Island, Krüger seemed to be doing fine.

In 1958, Thorsteinsson flew in and searched Cape Sverre but found no trace of Krüger.

■

Krüger's plans were as mysterious as his fate. Perhaps the official resistance to his early proposals taught him that the less said to bureaucracies, the better. Or maybe he just wanted to keep his options open. His original plans called for a five-year expedition, which he later reduced to one or two years, perhaps after meeting Hilda. A map Krüger left with friends in Germany suggests he wanted to investigate the old myth of land northwest of Axel Heiberg. At some point, he had even contemplated a suicidal crossing of the Arctic Ocean and had contacted Russian authorities for permission to land on their northern shores. The equipment on his sledge included a giant spool of piano wire, with which he hoped to find the edge of the continental shelf. If it dropped off too quickly, it would all but eliminate the possibility of undiscovered islands.

The timing between Krüger's three notes, however, shows that he turned south immediately after reaching Cape Thomas Hubbard. Although Hilda believed that he was returning to Germany in the fall of 1930, Krüger never ruled out the possibility of wintering somewhere around the Ringnes Islands. But his last destination, Cape Sverre, suggests that they were on a direct course back to Ellesmere Island when disaster struck.

■

Any unsolved mystery is an obsession waiting to happen. This one was made more tantalizing by the fact that all three expert travelers who had found Krüger's notes—Stallworthy, Hattersley-Smith, and Thorsteinsson—believed that his last camp will one day be found. I was less optimistic, but when Thorsteinsson offered me a new theory on Krüger's demise, I leapt at the chance to check it out.

By the time Krüger reached Meighen Island, Thorsteinsson pointed out, it is almost certain that he was critically short of dogfood. Three weeks' dogfood was all that one komatik could carry. Dogsled expeditions depended on bear, seal, or muskox, which are rare around western Axel Heiberg.

Early travelers of Axel Heiberg's west coast suffered serious food shortages, and none worse than Henry Stallworthy on his search for Krüger in 1932. Annotations on the hand-drawn map of his journey give a grim, cape-by-cape account of his march down that starvation coast: "Dogs hungry. 1 hare. Dogs hungry. 1 caribou. Dogs starving. Shot 6 dogs. 43 hours march: too weak to go on." If not for a food cache left for him by another patrol, Stallworthy would likely have joined Krüger as a missing person.

By the time he reached Meighen Island, even Thorsteinsson had been through such tough straits that half his party raced back to Axel Heiberg to hunt for game in a sheltered bay. Thorsteinsson believed that shortly after leaving Meighen Island, Krüger may have done the same, and singled out two bays on Axel's southwest coast. "I consider Good Friday Bay and Sand Bay . . . two of the least explored regions on Axel Heiberg," he wrote me. "These bays are about the only major bays on the island that I have not visited on the ground, and I know of no other member of the Geological Survey or anyone else who has been there."

What other excuse does anyone need to visit a place?

■

In July, 1999, my fiancée Alexandra and I found ourselves in Good Friday Bay, a ten-by-twenty-mile inlet named by Otto Sverdrup, who discovered Axel Heiberg in 1899, exactly a hundred years earlier.

Southwestern Axel Heiberg is exposed to weather from the turbulent west and northwest, so I was expecting to find only a few hardy lichens. Instead, arctic poppies reached their ten-inch stems toward the sun. Grasses sprang from the sandy soil and tiny, delicate flowers whose names I did not know greeted us at every step. A dry, corrugated crust of what looked like baked brain coral offered an almost ideal hiking surface.

This was only Alexandra's second arctic trip, but I found her presence reassuring. Both my earlier Krüger search attempts had suffered from unfortunate partner choices. First there was Larry, who quit after half a day on the trail. And in spring, 1999, a scientist with impeccable adventure credentials had to back out at the last minute because of a family emergency. When I carried on alone, I ran into bad snow that kept me from reaching the search area. Not only had Krüger's expedition been cursed, it seemed that my attempts to search for him were, too.

I had never expected to find a life partner who enjoyed arctic travel. My previous wife had suffered through my arctic awakening and hard travel phase. Although she was extreme in her own way, my exuberance oppressed her and made her feel conservative by comparison. She craved the artist's position in the relationship, not that of straight man. Besides, she wanted kids, which meant that the household needed one full-time breadwinner, and neither of us volunteered.

On an earlier trip to Devon Island, Alexandra had shown that combination of patience and mental toughness that arctic travel requires. She particularly loved the animals and had an eye for detail that I lacked. I saw many things for the first time through her eyes. At the end of the trip, we were still on such good terms that I proposed to her, at Truelove Inlet.

Likewise, I felt that Krüger's and Stallworthy's fiancées had been an important part of the story—Krüger's, because her love for him ended in tragedy for both, and Stallworthy's, because after he returned home from the search, they married and their love affair persisted until Stallworthy's death.

From our small base camp on the north shore of Good Friday Bay, we launched one-week trips to different points of the compass, covering the shoreline as we went. Krüger's last camp would almost certainly be on the coast. Explorers might hunt inland, but they always camped near sea ice—the arctic highway.

The route to Sand Bay led us over what earth scientists call a peneplain, a tableland sliced by erosion gullies. These arroyos and badlands were, at least superficially, reminiscent of Alberta's Dinosaur Provincial Park.

Sand Bay did not look like a suitable spot for Krüger's last camp. Flat coastline was scarce. Still, we hiked almost the entire coast in order to be sure.

To the west, the specter of Amund Ringnes Island in the distance taunted us. This big, flat island, named after a Norwegian brewer, should be in the record books as Most Dully Named Island of All Time. Places such as Stratigrapher River, Structural River and Geologist Bay showed that not all arctic scientists were imaginative. Cape Sverre was out of sight far to the north, but as I looked at Amund Ringnes I kept thinking, "Krüger died before reaching you."

Back at Good Friday Bay, the sunny, windless weather that we'd had for a week showed no sign of changing. It was warmer in Good Friday Bay than it was for most of that summer in Vancouver. Not a single mosquito came between me and the T-shirt I sometimes wore as late as eleven p.m.

This was the second balmy High Arctic summer in a row, and by early August the ice in Good Friday Bay was breaking up. But we still managed to travel by hopping from floe to floe, and even to camp on the free-floating ice, something I'd wanted to do since reading how Thoreau sometimes slept in the bottom of his drifting canoe, because he liked not knowing where he'd wake up in the morning. A day later, on shore again, we heard a tinkling as we fell asleep. "Like a store full of wind chimes," Alexandra had said. When we awoke, the ice was gone. Since we had a kayak, this made our exploration of Good Friday Bay simpler.

A sandy delta yielded several unusual items, including a fifteen-foot log that had drifted here from Siberia. This big piece would have been a great find for the Thule people, who used driftwood in houses, weapons, tools, everything. Nearby lay something even stranger: a weathered piece of wood, bark-like, about three feet long and three inches wide, with several drilled holes, and grooves that connected four sets of the holes. It looked like an old sled runner. The grooves allowed the lashings to lie flush.

I later showed a photo of the piece to Peter Schledermann, an archaeologist with the Arctic Institute of North America. He agreed it was from a sled, and was the first Thule artifact found on western Axel Heiberg. Amazing, since, even the Inuit historically avoided this starvation coast.

Scanning with binoculars that evening, we spotted something man-made directly across Good Friday Bay. Kayaking across, we found forty-three discarded drums, four propane tanks, over two hundred tin cans, shreds of brittle vinyl and sunbleached two-by-fours. Plants had already begun to grow over everything. The site looked like an oil exploration camp from the 1970s. The energy crisis of that era had companies scrambling for new sources of petroleum. One company had evidently based itself in Good Friday Bay. From the look of things, they'd spent some time here.

Government geologists such as Ray Thorsteinsson could not have known of these private explorations. Nevertheless, it was clear to us that the environs of Good Friday Bay had been well looked-over, at least by air.

Subtle items might have eluded these modern visitors, however, so we continued our ground search. Much of the shore on this south side was sloped and unproductive. No place for a tent or komatik. Large seracs hung from the leprous snout of the glacier at the head of Good Friday Bay. Mesmerized, I drew near, poised to flee should one of those monoliths of ice topple. Even the meltwater river between us was terrifying. The brown water didn't just flow, it exploded. Deep rumbles, and hydraulic burps punctuated the general roar. The river gushed into the sea like a giant fire hose, creating three-foot standing waves that stretched a mile into the bay.

Definitely not a river to consider fording. I'd never seen a place more suited to swallowing up humans, but this was not a place to look for them. After a few hours' sleep, broken by the terrifying noise of falling seracs, we kayaked back to base camp.

By now it was mid-August and autumn was approaching. By midnight, frost coated the shady side of the tent. Warbling snowbirds on their way south replaced the silence. Eider chicks tried out their sea legs. "A general hubbub is in the air," Alexandra noted.

The plane showed up for us a day early. We hurriedly broke camp. Combining our pickup with other business, the pilots took us over the ice cap of Axel Heiberg. If that inscrutable sea of ice held any answers to the Krüger mystery, it would not soon release them.

■

When Krüger failed to return to Bache Post by early 1931, a worried Corporal Stallworthy tried to reach Axel Heiberg Island, but failed to get through Sverdrup Pass. The energetic searcher then made a "small" 600-mile roundtrip to the abandoned RCMP post at Craig Harbour, on the south coast of Ellesmere, but found no sign of him.

Long dogsled journeys can only be made in the brief window between the return of the sun in mid-February and the flooding of the sea ice in mid-June, so a thorough search had to wait until the following spring. In March, 1932, Stallworthy crossed Ellesmere and sledded counterclockwise around Axel Heiberg Island. At Cape Thomas Hubbard, he and his three Greenland partners found Krüger's casual-sounding note. Spurred by a shortage of food, they rushed down western Axel Heiberg, traveling eighteen to twenty hours a day. By the time Stallworthy reached Good Friday Bay, his dogs were so weak from hunger that he had to lift them to their feet every morning to get them started.

His safe return to Bache after covering over 1,400 miles in sixty-five days is one of the great sagas in the annals of the Royal Canadian Mounted Police. Two other RCMP searches scoured the more southerly islands and came back empty-handed. Officially, Krüger was presumed dead and the book was closed on the case.

Back in Germany, the news must have crushed Hilda Schad von Mittelbiberach. An emotional letter she wrote to her missing fiancé in 1931, when hope was still high, hints at her desperate need to believe that he was alive: "I think of those never-ending peaceful afternoons when I was at your place and had a headache or was tired," she writes. "And then I was put on the sofa, and you would wrap me in the blanket so warmly and tenderly, that wonderful soft warm blanket, and then you would give me a kiss and say, 'Now sleep.' And then I would lie really, really still, above me the slow movement of the pendulum clock, and you not far from me at your desk, your left leg dangling over the armrest of your armchair, a book in your hand and a pipe in your mouth. And then this tranquility, only the beating of the clock, and then the very, very quiet short little puffs from your pipe, and every now and then a little bird sound from the garden. Everything is so quiet and dreamy and good and safe. . . . "

Her thoughts then take a desperate turn: "It is so important that you come back, Dad! My ability to be alone is not very great and I'm very lost and helpless. Various inferiority complexes are growing."

Hilda never married and committed suicide by taking poison in 1946, at age forty-four. Although it is impossible to say what other troubles she faced in post-war Germany, a friend of hers told Ray Thorsteinsson over ten years later that she killed herself over Krüger's disappearance. Perhaps coincidentally, Krüger was also forty-four years old when he died.

■

With our failure to find any trace of Krüger in Good Friday Bay, I felt as if my book was finally closed on the case, too. But if they didn't come here, and they didn't reach Cape Sverre, what did happen to them?

Though a long shot, it is possible that Krüger's party did reach Cape Sverre and perished later. No note was found at Cape Sverre because Krüger had not left one.

But if he did reach Cape Sverre, where did he go from there? Cape Southwest on Axel Heiberg was the logical next stepping stone on the way home. Krüger would certainly have left a note at that historic cape, but the RCMP had searched and found nothing. Besides, the hunting improves beyond Cape Southwest and the route back to Bache Post is straightforward.

Another distant possibility: Krüger headed west to Ellef Ringnes Island, with the intention of overwintering there or on nearby Loughheed or King Christian Islands. This had been one of the many options he was turning over in his mind during the planning stages. They simply may have starved during the winter of 1930-1.

This theory, which I call the Westbound Theory, rests on how much faith Krüger put in Akqioq's advice. Akqioq had twenty years' experience guiding white explorers. He had even been to King Christian and the Ringnes Islands years earlier with Donald MacMillan, where a shortage of dogfood forced them to retreat. So Akqioq knew how empty that region was.

However, Krüger was "the sort to whom you could tell nothing," according to some. If a headstrong Krüger had started quoting chapter and verse from Stefansson on how easy it was to survive by hunting seals, Akqioq, like most native guides of that era, would have held his tongue.

If they perished overwintering in that region, their last camp would be on the coast. Given our own experience in Good Friday Bay, and from what I have subsequently learned about the vigorous search for oil in the 1970s, and with all the traffic centered around a since-abandoned weather station on Ellef Ringnes Island, it is hard to imagine that any coastline escaped helicopter flyovers. The High Arctic is so naked, so uniform, that unusual objects are hard to miss. On Axel Heiberg, our own bathtub-sized tent stood out clearly from ten miles away.

To my mind, the only likelihood that the Westbound Theory is correct is if Krüger's party died while taking a shortcut across one of those flat islands later in the spring of 1930. Far from any coast, their remains might have gone unnoticed in the vastness of Nunavut.

In his 1993 paper, William Barr speculated that they may have died on a tiny island between Meighen Island and Cape Sverre. This remote speck is a tantalizing landfall to a party in trouble. But in 1995, Pen Hadow, a British organizer of polar expeditions, landed on the island on the way back from a Magnetic Pole journey. He searched it, but found only some old fluorescent material used as guidelines in the making of air photos.

This leaves only two likely solutions. Both possibilities conclude that they died on the ice between Meighen Island and Cape Sverre.

They might have died in their snow house of carbon monoxide poisoning. Most camping stoves give off this colorless, odorless gas, which is a byproduct of incomplete combustion. Defective stoves emit greater amounts of carbon monoxide. Often there are no symptoms: The victim suddenly loses consciousness and never wakes up.

The sensible thing to do is never to cook in a closed tent or igloo, but most arctic travelers flirt with carbon monoxide to some extent. Cooking inside gives some relief from the unrelenting cold. A little ventilation provides an adequate margin of safety.

Krüger's guide, Akqioq, would have known the importance of ventilation, but so did two almost equally experienced modern travelers, who barely escaped with their lives. In March 1963, paleobiologist Richard

Harington was in an igloo off Bathurst Island with his Inuk partner from Resolute. Harington dozed while the other man tended their stove. The next thing Harington knew, he woke up violently ill. His partner was comatose on the floor. Harington couldn't wake him, and dragged his friend outside, where both slowly recovered.

"The heat must have sealed the air hole and glazed the inside of the igloo at the same time," said Harington. "I still wonder how I happened to wake up."

Ray Thorsteinsson also had a close call in a snow house. "My assistant was lying in his sleeping bag, waiting till I had the porridge and bacon and eggs made. I didn't see him reach over to plug the airhole to keep warm. I bowled over. My assistant kicked out a snow block to let in air. When I came to, I had the worst headache of my life."

If a blizzard prompted Krüger or Bjare to plug up a draft in their shelter while Akqioq wasn't looking, all three could easily have perished together. The ice beneath them may have broken up that summer, or their bodies may have drifted southward on a old pan of ice for years.

Or they may have died, as I almost did in Labrador, by falling through bad ice. Most sea ice is five to eight feet thick, but just south of the little island that Pen Hadow investigated, right between Meighen Island and Cape Sverre, is a small patch of open water. In poor visibility, it is easy to miss the telltale signs of bad ice. It wouldn't have even been necessary for any of them to fall in. If just the sled sank, they were doomed. In early May, they would have needed the stove and fuel to melt water.

Nowadays, it is possible to verify whether they died between Meighen Island and Cape Sverre. For about $50,000, someone obsessed with this mystery could fly into the area, then, using snowmobiles, search the ocean floor from above with a side scan sonar. This device, about the size of a small fire extinguisher, can detect items as small as a flashlight battery or as large as a ship's mast. The distinctive shapes of Krüger's equipment would show up clearly.

But for me, that's an unsatisfactory solution. The lure of any mystery is not so much the hard facts. It's the peripheral human details. Were Krüger's final thoughts of Hilda? Who was the last to die? What did they say in their journals? Did they perish in a blind panic, the irritable Krüger screaming recriminations at whomever failed to notice the bad ice? Or did eternity quietly envelop them as comrades? No ghostly image of a rifle on the ocean floor could possibly reveal that.

With the obsession over the fates of Björling and Krüger behind me, I am still not at peace. I find myself turning my attention more and more to other unsolved High Arctic disappearances. Once inside the Arctic Triangle, it seems there is no way out.

Chapter Ten

Shores of the Polar Sea

I had never met a rock I knew before, but I knew that one. It stared at me from the watercolor that Edward Moss, assistant surgeon on the Nares expedition, had painted during a hike around Alexandra Fiord in 1875. The plate showed two men with rifles strolling past a big glacial erratic. Clumps of moss and grass flourished around the boulder. At the bottom of the watercolor Moss had sketched the plant life. "In many places, the ground was covered with a perfect garden of dwarf flowers," he noted.

This rock is the most distinctive landmark in the meadows of Alexandra Fiord. You might even say that it's the best-known rock on Ellesmere. In 1981, Toronto botanist Josef Svoboda wrote a paper on how the rock's dark surface absorbed the sunlight and fostered the rich growth. All over the meadow, small stones performed the same function on a lesser scale. In early July, Alexandra Fiord is a High Arctic rock garden of poppies, avens, purple saxifrage and heather.

Ellesmere Island is not an intimate place. You can never know it like you know your favorite stream or patch of forest. But seeing this familiar rock at a British archive was like bumping into an old friend six thousand miles from home.

The Nares expedition, the first true Ellesmere expedition, had been a disaster. But Nares's book reveals little. I was visiting the Scott Polar Research Institute at Cambridge University trying, without much success, to get a feel for what might have happened. This library, named after Britain's most beloved polar bumbler, is the world's premier archive for the Arctic and Antarctic. Its collection of original diaries and hard-to-find texts has unlocked many obscure doors. For days, I had lost myself in the papers of Nares and his officers; but while their technical mistakes were easy to spot, their emotional walls remained impenetrable.

Every morning at ten-thirty in the archive, a bell summoned staff and visiting researchers to share coffee in the downstairs lobby. Every afternoon at four, a different bell summoned us to high tea. It was very civilized, and as far away from Ellesmere Island as you can get, and the contrast was wonderful.

British expeditions of Nares's time followed similar protocol. Not for them, native food or native ways. Not for them, adapting to the Arctic. The proud British Navy carried its civilization with it. In the Arctic, the contrast between polar reality and tradition was not so wonderful.

■

Three years later. In a driving snowstorm on August 4, Alexandra and I set up camp on Floeberg Beach, where Nares's ship, the *Alert*, had over-wintered and launched its scurvy-shortened venture toward the North Pole. Just steps from our yellow dome tent, Nares's barrel hoops lay in rusted piles. The faint outline of Markham Hall, their large storage tent in case of fire, circumscribed one of the larger piles.

I had dreamt of visiting Floeberg for many years. This turf and shingle apron on the very shores of the Polar Sea is so difficult to reach, we were the first private travelers here. However, we were not the first visitors. The eponymous military base of Alert is just twelve miles away, and almost every year parties visit on foot or in large track vehicles.

A barrier of grounded floebergs paralleled the beach as far as the eye could see. Just beyond, the loose pack ice drifted at a walking pace, crunching, hissing, sizzling, plopping. In between the floebergs, there was a band of shallow water safe from the turmoil. Nares had managed to maneuver the *Alert* inside this barrier for safety. Sea ice has thinned in the last century, and our floebergs were much smaller than Nares described them and were grounded much closer to shore. Even Nares's seamanship could not have found a deep enough anchorage for the *Alert* today.

Despite dank weather, I could barely contain my enthusiasm. Two large cairns beckoned from the low hills behind our camp. The somber headstone of Niels Petersen's grave stood atop a knoll, just five minutes away. Ghosts rose from the permafrost, demanding inquiries into their demise.

At Petersen's grave, a wasp-waisted headboard poked into the leaden sky. Nares's men had found a large, flat piece of granite as a covering slab. It must have needed twenty of them to lift it into position. It also took them three days with picks and gunpowder to excavate a hole three feet deep in the frozen ground. One of Edward Moss's watercolors shows a ghostlike chaplain in white flowing robes leading the bearers of Petersen's body to its resting place.

"Look how short the grave is," said Alexandra. "Didn't Petersen lose both his feet to frostbite before his death?"

"Yes. But people were shorter then too. The British naval standards of the time were 5'5" to 5'8". Anything taller and you were considered to need more than your share of food."

Petersen's troubles began in March, when he and a sledge party from the *Alert* tried to reach their sister ship, the *Discovery*, seventy miles to the south. One day out, Petersen complained of stomach and leg cramps. His hands and feet became badly frostbitten.

"He [was] shaking and shivering all over and breathing in short gasps," wrote one officer. "There appeared to be no heat in him of any kind."

They retreated hastily to the *Alert*. Petersen needed both feet amputated. Although they didn't recognize the other symptoms at the time, he was likely suffering from the early stages of scurvy. He never recovered and died two months later, a victim of scurvy, the dread Disease of the Mouth, which killed two million sailors between 1500 and 1800. The world's most lethal occupational disease. Trying not to sully the pure blanket of snow around the grave, I stuck to a single pair of footprints while carefully studying the headboard. It consisted of four coarse-grained planks with a bronze face and edging. A pointillistic inscription, skilfully hammered into the bronze leaf with a nail, commemorated Petersen and another victim, George Porter, who had been buried on the sea ice thirty miles to the northwest. It ended with the hopeful biblical line that graces many old tombstones down south: "Thou shalt wash me and I shall be whiter than snow."

Alexandra returned to the tent to try to sleep off the flu she had picked up during the hectic days before our departure. Curtailing my desire to race to all the key sites in one besotted afternoon, I lingered around Petersen's grave, studying it against a copy of Moss's watercolor of the scene. The slate under the granite—stacked about four inches high in 1876— had settled under the weight of the slab and now lay level with the ground. The *Alert* cairn still loomed on the hill behind, but the original long staff had broken in two and its halves now protruded in a V from the top of the cairn. I trudged there through the snow, the last few steps up a slender dragon's back of shale. The keg that Nares had attached to the staff as a marker for distant sledge parties was now interred within the cairn itself, with part of its roundness peeking out from one side.

The snow stopped flying, the sky cleared and a west wind began to nudge the pack ice toward Greenland which, now visible in the distance, was all whiteness and quiet. It was eleven p.m., and the sun was too many diameters above the horizon to count. We were so close to the North Pole that as the hours called night advanced into the hours called morning, the sun kept roughly the same altitude. When I turned in around three a.m., it had just begun to climb subtly through the north-eastern sky.

■

The first explorers of a place don't have to be competent; they don't have to be dashing or heroic; they don't have to accomplish much; being first is enough to earn them lasting attention. A whaler named John Gravill first landed on Ellesmere in 1849. Inglefield named the island after the Earl of Ellesmere, a politician, in 1852. Three Americans, Kane, Hall and Hayes, pursued glory on the Greenland side, and Hayes even claimed to have sledded to Ellesmere in 1860, although in light of his descriptions of nonexistent mountains, it's doubtful he had actually done what he said. Nares was the first true explorer of Ellesmere.

Worming through gaps in the ice, Nares's ships first maneuvered into Buchanan Bay and sailed to its narrowing at Alexandra Fiord. They found an arctic oasis with the richest meadows on Ellesmere. Botanist Josef Svoboda and his successors have been studying this luxuriance for twenty years. Svoboda, a gentle expatriate Czech with huge hands from years of prison labor during the Soviet regime, had not known of Moss's study of the glacial erratic when he published his 1981 paper on the plants around it.

"Look at how the Twin Glaciers have retreated!" he exclaimed, when I showed him a copy of the watercolor. "In this picture, they're touching. Today they're separated by at least three hundred meters."

I had come to visit Svoboda at his office in Toronto's Erindale College because he was one of those Ellesmere old-timers whose life was interwoven with the island. I hadn't had much prior luck with botanists—I found most of them to be like fussy old ladies—but Svoboda exuded warmth and sensitivity. Like his arctic subjects, he had blossomed despite a long and hostile winter. In 1949, Czech secret police had imprisoned the twenty-year-old student for anti-Communist sentiments. Arbitrarily released nine years later, Svoboda took jobs as a surveyor, a zoo keeper, and eventually a lab technician. During a 1968 visit to his brother in West Germany, Soviet tanks rolled into Prague.

Svoboda and his brother won asylum in Canada. Almost forty years old, with no English or academic degree, Svoboda became a caretaker of the botany lab at a Toronto university. He studied English nine hours a day and found time to pass a biology course. Under the encouragement of professors who recognized his talent, he enrolled full time the following semester and obtained his bachelor's degree after one intense year. Four years later, at age forty-five, he completed his Ph.D. under Lawrence Bliss, a botanist who had done pioneering work on Devon Island in the 1960s.

In 1979, Svoboda chanced to land at Alexandra Fiord and discovered its idyllic meadows. He spent the next seven summers here, studying the local flora and investigating how hardy, fast-growing southern crops such as radishes grew in the twenty-four hour sunshine.

■

August 4, 1875 had been such a lovely day in Alexandra Fiord that many of Nares's men went ashore to hunt arctic hare. The meadows are easy trekking, but "one of the crew, miscalculating his power of walking in heavy clothing, had to be carried back on a stretcher," reported Nares in what is surely the comic high point of his two-volume account. Despite this mishap, Alexandra Fiord was "the nearest approach to an arctic paradise that we saw during our sojourn in the Polar Regions."

The steam engines on the *Alert* and the *Discovery* allowed them to ram through ice up to four feet thick. The ships could advance up to half their own length on each run. With a mixture of finesse, explosives, and muscle, they worked their way north. On the summit of Washington Irving Island, they discovered two mysterious cairns that were not native handiwork. Nares, who had a scientist's eye for detail, noted the lichen patches that continued from stone to stone, a measure of antiquity. "Probably erected by some enterprising and successful navigator who, if he ever returned home, has not published an account of his discoveries," wrote a puzzled Nares, not realizing he had turned up the first evidence of Vikings in the High Arctic.

In the genial arctic summer, Lady Franklin Bay is one of Ellesmere's more inviting corners, but by the time Nares reached it in late August, it "presented so desolate an appearance that we could not but compassionate her crew having to spend a year, if not longer, in such a place."

Noting the abundance of muskoxen, Nares ordered the *Discovery* to winter here while the *Alert* continued as far north as possible. They made another seventy miles to Floeberg Beach, where Alexandra and I were camped. I had often wondered how they came this far, considering the difficult ice, and how Robert Peary had also reached this same spot twice. But when we woke the following morning, I understood. During the night, the offshore wind had pushed the loose pack toward Greenland, and now a belt of open water miles wide lay between our grounded floebergs and the pack ice. Nares's observation confirmed my suspicion: the winds in this area were all offshore. "During our entire stay at Floeberg Beach, we never had a gale from an easterly direction," he wrote. If a mariner could slip past the bottleneck at Kane Basin and then wait patiently, an ice-free avenue was sure to appear. Perhaps the southern gales also common to this region explained the puzzling Big Lead that hindered Peary on his North Pole attempts.

We stayed two more days at Floeberg Beach while Alexandra's flu improved. Unlike many of my mileage trips, songs to perpetual motion, we had nowhere pressing to go. Floeberg was the magic place. Peary's presence was as strong here as Nares's. Typically, the competitive American had forced his ship one mile further north, built his cairn one hill further north. No one ever noted the distinction—history simply places both at Floeberg Beach—but Peary had clearly wanted to "beat" Nares, if only by a ten-minute walk.

■

My six-pound copy of Nares's sledging journals guided us during our days on the north coast. We didn't have time to trek from Floeberg Beach to Fort Conger, our original plan. This tantalizing route hadn't been done since a forgotten Dane named Godfred Hansen dogsledded from Thule to Cape Columbia in 1920 to lay depots for Amundsen's arctic flights. Before him, only Nares, Peary and Greely had skirted the "beetling cliffs" of that coastline. We decided to go as far as Cape Union, site of a cairn in which Nares's men left notes for each other. Because the cairn was not on top of a hill, it may have eluded helicopter parties.

These treasure hunts, in which you had to leave the treasure in place and the only joy was in the finding, nevertheless had all the excitement that I used to feel as a child pondering whether Captain Kidd's elusive chest of rubies and doubloons really did lie on some flooded sandbar off the coast of Nova Scotia.

Alexandra and I swung inland to avoid some boulder-strewn shoreline. The interior plateau was eerie emptiness in which fields of slate tombstones poked up in a kind of natural memorial to everyone who has died in quixotic wilderness pursuits. When the fog deigned to lift, we caught glimpses to the west of the peaks of the United States Range, eternally white and pure, and the blue headland of Cape Joseph Henry, beyond which "all is conjecture," as one of Nares's men put it.

We prowled this emptiness for three days, for the sheer pleasure of walking where no one ever had. In Byron's words, "And here on snows, where never human foot/Of common mortal trod, we nightly tread."

We found a mossy esker that was so sheltered and green and homey that we decided to camp here and race to Cape Union in a long day hike. A full day without heavy packs was better than a half-day with them. Two desolate streams trickled wearily through the landscape, and we followed one of them to the coast. The pack ice had returned, and its growlers and floes and bergy bits clashed together in a mesmerizing dance. Chaos in slow motion. A young wolf had unsuccessfully chased an arctic hare along the sand within the last few days, but otherwise animal tracks were rare.

The good walking over shale and hard black sand continued to Cape Union, when we had to clamber over boulders for two miles. Here, out on the ice, Niels Petersen had collapsed, forcing the sledge party to return to the ship "with a sad tale of woe and suffering." We continued over the rocks from one small point to the next but could find no sign of the Nares cairn. At last, we turned back empty-handed.

The midnight sun bore into our eyeballs as we trudged north along the strand. It was at that dazzling height that just peeks underneath a visor. Down south, this lasts minutes; here, it continues for five hours, as the sun creeps northeast at the same altitude.

I was tired and disappointed, not to mention half-blind, when we reached the tent after the fourteen-hour march.

■

Upper-class prejudices against the use of dogs and native techniques made many British sledding expeditions, including Nares's, caricatures of what not to do. Empty, Nares's oak sledges weighed a hundred and forty pounds. On some, the payload included a seven hundred pound boat. No one had skis; only two had snowshoes. Even more importantly, no one had ski poles. Ski poles improve balance and make long days less tiring. They also prevent countless wrenched knees.

Autumn sledging was, in their own words, "the very acme of discomfort." Ellesmere gets most of its snow in September and early October. After that, it gets too cold to snow and the same stuff just blows around all winter.

Fall snow is soft, and hell to pull through. Seven men in harness drew each 1,700-pound sled, while an unencumbered officer scouted the way, sketched maps or urged the men on. They had to resort to standing pulls: At the count of three, the haulers strained like horses dragging a cart out of knee-deep mud. The sledge reluctantly lurched ahead a couple of feet, then came to a dead stop. This went on all day. There is no pleasure in this sort of hauling, no rhythm, almost no progress.

Spillage problems made carrying water an ordeal. The water that didn't freeze in their pockets leaked. In the end, they gave up drinking except at lunch, when they had to stamp their feet for an hour and a half to keep warm, while their inefficient stoves melted a few swallows of water.

"On our first day's march, there was nothing to drink but icy cold raw rum," recalled Moss. The alcohol increased their water loss, while the salt meat increased their water needs. They couldn't have dehydrated themselves better if they tried.

At night they cooked in the tent. Traveling in the Arctic with some crazy Russians, I once experienced how quickly this practice, if not carefully managed, can destroy insulation. When the water boiled, steam filled our big tent like a sauna. We could barely see the person next to us. The vapor condensed everywhere—on sleeping bags, parkas, tent walls. Every morning, the stove melted this frost. Water dripped from the ceiling onto sleeping bags; everything then refroze. Within two days, our down bags were as flat as if we'd poured pots of water over them.

By the end of their autumn travels, Nares's thirty-two pound tent weighed fifty-five pounds, the floor cloth went from eleven to twenty-nine pounds and sleeping bags increased from eight to fifteen pounds. Clothing became "more like a piece of wood or sheet iron than an article of woolen material." Twenty-four men had forty-three frostbites. Three of them lost big toes.

In March, after a long winter in which condensation had also been the main problem on the ship—one officer rigged an umbrella over his chair so he could read without water raining onto his book—the sledging trauma began again. But now it was much, much colder, and pulling their gigantic sleds was like dragging heavy desks across the carpet. Their camp gear was not made for –40°F. Even –15°F in the tent, a comfortable temperature by modern standards, meant a night of shivering.

As for clothing, they had goose down jackets but didn't like them. Their parkas had no hoods. Some items sound Monty Pythonesque: mittens of fearnought covered with duck, helmet-worsted sleeping caps, cork-soled carpet boots. They needed a John Cleese to throw everything in the ocean, hand them a pair of Inuit kamiks and say, "And now for something completely different."

■

The Portuguese explorer Vasco de Gama first wrote about scurvy in 1498. For the next four hundred years, long voyages made sailors all too familiar with the disease. It began with loss of appetite, lassitude, and pains in the joints, progressed to swollen gums and bruised skin, and ended in death. It seemed connected with the absence of fresh food. In 1747, British naval surgeon James Lind demonstrated that citrus juices cured scurvy. Thereafter, British sailors became known as Limeys because of their lime or lemon juice rations. But the scurvy that unexpectedly befell Nares's expedition caused forty years of confusion and loss of faith in the lime juice remedy; even into the twentieth century, Fridtjof Nansen argued that tainted food caused scurvy.

Nansen's science was faulty, for once. Scurvy comes from a lack of what was first called "accessory food factor C." The confusion was understandable. First, Vitamin C is so fragile that antiscorbutic foods can easily lose their content and become useless. Second, if fresh fruits and vegetables prevented scurvy, as most assumed, no one could explain why the Inuit thrived on an all-meat diet. Finally, almost all mammals manufacture their own Vitamin C, so the usual dogs, cats, rats, and birds were useless as test subjects. It wasn't until 1907 that two Norwegians discovered that guinea pigs, like humans, developed scurvy. In dubious honor of their contribution, guinea pigs came to symbolize experimental testing.

Everyone needs ten to fifteen milligrams of Vitamin C a day. The body does not store it well; excess amounts are eliminated in urine, turning it golden. Nevertheless, the blood can hold about fifteen hundred milligrams. We thus have a grace period of about four months before the well is empty. That is often, in fact, when the first symptoms of scurvy appeared among the old seafarers.

Vitamin C was completely absent from the storable foods upon which long-distance expeditions depended. Butter, cheese, rice, dried peas, chocolate, well-cooked or preserved meat, and all flour products including bread have none. Wine and beer also have none, a fact accepted reluctantly by those hard-drinking sailors, some of whom swore by the medicinal value of hops. In the subarctic, cloudberries, scurvy grass, and spruce needles were time-honored preventives, but High

Arctic explorers had fewer options. The British Navy doled out concentrated lemon juice in one-ounce doses every day at ten a.m. As each crewman reluctantly downed the sour potion, an officer ticked his name off a list.

But wonky theories still prevailed. Experts blamed the disease on lack of sunlight, stuffy air, moisture in the bedding, ptomaine poisoning, and even depression, which prompted one captain to force his men to dance on deck every day, one of the stranger arctic tableaus.

Semi-scientific pundits buzzed around the answer. The tartness of traditional antiscorbutics suggested that the more acidic a food, the better. A prophetic few suggested that copper pots were harmful. There were so many theories. For every lime juice advocate, there were five soda water or carrot marmalade believers.

Until Nares, British expeditions had been scurvy-free for years. But a pernicious substitution had recently occurred. Around 1860, the Navy switched from time-tested Mediterranean lemons to West Indian limes, which were easier to obtain. In that era, the terms lemon and lime were used interchangeably. Probably no one even noticed the switch, except that the limes tasted slightly more acidic, supposedly a good thing.

After Vitamin C was isolated in 1927, researchers learned that lime juice had only two-thirds the antiscorbutic power of lemon juice. Gradually, the fragile and fickle nature of the vitamin became clear. Almost everything broke the molecule's weak bonds: cooking, long storage . . . and copper. After twenty minutes cooking, cabbage loses sixty-five percent of its Vitamin C in a copper pot but just eighteen percent in an iron pot. Copper tubing pumped the commercial lime juice of the day into the holding tanks. One experiment suggested that alcohol also affected the vitamin content. Nares's lime juice was premixed with "spirit" to hinder freezing.

As a result, British lime juice had minimal Vitamin C. Nares's crew was getting three to five milligrams a day. Some previous expeditions had accidentally escaped scurvy by living on fresh meat, another source of Vitamin C. The Inuit themselves typically averaged forty milligrams a day from their all-meat diet. The *Discovery* had some access to muskoxen and seals, but game was scarcer around the *Alert*.

In April, 1876, three sledging parties set out. From the *Alert*, Albert Markham struggled north toward the Pole, while Pelham Aldrich explored the lovely north coast of Ellesmere—a white world of eternal silence where toothy peaks erupted from the bony jaws of ice fields. Meanwhile, the *Discovery* sent a reconnaissance party across the frozen strait to Greenland. The travelers' intake of Vitamin C now dropped to zero. In one of those quaint naval protocols, daily rations of the hated lime juice were not required on land.

The bad snow, rough ice, and overloaded sleds made travel a task that the classically schooled officers might have called Sisyphean. At first, journal entries focused on the misery. "The sledge broke five times today." Or "The Sergeant lost a pair of spectacles in a snow drift and spilt the contents of a glycerin bottle in his pocket." Or "Travel exceedingly heavy . . . men working like horses." Or "Beastly chilly."

In one of their few good travel ideas, each man had sewn a unique design on the back of his holland overall, so the person behind him had something to rest his eyes on and think about. One man wore a large black anchor with the motto *Hold Fast;* another a locomotive engine; another, a Freemason's hieroglyphic. The great modern sledder Børge Ousland had one of his kids paint pirates on his skis for his wondrously fast trek across Antarctica.

Soon scurvy fell like a lengthening shadow over the sledgers. For a long time, they didn't realize what was happening. Aldrich became furious when one apparently lazy sailor could no longer keep up. Aldrich went back to look for him. "I found my gentleman lying in the snow [face down, Aldrich later admitted]. I touched him on the shoulder and said, 'Get up.' He got up. Confound his impertinence. I had half a mind to give him a welting with his drag belt."

Markham's crew, struggling over the Arctic Ocean till early June, fared even worse. "A more thorough break-up of a healthy and strong body of men . . . would be difficult to conceive," he wrote. By the end, only three of fifteen were able to walk, including Lieutenant Parr, whose heroic forty-mile dash back to the ship saved everyone except George Porter, who died on the ice of what is now Porter Bay.

Of the expedition's one hundred and twenty men, sixty came down with scurvy, forty-five from the *Alert* and fifteen from the *Discovery*. Four died, two from each ship. Recovery was slow for the invalids because of the poor lime juice. The Greenland party improved more quickly, thanks to an earlier explorer's four-year-old cache of superior lime juice, preserved in popsicle form in Polaris Bay. Still hedging their bets, they supplemented this with "cornflower, blancmange, and rum." Confused by the scurvy, discouraged by the hard travel, Nares returned to England a year early.

The British Arctic Expedition had left to crowds cheering on the docks of Portmouth. They returned to salvos of refined sarcasm. The expedition "went out like a rocket, and has come back like the stick," wrote the journal *Navy*. The "microscopic mileage" of the sledgers came under special disdain.

August doctors held post-mortems that would do the talking heads of CNN proud. A Dr. Buzzard opined that the "vegetable element in the sledge dietary" was "evidently exceedingly inadequate." Carbolic acid content of the air in the lower decks of the *Alert* was debated ad nauseam. Nares, whose political skills were far superior to his arctic leadership, survived the drubbing and like his lieutenant, Albert Markham, eventually rose to admiral. Markham weathered a second scandal twenty years later when he crashed his ship into another while performing a showy maneuver, killing three hundred and fifty-eight.

■

In late August, Alexandra returned to her southern job, while I followed the Nares route west toward Black Cliffs Bay. Every day, the weak sun edged closer to the horizon. The temperature was now below freezing at noon. I hurried to finish my trek before winter set in.

Driftwood from Russia lined the beach of Hilgard Bay. Ellesmere rocks are usually algae-free, but the north coast dampness made the shale greasy and treacherous. I was mentally congratulating myself about what a competent traveler I was compared to the British when I got lazy with my ski pole and my feet squirted out from beneath me. I crashed down hard on the rocks. Woozy from pain, I sat down for ten minutes until my head cleared. I was grateful for this lesson in humility and glad that it hadn't included a broken hip.

I woke up the next morning to a south gale that sent whitecaps flying across the half-mile lake beside which I had camped. At least it was a tailwind. I decided to leave camp set up and walk the ten miles to an old Nares depot at Cape Richardson.

The gale pounded at my back. A dangling ski pole fluttered horizontally, indicating a wind of almost fifty knots. My parka hood cracked like a nylon whip, but I was warm inside my multi-layered cocoon.

The offshore wind had blown the floes out to sea, but a few grounded blocks clung to shore, lashed by freezing surf. Although the Inuit call this place "beyond the land of the people," their own daring explorers had probed even this edge. At the mouth of the Wood River, a circle of paving stones outlined a two-thousand-year-old tent site. I looked around cautiously for polar bears. To travel light, I had left my gun behind. Even the fuel bottle, which could serve as a Molotov cocktail, was back in the tent. At least polar bears were rare on the north coast, because so were seals. Those ancient Inuit explorers also realized this, and eventually abandoned this marginal land.

The Nares sledging journals guided me to several spots where I might find something. I don't understand why, in recent years, I have become obsessed with exploration garbage, except that it somehow brings these people to life and validates the countless hours I spend poring over their dull books, thinking about them.

Aldrich camped at Knot Bay on June 4, 1876, but the long gravel spit yielded nothing. On September 25 of the previous fall, Markham explored the south shore of Victoria Lake, a craterlike pond bordered on its north end by a slender causeway, beyond which the dark sea raged. Causeways intrigued me. As a kid, I had recurring dreams of them. They bridged unexplored lands of good and evil. Here, hostile forces pursued me relentlessly. The stakes were high, the calls were close, but I seemed to be just slippery enough. I don't know whether I have ever seen the causeway that served as the model for these nighttime escapades. Some would call them nightmares, but I loved them. Like hard adventure, they gave life intensity and meaning.

The causeway led into what Nares's men had ominously called the Frostbite Range but what was really, even in a screaming gale, just a couple of gentle hills. I had already been walking nonstop for eight hours and was tired and dreading the return trip into the wind. How many fourteen-hour days did I have to put in before finding something? It hadn't been this hard for 1950s greats Geoffrey Hattersley-Smith and Ray Thorsteinsson. For them, treasure lay on almost every point of land. I was fifty years removed from Wilfred Thesiger's gasp of relief, "To have been there just in time."

I trudged south from Cape Richardson along the hard sands. The wind was taking breaths now, not just blowing with infinite lung capacity. Under the gray sky, the landscape had a sameness which lay somewhere between monotony and softness. I remembered a science writer telling me how our brains were made to process scenes of one or two pixels, not the riot of urban lights and sounds and movement. This drab gray one-pixel landscape was somehow calming.

Suddenly, a second pixel intruded. A small but obvious manmade shape jutted into the monochromatic sky. "That's something!" I said out loud, finding new legs. When you see nothing but curves for weeks, the angularity of a wooden box is unmistakable.

Nares's cache! Not much remained. The ancient box, bleached and pulpy, now served as a planter for moss. Rotten cans, whose edges were as soft as wet crackers, likewise imitated garden pots. I didn't want to disturb the moss—it had taken a hundred and twenty-five years to get this far—but I lovingly admired the rusted debris. On a terrace near the beach, the British had placed their tent. A few inconsequential items lay about, splinters of wood and bully-beef cans three-quarters of the way to becoming turf. I scanned around. No polar bears. The wind was definitely dying down. Drawn by a low pile of rocks that was maybe natural and maybe not, I wandered upslope. A small cairn. I peered inside. Something there! I reached in and withdrew a russet metal can. Aldrich?? The white stenciling was faint, but I could make out, "Kjöbenhavn."

Sigh . . . not the Holy Grail, not an original Nares tin. The russet color and Kjöbenhavn identified it as one of Godfred Hansen's Royal Danish Navy tins from 1920. Three explorers had traveled this coast on foot: Nares, Peary, and Hansen, on that grand dogsled journey from faraway Thule, leaving supplies for an Amundsen flight that never took place.

I opened the lid. Inside was a note, badly pulped from leakage through a BB-sized hole in the bottom of the tin. I left artifacts *in situ*, but rotting notes, as far as I was concerned, were fair game. This one had only a few years left. I popped it in a Ziploc bag and put it in my day pack. A note from Hansen was a respectable find.

The next six hours flew. My fatigue disappeared. So had the wind. How often does a tailwind die the moment you turn into it? I gave silent thanks to whatever, and hurried back to camp.

I was so exhausted after the fourteen-hour trek that I fell asleep without eating or reading the note. I woke to a cool, foggy day. New snow dusted the hills. Delicately I unfolded the note, dry as tinder. The penciling was faint, but as soon as I read the word "Blackader," I felt the same letdown as when I had seen "Kjöbenhavn." In 1953, Geoffrey Hattersley-Smith and his companion Bob Blackader had dogsledded from Alert to Ward Hunt Island. This excellent traveler had found the Hansen/Nares cache and had even, I found out later, sampled Hansen's rum. On closer inspection, I made out Geoffrey's signature.

The note was almost fifty years old, and I admired everything about Geoffrey, but I wished he'd missed this one. Just this one.

■

Later, I did make a small Nares find. I was at Fort Conger, where the *Discovery* had wintered. Two able-bodied seamen, Paul and Hand, had died on a sledging trip, and a wooden memorial to them overlooked lonely Fort Conger. The original plaque was now in a museum, but this replica was exact, down to the crack in the wood.

Fort Conger is one of the few places on Ellesmere that has been closely studied. Several papers have been written about it. The national park has an inventory of all its remains. In a binder at their Tanquary Fiord headquarters, numbered four-by-six color prints map the artifact-rich turf. Every year, wardens made a quick visit to compare the binder photos with what's on the ground. If something has been taken, they have a good idea by whom. Maybe two groups a year visit Fort Conger.

I camped here for days, communing with the sunshine and the ghosts. Some of the same russet cans from Hansen's expedition lay on the ground and in one of the tiny cabins built by Peary.

There were so many muskoxen in these hills, but Nares's men had disliked the meat. They had also killed the animals during the rutting season, when the male's flesh has a very musky taste. They had fried the hell out of the meat to kill the muskiness, inadvertently killing the Vitamin C.

A plane was coming to drop off a few tourists and to pick me up. I packed my gear for the trudge to the rough airstrip a mile away. The sun blazed. Grass was green. All seemed well. I made a farewell tour of the site. Within fifty steps of the memorial to Paul and Hand, the gentle beach gave way to a kind of clumpy ground called hummocks that is like walking on the backs of tortoises. A good place to turn your ankle, and I watched my step carefully. I couldn't believe what I saw. On the sides of each hummock grew dense clumps of *Oxyria digyna*, wild rhubarb—the richest source of Vitamin C in the High Arctic.

Chapter Eleven

On High Alert

From a long way off, the tail of the downed Hercules stuck out of the tundra like a shark's fin. We trudged over to the wreckage, two tiny figures lost under mountainous backpacks. Jagged pieces of aluminum from the almost unrecognizable fuselage groaned in the wind; rags of insulation flapped mournfully.

"We're treading on someone else's nightmare," said Alexandra uneasily.

Of Ellesmere's nightmares, this was the most recent. On October 30, 1991, a military transport plane with eighteen passengers and crew was making the one hour and twenty minute shuttle from Thule, Greenland to Alert. It was part of Operation Boxtop, a series of back-to-back flights that, two or three times a year, resupplies this northernmost settlement on earth with everything from corn flakes to heating fuel. This was a fuel flight. Two weeks earlier, the sun had set for the winter. It was 4:15 p.m. and pitch dark, but the approaching aircraft, known as Boxtop 22, could make out the twinkling lights of Alert.

On this clear night Captain John Couch decided on a visual approach. Although Couch was considered a veteran flier, his 3,500 hours paled next to the 20,000 to 30,000 hours of Resolute's masterful Twin Otter pilots. His co-pilot and navigator were relative newcomers to the Hercules.

Lured by the lights of Alert, which looked closer than they were, and fooled by an arctic radar phenomenon that made the crew believe they were over the ocean, Couch took the plane below a thousand feet for his final approach. Suddenly, the lights of Alert disappeared from his port window. He dipped the left wing for a look, and the plane hit the ground. It skidded 1,600 feet on its belly, broke into pieces and spewed fuel everywhere. The crew scrambled out an emergency hatch before the fireball erupted. The passengers were thrown free. Two died immediately, two shortly after, but incredibly, many escaped with just minor injuries.

The Hercules is a military workhorse, transporting everything from troops to tractors. Its interior looks like the space ship from the movie *Alien*, full of dark corners and pipes running along the ceiling. A row of firefighters' masks above the seats could be space helmets. Passengers sit lengthwise on benches of red nylon webbing, facing each other. En route, experienced troops doze or pass the time with 700-page novels. A Hercules has fewer windows than a passenger aircraft but more foot room, and the box lunches are heartier. Instead of a choice of chicken or pasta, the boxes hold slightly different combinations, and a lively swap of one's apple for a neighbor's packet of Oreos is SOP, in military jargon, Standard Operating Procedure.

The twisted wreckage of Boxtop 22 recalled our own uneventful Hercules flight to Alert. I recognized the little packet of Chiclets on the ground; on our flight I had bartered mine with Alexandra for her second drink box. This yellow gum packet was the lone splash of color in the scene. The impact had cracked the hull open lengthwise and forced the halves together like aluminum jaws. The red sling benches were bitten and crushed; it was hard to believe that anyone survived. A spaghetti of wires littered the inside of the detached tail section, where the survivors took refuge. The landscape looked like a black-and-white vision of Kansas after a nuclear blast.

■

Alert is the hardest place in Canada for an ordinary person to reach. This makes it extremely attractive to a traveler. Travel is largely the art of penetrating the forbidden before it opens up, of witnessing primitive customs before they become a show for tourists.

Alert is not just a military base. It is a large electronic ear cocked toward Europe and Asia, traditionally Russia, but now also such geopolitical messes as Bosnia and Pakistan. Signals intelligence might include eavesdropping on a Serbian general on his cell phone or intercepting an exchange between two Russian MiGs. Sonar cables along the north coast also listen for passing submarines. To travel in Ellesmere is wonderful enough, but to infiltrate a spy post on the remotest corner of the island is the stuff of dreams.

Civilians do occasionally get inside. Alert was established in 1950 as a weather station and two federal meteorologists still gather data year-round. A wildlife biologist known in Alert-speak as the Birdman returns every summer to survey the turnstones, knots, and other shorebirds. Song-and-dance troupes twice disrupt the winter blues. Once a year, the Department of National Defence holds a media day, when journalists can ask the same questions and be given the same vague answers. Otherwise, Alert is off-limits, and private aircraft asking to land are invariably refused. Alert hadn't hosted adventure since Sir Ranulph Fiennes flexed his Buckingham Palace connections during his Transglobe Expedition back in 1982.

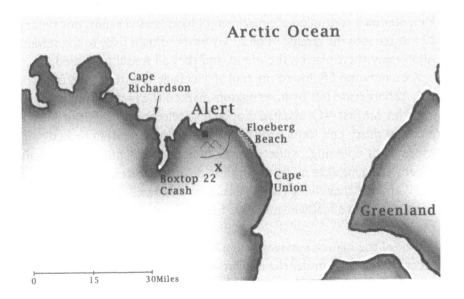

My only link with Buckingham Palace was an unsuccessful attempt at age sixteen to make one of the bear-hatted guardsmen crack a smile, but a military friend suggested that I try appealing directly to the Minister of National Defence. By then I had traveled just about everywhere else on the island, with everyone from Inuit hunters to the Coast Guard. To my astonishment, my request was approved.

I wanted to see the base itself, but I was also drawn to the tragedy of Boxtop 22. It had already been analyzed in a book and dramatized in a television movie, but only the military had been to the site. So I arranged to spend a month at Alert, of which most of my time would be out on the land.

An airplane crash is nothing new in the north. Rare is the arctic village that does not have crumpled aviation wreckage on its outskirts. Resolute has had five crashes; Grise Fiord and Eureka, one each. Boxtop 22 was one of three at Alert. It is the cost of doing business in the north, just as ice claimed a regular percentage of nineteenth century whaling ships.

What made Boxtop 22 different is what happened after the crash.

■

Previous accounts stated that the plane clipped a hill, but this was the flattest natural ground I had ever seen. There were no rocks, and even the expansion cracks in the frozen mud were too shallow to catch a wheel. A Hercules on a controlled approach could have landed safely, but Boxtop 22 just ran into the ground. The survivors owed their lives to the terrain. Almost anywhere else on the island, and they all would have died.

Alexandra and I followed the trail of wreckage 438 steps back from the tail. A short stake left by investigators marked the point of impact. The left wing hit first—Couch had dipped it to relocate the lights of Alert— followed thirty-one steps later by the rest of the aircraft. The body and wings went spinning, while the tail broke off and ploughed straight ahead. The long skid made no impression in the frozen earth.

"Why were they flying east?" Alexandra wondered. I didn't know, unless Couch had already begun what he imagined was the final circuit to the runway.

One of the injured survivors was a hair stylist, and an exploded can of Alberto mousse lay under the remains of one wing, from which hung gobs of melted aluminum, congealed in mid-ooze. Jagged metal soughed constantly in the wind. Used magnesium flares from rescue aircraft lay up to three miles away. On this cold August afternoon, a survival pouch of water resembled a small freezer pack.

The survivors were not trained to survive under extreme conditions. They were radio technicians, for whom Alert existed, and the support personnel who cut their hair, diagnosed their ailments, and sold them bars of soap at the little PX. Indoor workers all. Flight crews are better trained, but the air force survival school that I attended as an observer one year focused on treeline skills such as building lean-tos and signal fires. Arctic training used to take place at Resolute, but there were so many cases of frostbite that the program was eventually stopped. Six weeks before Alexandra and I arrived, a June survival exercise at nearby Floeberg Beach had ended disastrously: The group had managed to place its tent on a spot that flooded at high tide, no easy feat in this region of small tides. "They woke up blowing bubbles," said Master Corporal Joe McDonald, who led the convoy of vehicles that picked up the hypothermic group after their call for help.

Despite their marginal training, the Boxtop 22 survivors did everything right. They stabilized the two injured members who could not be moved, then huddled together in the tail section to wait for rescue. A second Hercules had already pinpointed their location from the fires. They were twelve miles from Alert. The temperature was 0°F, the wind was calm and a half-moon burned in the sky. A long-range forecast showed a storm moving in from the north.

Al McDonald, the bush pilot, was in Eureka when the accident happened. "We offered to pick up the survivors, but the military wanted to handle it themselves," he said. With flares to light the ground, McDonald's Twin Otter could have landed beside the downed aircraft within two or three hours. Instead, the military summoned search-and-rescue technicians from Edmonton and Nova Scotia, over two thousand miles away. By the time they arrived, the storm had moved in and parachuting onto the site was impossible.

Twelve miles isn't a lot, even in the dark, and I wondered whether it would have been possible to ski to the survivors before the storm. Alert had no speedy snowmobiles, but after the crash, volunteers had driven enclosed track vehicles six miles south to what the maps call Dean Hill, but what is better known as Crystal Mountain, a popular destination for summer rock collectors. As Boxtop 22 made its misguided approach, 1,300-foot Crystal Mountain is likely what blocked the lights of Alert from the pilot's view. The track vehicles kept breaking down, but the main obstacle was the Sheridan valley, an impenetrable gorge, the rescue party had reported.

Yet there is no valley on Ellesmere that a hiker cannot cross. Tiny creeks sometimes forge slot canyons, but they open up quickly. The Sheridan is frozen solid by late October, and like other Ellesmere rivers its banks are mostly gentle. If you chose your descent route with the same perverse skill that the Floeberg trainees chose their flooded campsite, you might go for a tumble. Otherwise, "I don't understand what the fuss was about," said Alexandra, as we scrambled up and down the Sheridan valley in several spots.

Nowadays, vehicles do cross the Sheridan, but in the dark, with cranky engines, it was asking a lot. Although they could see the pot fires flickering just four miles away, an hour and a half on foot, the rescuers rumbled back to Alert. By now the storm had arrived and a Condition Two warning confined everyone indoors until further notice.

After rock-hopping across the Sheridan, Alexandra and I camped at the foot of Crystal Mountain. It was one of the few perfect afternoons of that cool summer. We dozed with our bare feet sticking out the tent into the sunshine. Two hours later, we woke to a rising storm. I hurried outside to shore up the tent with rocks as the south wind gained momentum. Ellesmere is not particularly windy—Alert is less windy than Vancouver—but gales do occur. An eighty-mile-an-hour wind once blew for seven hours at Alert, and Greely recorded gusts up to a hundred miles an hour at Fort Conger. Our own storm, we discovered later, approached fifty miles an hour. You can travel in such a tailwind, but we decided to wait it out. For the next day and a half, we slept, read and sipped hot chocolate. Boring but cozy. However, I would not have wanted to spend that time inside a metal hull in late October, wearing gasoline-soaked clothes, with just a package of Chiclets to keep me warm.

Thirty-two hours after Boxtop 22 went down, the storm abated and rescuers reached the half-frozen survivors. Of the eighteen people on board, thirteen were still alive. The only person who would have benefited from a quick rescue was John Couch. The guilt-ridden pilot gave his own coat to one of the passengers and kept checking outside on the pair who were too injured to move. They survived, but Couch died of hypothermia. For me, Couch exemplified the best and worst of the military: They often screwed up, but their hearts could be huge.

■

We reached Alert at three a.m. and stomped into the coatroom, where parkas hung neatly on pegs and overboots sat in formation on wooden shelves. We were suddenly aware how ripe we smelled after two weeks on the land. Luckily most of the station was asleep. Self-consciously, I unloaded the gun we carried for protection from polar bears.

Overlooking the Arctic Ocean, Alert is a daisy chain of trailers linked by passageways that can be bulldozed in the event of a fire. The social center is the Beach, an airy foyer of patio tables. The cafeteria, store, clinic, and command center all lie within steps of this informal café. On the second floor, a 250-seat auditorium, amateur radio station, bar, pool room and library further centralize the base.

Doors on either side of the main corridor lead into the residence hallways. Each profession lives together, in fraternity houses with their own initiations, secret rituals, and bar/common room. In our unaccustomed role as VIPs, we were given spacious quarters in Hut 53, home of the senior staff. Mechanics lived in the Monster House (guarded by a coffin and Frankenstein dummy), cooks in the House of Chefs, and radio technicians in the lively Zoo, decorated with multicolored stuffed animals whose names, apparently, were also top-secret.

There used to be 220 people at Alert. The signals were gathered, analyzed and sent south every week in an attaché case flamboyantly handcuffed to the messenger's wrist. Nowadays, the signals are simply coded and sent south by satellite to the analysts at Leitrim, near Ottawa. Currently, sixty-nine people, including half a dozen "techs," live at Alert for three- to six-month stints.

Marc Bastien, the head radio man, had a cheerful way of deflecting questions about his work. He was an easygoing technician who kept the equipment tuned to whatever frequency or country the higher-ups required. "I'm like M in the James Bond movies," he explained.

Bastien, whose wife was one of the analysts down south, worked in the Ops, or Operations, area in a distant corner on the second floor. Only those with the highest security clearance, half a dozen people on the base, were allowed to ascend the mystical stairway to Ops that lay behind locked door number 150. Nearby, security posters on the wall reminded everyone to "protect your piece of the puzzle" and to "evaluate the need to know." One non-military person I knew had seen the inside of Ops, but before his visit they had draped the machines with bedsheets, "as if they were painting the place," he said.

My need to know was curiosity, not espionage. I was impressed by how they denied their interest in submarines even when the locations of their sonar cables were pointed out to them. On the roof of the Ops building stood the most interesting array of antennas I had ever seen. They had a whimsy that was almost beautiful. One looked like a teepee; another like a dunce cap; another like the discombobulator with which Martin the Martian zapped Bugs Bunny. The array was classified, and photographing it was forbidden. I was in love with the array and studied it in admiration every day.

Other Ellesmere presences seemed to regard the military as a wealthy redneck cousin: Its behavior was sometimes embarrassing, but it had the resources to do a lot of good, if it chose. The relation between the young national park and the military was particularly strained. "We have a memo of understanding," one defence official told me primly, when I asked whether the two groups often communicated. A park warden answered the same question with a zinger: "They're supposed to be a listening post but they never hear you on the radio."

Alert disliked the park's mincing objections to the freedoms they had previously enjoyed, helicoptering to Lake Hazen for a day's char fishing, for example, while the wardens found themselves sharing the island with yahoos who still threw cigarette butts and wrappers on the ground, picked up artifacts as souvenirs, and fed the foxes and wolves. The military now discouraged the feeding of wildlife; "We are environmentally conscience," as one spokesman put it. Nevertheless, they remained on the defensive, and park officials hoped eventually to annex much of the area around Alert, especially historic Floeberg Beach.

Yet the individual servicemen and women at Alert had the same admirable qualities that made hunters and anglers generally better company than hikers. Alexandra and I felt it the moment we arrived, an open-armed, unreserved hospitality. They accepted us immediately, welcoming us warmly into their lives. When high cost made us reconsider accepting a ride to our base camp, several people offered to drive us themselves, unofficially. One volunteered to take up a collection on our behalf. Another assured us that he was going to give the commanding officer a piece of his mind about charging us for such a small favor. I was in awe of how generous and unselfish they were. As long as you weren't stuck up, they treated you like an old foxhole buddy. The only others I'd met whose hospitality compared were the Russians.

■

Everyone at Alert still referred to their former nemesis as the "Soviets." The new Russia remained one of Alert's prime eavesdropping targets. In 1988, I had been at Eureka when the Soviet-Canadian expedition came through after their ski crossing of the Arctic Ocean. Eureka maintains a small military base in the summer called Operation Hurricane. Its job is to service the five communications dishes on Ellesmere hilltops that connect Alert's telephones to Eureka, from which the signals go by satellite to land lines down south.

Before the expedition arrived, the head of Operation Hurricane came to the weather station and removed from the walls some topo maps that a Soviet attaché could have purchased at any map store in Ottawa. He then advised us to "keep our eyes open." The following day, as the Soviets and Canadians milled around, savoring their first warm building in three months, he mingled in plain clothes, no doubt keeping his eyes open.

The Soviets, of course, knew about Alert, and everyone knew that the Soviets knew about it, and the Soviets knew that. One winter in the 1960s, an empty building by the runway in Alert caught fire. It was the polar night and no one was outside to notice the flames. Then the phone rang in the commander's office at Alert. It was Ottawa.

"There's a fire on your airstrip," said the voice.

"How do you know?"

"The Soviets told us."

After the collapse of the Soviet Union, many of their old icebreakers were converted into cruise ships for wealthy capitalist tourists. The icebreakers show up every summer in Resolute, rusted hulks with what look like new highrise apartments grafted onto their foredecks. The largest icebreakers, such as the nuclear-powered *Yamal,* remain the best in the world.

A few years ago, the Department of National Defence in Ottawa received a tempting offer from Russia. "Perhaps our icebreakers could resupply Alert?" Although it would have saved hundreds of thousands of dollars a year in Hercules flights, Ottawa declined. It's hard to relinquish a good enemy.

■

A day at Alert began with a seven a.m. breakfast at the Igloo Gardens cafeteria. Food was basic 1970s: Bacon and scrambled eggs held sway. Yoghurt had arrived, but not the espresso machine. A cook's helper named Tiny, so-called because of his gargantuan biceps, doled out the portions. "You can leave Alert a hunk, a chunk, or a drunk," someone said, and Tiny had made his commitment clear.

Like a pro sports team, everyone had nicknames: It strengthened the group identity. At eight a.m., Sawdust the carpenter went to his workshop. Zippo fueled the vehicles while Smokey the fire chief and Puff his assistant stood by. Pack Rat dived into requisition forms at the supply warehouse. H20 checked the water tanks. The personnel turned over every six months, but the nicknames never varied.

I had always feared absorption in the Borg Collective. Nietzsche's "I hate to follow and I hate to lead/Obey? Oh no. And govern—No indeed!" was more my style. Afraid that they would see through my feeble attempts at mixing, I clung to Alexandra, who is one of the world's friendliest people. Everyone automatically assumed I was friendly when I was with her: I just had to grin and nod. Then they relaxed and said things while I listened carefully.

Alert brought back memories of the battle I'd waged against my soccer team at the age of eighteen. During a tournament in Spain, a shaving cream shampoo became the team initiation. I eluded ambush after ambush until finally I was the only holdout. On the last evening, the entire team ganged up. My roommate slipped the ringleaders the key to our hotel room, but I barricaded myself in with the chair-against-the-doorknob trick and locked myself in the bathroom. It seemed vital not to succumb. They broke down the outer door and picked the bathroom lock, but I managed to hold the door shut by jamming my legs against the far wall. The hotel room was destroyed but I had won. Eventually they wandered away. Alone in my bathroom, I felt disappointed that they hadn't persisted a little longer. It was lonely in there.

I envied the good people at Alert their sense of belonging. The entire station gathered to cheer every new recruit coming in the door. At the end of their tour, they filed out one by one to an ovation that sounded like the introduction of the starting lineups at the Super Bowl. Many spent their evenings in the "house" to which they belonged. Part bar, part television room, these lounges had the air of college fraternities, except that most members were in their thirties. With twelve bars for seventy people, it was easy to leave Alert more drunk than hunk, if you were so inclined. A Prohibition-like experiment some years earlier had failed miserably.

Alert's reduced manpower made the station feel like a New York with only a million residents. The former curling rink, with its artificial ice, a lovely irony, was boarded up. Only a soft glow behind the distant pins lit the two-lane bowling alley. In the full-sized gymnasium, perhaps one dedicated figure shot hoops in the semi-darkness, the ball echoing every time it hit the floor. Bedsheets covered the shelves in the library. Game rooms lay vacant. I never saw a soul in any of the well-equipped photography, carpentry and lapidary clubs. The only regular draw was the computer games room and a well-stocked video lending library.

Every week, new arrivals from Trenton, Ontario, gathered in the auditorium for orientation. This was the first and last time they would see a salute during their tour. The heads of the departments made a formal entrance, followed by the commanding officer, Major Stéphane Marcoux, as the recruits sat at attention. Here they learned the rules, which were few: No muscle shirts beyond the main entrance; no photos of the array; and, for reasons no one could explain, no smoking outside. (Smoking inside was permitted.)

Alert's informality was partly an attempt to address the isolation and partly Marcoux's own easygoing style. I wondered if this was a prerequisite for Alert commanders, but one recent CO had insisted on maintaining strict stand-by-your-bed inspections and regular drills.

While the radio technicians rotated between Ottawa, Alert, and similar bases in British Columbia and Newfoundland, the support staff were often veterans of international peacekeeping missions, Somalia one year, Bosnia the next. Many of these thirty-somethings were already closing in on their pension. For most of them, the hardest part was separation from their families. "My wife gives our two-year-old a gummy bear every day," said one man. "He knows his father will be coming home when the jar is empty."

"It's funny," said another, "but I really miss mowing the lawn."

Summer temperatures at Alert were typically between 32° and 40°F, with a lot of fog and overcast. But the constant daylight was cheering, and occasional day trips broke the sense of confinement. Walls were so thin that when a man and woman craved a little privacy, they spent a weekend at a nearby fishing hut known as the Love Shack.

Women had worked at Alert since 1980 and now made up ten percent of the station. Adapting must not have been easy. All the women had cultivated that needling banter which so often passes for communication among men. In the Zoo, Alexandra and I chatted with a newly arrived technician in her twenties. She assumed we were military, and within a few minutes she was explaining why she preferred the word "cunt" to "pussy." Meanwhile, a gawky Newfoundlander tried to impress us with misogynistic jokes that even I, not known for moral outrage, found distasteful. As he aired his prejudices, the women just rolled their eyes good-naturedly. And at basic training, one woman had a hard time saying "fuck," so her entire unit were ordered to do pushups until they fainted, and when they recovered, they had to do more pushups until she finally squeaked out the word.

Alert lay on a historic corner of Ellesmere, yet the lack of staff continuity made them strangers in this strange land. One man, a civilian now, liked the place so much that he kept coming back and performing his old duties on contract. But for the rest, it could have been Germany or Saudi Arabia or anywhere else in the world. A servicewoman at Eureka once told me, "They send us up here as a punishment or slight, and when they find out we like it, they never send us back."

One person who was a true part of the Alert and Ellesmere tradition was George Stewart, the crusty sixty-two year old organizer of Operation Boxtop. One night we sat down at the Beach and talked for hours. A restless man, he kept crossing and uncrossing his legs as we spoke, as if sending Morse code messages to hidden cameras. He knew Ellesmere, its old-timers, its stories, its rumors. He had been involved in Alert since the 1950s. When Boxtop 22 crashed, he was in Thule. "I was supposed to have been on that plane," he said.

It was Stewart who later identified the bodies. One woman had been so badly burned that he recognized only the distinctive ring she wore, and the rank patch on her uniform. He bluntly answered a lot of my questions, although he insisted that I not take notes. During the Boxtop 22 crisis, he developed a dislike for what he called the bloodsucking media. Maybe Stewart didn't like what I did, but I found him charming, and I especially liked something he said about the press. Notes or not, it was impossible to forget: "I'm not a journalist, so I'm not in the business of gathering information that is none of my business."

Chapter Twelve

They, the People

The angry October sea pitched the Zodiac around as we approached Button Point, on the southeast corner of Bylot Island. Flurries of kittiwakes skimmed above the bobbing icebergs. Snow flew, and the dampness penetrated even our floater suits. Through his headset, first mate Marc Thibeault kept the mother ship informed of our condition.

Most places look best in sunshine, but extreme spots need extreme weather. Who wants 75°F in Death Valley? Who wants calm seas during a first crossing of the Shrieking Sixties? Extreme weather even flavors ordinary places. Montreal ice storms, Kansas tornadoes, California earthquakes: The earth roars, and we feel proud to be part of something bigger than ourselves.

I had hoped to land to search for signs of ancient Inuit, but Bylot Island was a bird sanctuary and no one was sure whether the summer restrictions against landing also applied in fall. The real mise-en-scène, anyway, was the icebergs. Like the kittiwakes, we circled round and round one that erupted from the sea like a canine tooth. My eyes glazed over as I imagined the pitched battle that had taken place here.

It was spring, around 1850. During that season, the sea was frozen. Some Inuit led by a shaman named Qitdlaq were seal hunting near the icebergs rooted off this Baffin Island satellite when they saw a larger party dogsledding toward them. Qitdlaq had reason to be suspicious. A dynamic but ruthless leader, with a bald head rare among Inuit, he had left southern Baffin Island to escape the family of a man he had killed. He had made enemies in north Baffin too. Now he and his men retreated to a steep iceberg, cut steps into its glassy surface and climbed high to await the attack.

The iceberg shielded Qitdlaq's group from the hail of arrows. Eventually the attackers withdrew. Although Qitdlaq did not hesitate to murder a rival, he disliked the consequences—always having to watch his back. After the Battle of the Iceberg, he and his followers moved near what is now the village of Igloolik. But this was not enough for the restless *angekok*, or shaman. He wanted to put a more formidable barrier between himself and his enemies. He convinced the others to follow him across Lancaster Sound to the little-known islands to the north. No one liked Lancaster Sound because a floe could break off without warning and drift into open Baffin Bay. The Inuit of the region still say that, "If you took the caribou parkas of all the men who've died on the ice, you could build a bridge from Igloolik to the mainland."

By 1853, Qitdlarssuaq, the Great Qitdlaq, and forty or fifty others had crossed the Sound and settled on the southeast coast of Devon Island. Darkly streaked cliffs give Devon its Inuktitut name of *Tatlurutit*, Tattoos of the Chin. (Chin tattoos, using caribou sinews coated in lamp soot and run through the skin with bone needles, were a common adornment among women.)

Today, Devon is the world's largest uninhabited island. Its modest human history amounts to Qitdlarssuaq's colony, Frederick Cook's overwintering in 1909, an RCMP post in the 1930s and a thriving biology camp in the 1960s. In recent summers, the Haughton Crater on the west side has hosted a quasi-scientific circus of Mars aficionados, running around in moonsuits and erecting jazzy-looking structures, supposedly prototypes of Red Planet housing. The entire High Arctic has a Mars-like flavor, that's part of its appeal, but this particular site was chosen mainly because "crater" sounds sexy and extraterrestrial.

For several years, eastern Devon's bird and mammal colonies supported the settlers. For practical and perhaps political reasons, they split

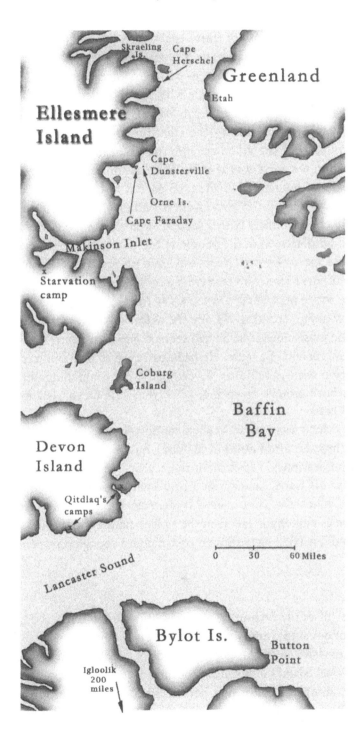

Skraeling Is. Cape Herschel

Greenland

Etah

Ellesmere Island

Cape Dunsterville

Orne Is.

Cape Faraday

Makinson Inlet

x
Starvation camp

Coburg Island

Baffin Bay

Devon Island

Qitdlaq's camps

Lancaster Sound

0   30   60 Miles

Bylot Is.

Button Point

Igloolik
200
miles

into two camps of twenty or thirty each—one led by Qitdlarssuaq, the other by an influential man named Oqe. They may have remained on Devon but for two chance meetings with passing explorers. In 1853, Edward Inglefield met Qitdlarssuaq in what is now called Dundas Harbour. Through an interpreter, he told the *angekok* about a people like themselves in northern Greenland—the Polar Inuit.

Qitdlarssuaq did not act on the information at first. In the meantime, his reputation as a great *angekok* grew. When a walrus overturned his kayak within sight of his horrified wife, she gave him up for dead. But that evening he walked into camp and went to bed as if nothing had happened.

In 1858, an encounter with a second explorer, Leopold McClintock, reminded Qitdlarssuaq of the people to the north. Although he was well into middle age, unknown Greenland lured his restless spirit, and he incited the others to join him on a great journey northward: "Do you know the desire to see new lands? Do you know the desire to see new people?" Never shy about boosting his oratory with a little charlatanry, he described the mysterious tribe he had seen on one of his spirit flights. That is the Inuit version of events. He had neglected to mention to them his conversation with Inglefield. Nevertheless, his compelling personality won over both groups. In spring, 1859, they left Devon Island for the promised land.

The distance was not far. In good conditions, a light party could dogsled the three hundred miles in ten days, but with children, kayaks and all their possessions, it took them three years. In 1861, they spent the winter just off Cape Faraday, on a tiny island labeled Orne on today's maps but which the Inuit called *Ingersarvik,* the humping place. The Inuit were as raunchy as sailors in their place-naming, and countless Shit Brooks and Tit Hills have slipped past modern topographic censors.

■

Since the "h" at the beginning of words is silent in French, the Quebecois crew of our ship weren't sure whether I was being raunchy myself by lobbying to visit "Horny" Island, the scene of Qitdlarssuaq's greatest crisis. On Orne Island, a showdown occurred between Qitdlarssuaq and Oqe, the group's other strong personality. Many of the migrants, including Oqe, were fed up with this eternal wandering and wanted to return to their Baffin homeland. For once, Qitdlarssuaq's powers of persuasion failed. More than half turned south with Oqe, while about fifteen remained loyal to Qitdlarssuaq.

On a foggy September afternoon, our ship's helicopter lifted off for the ten-mile flight to Orne Island. We flew low, and the grey pack ice flashed past. We couldn't yet make out the low-lying island, lost against the ice cap behind Cape Faraday.

"Polar bear!" said the pilot, banking sharply.

We peered out the port window. A whitish bear, disturbed by the noise of the rotors, trotted evasively over the rubbly pack. Orne Island's location near what Inuit call the *sina* (she' na), or floe edge, gave it perhaps the best hunting on the southeast coast of Ellesmere, a good reason for Qitdlarssuaq to winter there. In the poor light we continued to have trouble finding the island, but eventually we landed on a knoll that looked right. The pilot left me with his shotgun and hastened back to the ship, promising to return in two or three hours.

In 1975, a Maryland banker named Norman Brice dogsledded from Qaanaaq to Grise Fiord with some Greenland guides. Brice's hobby was archaeology and his unpublished inventory of sites, though quaint in its interlacing of science and anecdote, has proven surprisingly useful to professional archaeologists. Brice was thorough and he drew great sketch maps. He seemed able to visualize what each site looked like from a hundred feet in the air.

I had Brice's sketch of the Orne Island sites with me, but something was wrong. The island I was on did not look anything like Orne, yet Orne was the only island in the area. Cape Faraday seemed much too close. I wandered for half an hour amid old meat caches and remnant *qammaqs*, or winter sod houses, that poked above the September snow. I was totally confused. Finally, I had to conclude that this was not Orne Island but Cape Faraday itself.

It was as if the spirit of the great *angekok* had thrown magic dust in our eyes and prevented us from seeing the island. Or he had appeared in the shape of a bear off our port side just as the difficult-to-spot island passed to starboard. I wandered around Cape Faraday, dwelling happily on this almost supernatural event.

By the time the pilot picked me up, he too had realized his mistake but had still failed to spot the real Orne Island. Had Qitdlaq transformed it into one of the many island-like icebergs floating in Baffin Bay, just as he had transformed himself into some animal for his spirit flights? Only when we ignored our eyes and followed the latitude and longitude on the navigation console did we track it down. It looked like an ice floe. It was low, small and completely snow-covered. No dark outcroppings of rock to give it away. We circled over the western promontory that had probably been Qitdlarssuaq's camp, but we did not land. I did not want to.

A further oddity surfaced that evening when I checked my notes. There is some doubt whether the schism with Oqe occurred on Orne Island or at Cape Faraday itself. Inuit legend says Orne, but archaeologists have discovered at Cape Faraday two coeval winter camps, separated by a polite distance, that might have belonged to the two factions. So perhaps I did visit the site I was after, without knowing it.

Meanwhile, the story of the missing island spread throughout the ship. "It's like Avalon," said Lisa, one of the passengers.

"What's that?"

"The island lost in the mists when Britain embraced Christianity."

■

After the separation, Qitdlarssuaq and his remaining followers continued north and reached their promised land at last in May, 1862. They settled near Etah, an occasional hunting camp that was also a base for the white men who were now exploring these latitudes more frequently.

No Greenlanders visited Etah that year, but Qitdlarssuaq remained over the winter, taking advantage of the good hunting. The following spring, he finally met the mysterious Polar Inuit. The first man he saw was a hunter who had lost a leg in a rockfall and been fitted with a wooden one by a surgeon from one of the explorers' ships. Qitdlarssuaq wondered whether all people in this strange land had wooden legs.

Qitdlarssuaq must have felt great joy that his decade-long quest had succeeded. Although the dialect was different, the two groups could understand each other. The hundred Polar Inuit had been isolated for a century by the near-impassable coastline of Melville Bay. During that time, they had forgotten how to make such vital tools as the kayak and the bow and arrow. No doubt they looked on Qitdlarssuaq's technology as marvellous, and it would be surprising if the *angekok* did not modestly admit that his magic had created them. The two groups mingled, intermarried, lived together. After six years, they were one community.

But peace continued to elude Qitdlarssuaq. He had a falling out with a friend and fellow *angekok* named Avatannguaq. Thereafter, disturbing portents, voices from the ground, gyrfalcons out of season, caribou that turned into rocks, suggested that Avatannguaq was showing his displeasure. Several worried migrants, plus some Polar Inuit, urged Qitdlarssuaq to rid them of the rogue conjuror.

Qitdlarssuaq was old by now and did not want to murder again. But he reluctantly agreed and stabbed his former friend in an ambush.

Not long after, Qitdlarssuaq fell ill with what sounds like stomach cancer. Like many lifelong wanderers, he became obsessed with dying in his homeland. He had lost none of his authority, and most of the original migrants plus some Polar Inuit agreed to accompany him back to Baffin Island. But soon after they had crossed to the Ellesmere side, Qitdlarssuaq died. The year was 1868. The last great Inuit shaman, leader of the only Inuit migration in historic times, was buried either on the ice or in the pass behind Cape Herschel. This was the same windy neck where, fifteen years later, Greely's unfortunate sergeant, Joseph Elison, would irreparably freeze his hands and feet.

I've looked twice for Qitdlarssuaq's body. Steep hills flank Elison Pass, and there are few suitable places. Today there is what may be the outline of a grave on the narrow causeway, but an archaeologist who stopped there for a look believes it's just a broken-down meat cache. However, Norman Brice met some Swiss scientists at Cape Herschel who reported finding a skull in the pass in 1973.

■

Part con man, part inspired leader, Qitdlarssuaq's spirit still infects those susceptible to its spell. A Roman Catholic priest from Pond Inlet, who became a world-class scholar on Inuit history in his spare time, published the story of Qitdlarssuaq just two years before dying in a fire. And in 1987, an Igloolik schoolteacher named Renee Wissink retraced Qitdlarssuaq's route by dogteam.

Two years previous, Wissink and I had skied a hundred miles on Baffin Island together. He spoke of organizing a big expedition but he seemed more dreamer than doer. Nevertheless, with a team of five, including three local Inuit, he covered Qitdlarssuaq's route from Igloolik to Qaanaaq in a single season.

Near the end of their trip, they met some Greenland dogsledders near Cape Herschel. In a chilling reenactment, one of the hunters died of a stomach ailment before their eyes. A few years later, one of Wissink's partners, a Baffin descendent of Qitdlarssuaq, succumbed to stomach cancer at the age of forty-two. Little wonder that some Inuit believe that Qitdlarssuaq still exerts shamanistic power from beyond the grave.

By 1995, Wissink had become Chief Park Warden of Ellesmere Island (now Quttinirpaaq, or Top of the World) National Park. We spoke over the phone for the first time in years, and he invited me up that summer. To my surprise, my former partner had evolved into total stranger. His knowledge of the island was profound. His self-assurance made me wonder if this was the same person. Vaguely I recalled that the article on his Qitdlarssuaq expedition, about the only thing he'd ever written, had won a National Magazine Award.

In his laid-back way, he seemed fearless. He fought articulately against the pencil pushers in Ottawa. Once he noticed a visiting politician snitching an artifact and forced him to put it back. He had loved kids from an early age and was beginning another family with his second wife. He reminded me of what Peter Freuchen had said of Knud Rasmussen: "Knud is a whole man; I am only half a man." The Inuit, for whom anyone without kids was incomplete, would have agreed. During his expedition, something of the magic of Qitdlarssuaq had turned this quiet man into one of Ellesmere's great ones.

■

After Qitdlarssuaq's death, the most harrowing part of this Inuit Odyssey began. The nineteen survivors continued toward Baffin and soon reached Orne Island, where they again overwintered. The following spring, drawn by the promise of good game, they moved into Makinson Inlet. They spent the summer combing the area but failed to stock up for the winter. Open water prevented an early return to Orne Island, so they built their winter camp by a small lake deep inside the inlet. Many starved. Survivors ate the remains, then two of the less scrupulous began to murder their fellows for food. During a moonless period, one desperate family managed to escape this death camp to the outer part of the inlet, where they survived on a couple of lucky seal kills.

In spring, they managed to catch a young bear in a stone trap. These traps are about nine feet long and made of piles of heavy rocks, with a narrow chamber through which a bear, even a human, can hardly wriggle. Drawn by bait at the far end, the bear crawls inside. When it pulls the bait, a traprock slides down behind it. In these tight quarters, the bear can neither back up, turn around nor swing its paw to knock an escape hole. The hunters eventually come, remove part of the roof and spear the bear through the hole. There are ten known bear traps in the Ellesmere area, including this one at Cape Dunsterville, just north of Orne Island, to which the survivors owed their lives. The five of them, including one young girl, eventually returned to Greenland. Today, the descendents of Qitdlarssuaq and his band make up one-third the population of northwest Greenland.

■

In Qaanaaq, I met the great-granddaughter of that young girl. For me it was like meeting a queen, because she was also the granddaughter of the greatest of all Ellesmere travelers, Nukapinguaq.

Qaanaaq overlooks the useful and beautiful icebergs of Inglefield Bay. When I arrived, a storm was brewing and fishermen were prudently dragging their vessels ashore on a slipway of iceberg pieces. Although there was running water, many homes kept a chunk of iceberg on the porch for drinking. As in most Greenland towns, sled dogs outnumbered people. Because of the danger to kids and drunks, they were all chained. Some slept as I walked past; others studied me with vaguely Slavic eyes.

An impromptu celebration that evening drew most of Qaanaaq to the school gymnasium. Disco lights threw roving multicolored polka dots on the stage while a delightfully off-key choir sang the Greenland anthem, using crib sheets to remember the words. With the disco lights passing over them, two old men in polar bear skin pants then chanted ancient songs while beating a sealskin tambourine. Kids of all ages wandered, crawled and ran underfoot. Of Qaanaaq's 649 inhabitants, 500 of them seemed to be under ten years old. Most adults watched quietly from the sidelines like pre-teens at their first dance.

When the old men had done their numbers, I approached them and, feeling glaringly *qallunaat*, booted up my laptop. From the hard drive I opened two old portraits and asked whether they recognized either of them. The photo of Peeawahto on Eureka Sound wasn't familiar, but the second black-and-white image made the eyes of one old man flicker.

"Nukapinguaq," he said. "His granddaughter is in this room."

He led me to Inalunguaq Joelsen, a slender woman of fifty-six with square black glasses. She listened politely as I raved about her grandfather, Nukapinguaq. Just then a rock-and-roll band struck up, ending conversation, so Inalunguaq invited me to come to her home the following morning.

The next day, onyx clouds and a steel grey sea. No wind. Inalunguaq's living room was spic and span, with a new coffee table of blond wood and several closed doors, behind which things probably weren't so neat. Old family photos covered three of the four walls.

Inalunguaq sat at a little sewing table, hands folded primly, braced for what she imagined was a serious interview. Her father had been one of Nukapinguaq's three children with his first wife, Vivi. I mentioned my love of travel and the High Arctic and its great figures and my conversations with the niece of RCMP Sergeant Stallworthy, one of her grandfather's best traveling companions.

Most of her contribution to this awkward conversation was a foggy recollection that the Canadian government had promised her grandfather some payment that he never received, and how a Canadian ship once landed with a load of supplies for Nukapinguaq, which the entire community helped itself to. This story went on for so long that I wondered whether she was hoping I'd right this ancient grievance by arranging to have large amounts of lumber and cash deposited on her doorstep.

Inalunguaq was thirteen when her grandfather died, but it was soon clear that her best memories of him would not come forth in this conversation. Most Inuit do not talk freely to white people. A few words here and there, with pregnant pauses that seem to end the thought but are really just minute-long punctuation marks. If you can ride out the silence, the conversation may resume.

Forgetting Nukapinguaq, I took out the computer and showed her some of my own family photos. She laughed when I brought up one of Alexandra kissing a pet chameleon. As I left, Inalunguaq gave me a tiny pair of toy kamiks as a memento. "Please say hello to your wife for me. And pass on my greetings to the niece of Stallworthy."

■

Nukapinguaq was one of the most celebrated of all Greenland guides, a Tenzing Norgay of the High Arctic. Almost every major expedition between 1913 and 1938 engaged the five foot six Nukapinguaq. His prime coincided with the era of great long-distance expeditions. In one five-year period, he traveled 5,500 miles. Thanks to his legendary hunting skills, no one went hungry. He could pick the best route through rough ice and judge the safety of newly frozen leads at a glance.

Nukapinguaq knew he was good, and his self-confidence did not sit well with everyone. "A young man spoiled by an old mother," complained one explorer in 1913, when Nukapinguaq was twenty. Another remarked that his employee was "not contented unless he is doing just as he pleases and is inclined to be very sullen." But by the following year, the two had become friends.

In 1925, Nukapinguaq began working for the Royal Canadian Mounted Police, hunting for the post and assisting on spring sovereignty patrols. Special Constable Number 1718 was paid just three hundred dollars a year, but the work suited his wandering temperament. A superb craftsmen, he could carve exquisite miniatures out of walrus ivory or jury-rig a broken sled on the trail. Inalunguaq showed me a *kamiut* for softening sealskin boots that her grandfather had made, a vertical wooden stick with a metal tongue on top and an ingenious T-joint on bottom for steadying with the feet. The T-joint was firm but as flexible as a komatik and had worked for decades without breaking.

Although Nukapinguaq's name means *small nice bachelor,* he married three times. His first wife, Vivi, was Inalunguaq's grandmother. His second wife seems to have been an Inuit femme fatale who began as his father's young consort. Nukapinguaq liked her so much that father and son stopped speaking. When Nukapinguaq's father died, the widow promptly moved in with the son. Her name, coincidentally, was also Inalunguaq, but explorers called her the Duchess, because of her airs. The two had no children. Eventually, this small nice bachelor married a third time.

Nukapinguaq worked for the RCMP for ten years, as posts opened, closed and reopened in time with spasms of angst about sovereignty. In 1953, at age sixty but still "extremely spry," he and his third wife spent the winter at the first magic spot I'd seen on Ellesmere, the Thorvald Peninsula. On calm summer evenings, a thin glacier slides down to the water's edge and forms a perfect zigzag with its reflection. Rich meadows overlook an ethereal seascape of floating ice mushrooms. I thought I'd died and gone to Mars. Nukapinguaq lived in the RCMP hunting cabin, a mere framework now, until the summer, when a new generation of Mounties established a post at nearby Alexandra Fiord. In a bitter irony, they reminded Nukapinguaq that it was illegal for Greenlanders to hunt in Canada.

Still, his decade with the RCMP remained the glory years of his life, and as he lay dying at Thule in 1956, he asked that a member of the RCMP be present. "Knowing Nukapinguaq's feelings toward the Force, this would be an expected request of him," police records state. To their credit, they sent a constable from Resolute. So died the man who was really the Last King of Thule.

■

History may be an open book on Ellesmere, but even a studious traveler can only faintly taste its archaeology. Almost every point of land has a circle of rocks where some Stone Age family pitched their tent, but the real stories usually lie beneath a foot of topsoil. These ancient people often lived partly underground, beneath a cantilevered roof of bone and driftwood covered with sod. When they abandoned the house, the roof collapsed and the sod regrew and covered everything. Only archaeologists who excavate the ruins can truly touch the daily lives of prehistoric Inuit.

In 1958, archaeologist Moreau Maxwell investigated an old house first mentioned by Greely, where the Ruggles River flows out of Lake Hazen. Maxwell compared its artifacts with similar Greenland ones and concluded that the house was built around 1300 A.D. and lived in for one winter. A hundred years later, another family moved into the House on the Ruggles. They stayed for three winters. In summer, for a change of air, they moved to a skin tent a few feet away.

The Thule people depended on the sea for food, so these heartlanders were daring, perhaps desperate. Yet of all interior Ellesmere, this was the best place to try to make a go of it. The Ruggles River stays open all winter, and its arctic char will rise to anything. On the far side of the lake, caribou and muskox thrive in a polar oasis.

Nevertheless, the Ellesmere interior cannot indefinitely support even a single family. Tragedy ended the experiment of these pioneers. The man died, and his wife buried him beneath a pile of rocks in their former summer home. The young widow was not able to fend for herself, and was too far away from her homeland to return. The loneliness of her last weeks can hardly be imagined. Maxwell found her skeleton and some dog bones on the sleeping platform of the winter house. "Presumably," he wrote, "[she] had been left with no alternative but to eat the last of the sled dogs, and finally to die of starvation as she lay alone on the sleeping platform." Not surprisingly, archaeologists came to classify northern Ellesmere as a "cultural cul de sac." It is the most extreme environment in which humans have ever lived.

■

Around 2500 B.C., the first people reached Ellesmere from Alaska. Perhaps the same mixture of wanderlust and practicality that drove Qitdlarssuaq inspired them. They had hurried quickly through the more barren islands to the west, but once they reached the east coast of Ellesmere, they put down roots. Their earliest known home was Skraeling Island.

Skraeling is one of the most visited spots on Ellesmere, which means it gets about forty visitors a year, mostly kayakers and botanists based at Alexandra Fiord. It is four miles away from the place where Nukapinguaq spent his final winter on Ellesmere, before being ignominiously shooed back to Greenland.

In August, 1875, George Nares became the first white man to see Skraeling Island. He called it the Three Sisters, after a trio of prominent peaks visible from the east. In fact, one of the peaks belongs to a nearby island, and in 1898, Otto Sverdrup renamed the island Skraeling, after noting its many Thule ruins. Skraeling is an old Norse word for the Inuit, meaning *weakling*.

Skraeling Island looks like a two-mile-long snake that has just swallowed a very lumpy mouse. In late April, mist from a nearby polynya plays about its contours in the cool of evening and makes it seem like another Avalon.

Intrigued by Sverdrup's name for the island, Calgary archaeologist Peter Schledermann visited it in 1977 and discovered a rich trove of artifacts and houses spanning centuries that have made Skraeling Island the Macchu Picchu of Ellesmere, its prime archaeological treasure. For the next fifteen summers, Schledermann and his team excavated the ruins. Most intriguing of all, they turned up a piece of chain mail, some woven wool, iron boat rivets . . . in all some thirty-seven Viking artifacts from Skraeling and the neighboring fiordlands. These items might have come from southern Greenland through trade with other natives, but the unexplained pair of cairns discovered a few miles away by George Nares makes it likely that a Viking ship was shipwrecked here around 1250 A.D.

Despite conflicting interpretations, the main points of arctic prehistory seem clear. Ellesmere was occupied from 2500 B.C. to 500 B.C., with a gap between 1500 B.C. and 1100 B.C. God knows how these early Stone Age cultures survived. Their life was so marginal that they had to keep hunting even during the polar night. Signs of their presence are common but subtle, a half-buried square of stones marking an ancient hearth, or a tent circle so faint that the manmade pattern appears only in certain light.

Around 500 B.C., the climate became colder and an already difficult life became impossible. For the next twelve hundred years, the High Arctic lay empty. Then around 700 A.D., a new wave of settlers moved east from Central Arctic shores. They were able to stockpile enough food to pass the winter in communal dwellings, in sociable hibernation, drumming, telling stories and sleeping a lot. The Dorset, or Tunit, ruled the High Arctic for five hundred years. They lacked dog teams, but they were magnificent craftspeople. Their tiny tools and sculptures are triumphs of miniaturization. "They could have been used by human-like creatures only a foot tall," writes one appreciative researcher. Life must have been good, because they left behind more art than tools. Given their skills, it is strange that the Dorset never learned to drill in bone or wood, they gouged grooves until a hole appeared. Any artifact with a round hole comes from their successors, the Thule, and is at most nine hundred years old.

No one knows whether the Dorset vanished because of clashes with the Thule during the hundred years, from 1100 to 1200 A.D., when they both lived in the same region. But by 1200 the Dorset had either died out or disappeared through intermarriage with the dominant new culture. Oral Inuit tradition remembers the Dorset as a race of supermen. According to legend, Button Point, where Qitdlarssuaq survived the Battle of the Iceberg, was the Dorset's last home.

The Thule, like the earliest arctic peoples, came from Alaska. Their boats, kayaks and dog teams equipped them for long-distance travel. Their bows and arrows allowed them to hunt caribou. They are the direct ancestors of the modern Inuit. Thule simply refers to the Inuit before they were discovered by John Ross in 1818. After 1818, the prehistoric Thule become the historic Polar Inuit.

■

Ice caps cover one-third of Ellesmere, but the early migrants could cross the island through five passes without resorting to glacier travel. One of the passes, from Cañon Fiord to Copes Bay, is difficult and usually overlooked, but when my partner and I skied it that warm May, we found a bone sled piece with a hole neatly drilled through it. It lay on a rough slope which was claiming pieces of our sleds, too.

A second pass followed what Danish anthropologist H.P. Steensby called the Muskox Way. He claimed that northern Ellesmere was a highway for the earliest people, who depended on muskoxen. The catchy phrase, "Muskox Way," has outlived the theory itself. Although the Muskox Way was a secondary route, it is now the only commonly walked trail on Ellesmere.

The Muskox Way begins near Tanquary Fiord, headquarters of Quttinirpaaq National Park. I hiked it one summer with a group of adventure tourists. Mountains and ice caps overshadowed our route, but the terrain was flat and easy. Yet for me, it was still an extreme journey, because I had chosen to carry thirty-five pounds of camera gear in addition to my share of supplies. A big tripod and a 500mm lens were my weapons for hunting muskox. Dragging 115 pounds on a sled is easy, but backpacking that weight for seven to ten hours a day is grim. Even expedition packs are not made to bear that much. The vaunted suspension system turned to mush and I had to bend sharply at the waist. Eyes pointed at the ground, I saw little of the country. Friction sores in the small of my back and sciatic pains that radiated down my legs made it hard to sleep. I took just one good muskox photo in the seventy-five miles between Tanquary Fiord and Lake Hazen, but at least I had successfully hunted the Muskox Way.

By mid-July at Lake Hazen, the ice has rotted vertically into foot-long candles which bond loosely together. They tinkle and break as the wind nudges them against the shore. This yearly scouring bulldozes the shallows and makes Hazen one of the most sterile lakes in existence. Some years, the surrounding land gets less precipitation than Death Valley. Yet wildlife love it. Insouciant arctic hares nibble the cottongrass; Peary caribou roam the high meadows; nesting terns protect their air space with swoops and occasional head pecks.

It is another seventy miles from Lake Hazen to the east coast and the end of the Muskox Way. I would do this section alone. I could not bear another week with such a pack, but since I planned to linger on the coast and then possibly hike back, I needed three weeks' food. By leaving most of my camera gear and research papers behind, I managed to reduce the weight to about ninety-five pounds. This was heavy but not as physically destructive. As I lumbered off, Bill King, a Toronto vascular surgeon who was hiking the Hazen area, advised me that the number one cause of death among the old voyageurs was strangulated hernias.

Hazen to Discovery Harbour is one of the easiest extreme wilderness hikes in the world. Hard, flat ground skirts the foot of bare café-au-lait hills. Little wonder that Greely was able to drag his little rickshaw over most of it and record in his journal, "Pace 3 mph" or "3½ mph."

No wilderness hike is complete without losing the way at least once and having to struggle over boulders. Donning neoprene booties, I tried to wade through Hazen's ice water, but razor-sharp candle ice sliced open my shins, and the unnerving sight of streamers of blood in the water drove me ashore again. After taking nine hours to cover four miles, I camped on a sunlit meadow beside a small stream. Ineffably pure water, as if freshly mixed from hydrogen and oxygen, splashed past my tent. I rested my sore bare feet in the cool grass and watched the midnight sun swing round to backlight the yellow poppies. I didn't seek 70°F weather but I didn't mind when it sought me out. There were even mosquitoes, a rarity on Ellesmere. Lake Hazen and Alexandra Fiord are the only places warm enough for them.

Just before the Gilman River, I crunched over a beach twinkling with orange jewels inset into fragments of coal. Amber, the only source on northern Ellesmere. I pocketed some as a souvenir, just as the ill-fated man from the House on the Ruggles had done for his teenage wife. Among her few possessions on the lonely sleeping platform where she died was an amber necklace.

1998 was one of the warmest High Arctic summers on record, and the glacier-fed Gilman River was high and dangerous. I waited till five a.m., when the water was lowest, and waded cautiously across. High Arctic rivers are not broad liquid ribbons but three or four narrow channels separated by gravel bars. None of river's main braids was more than twenty feet wide, but the thigh-deep rapids were almost too powerful to manage alone. The mind is rarely as focused as it is when wading across a river on the verge of sweeping you away. For half an hour, I forgot about the pack. Safely on the other side, I felt exhilarated, intense.

Nevertheless, the humdrum route across the bogland, past Lake Hazen and down Black Rock Vale, was boring compared to most of Ellesmere. I pitied the tourists who trustingly shelled out five thousand dollars for the experience. Outfitters worked the route because it was easy, it was in a national park, and planes could land at both ends without special permission. Tanquary-Hazen, the first half of the Muskox Way, at least had good scenery and wildlife.

By the end of the seven-day trek, I looked like a veteran staggering home from the wars. No hernias, I was just out of steam. In most travel, the meaning comes along the way, as it should, but once in a while, it's okay if the way is just an obstacle between you and the goal. When I saw the lovely blue water of Discovery Harbour, bathed in sunshine and silence, I threw the pack to the ground and sat on it, bouncing up and down like a happy kid. I knew how the Thule must have felt at the end of their long journey.

Chapter Thirteen

Tours de Force

Like most things, Grise Fiord looks best from the outside looking in. From the outside, great cliffs beautify the row of bungalows even as it makes them look small and insignificant. Dogs howl when the church bell rings. Kids on bikes do tricks off natural ramps of sastrugi. From the inside, Ellesmere's one village faces south onto the white nothingness of Jones Sound. A hundred and sixty-nine people live here. Most are Inuit. The dozen whites come for a year or two as policemen, nurses, teachers and store managers, but they leave before their kids reach school age.

The sky is the only canvas for vivid colors in the Arctic, and in March, the sun's brush is at its most expressionistic. Even the snow is soft ivory and blue and orange, not yet blinding white. A few hours of twilight, even night, are to be savored, for from April till September the ceiling bulb is always on. The cold bites like a snake, but you get used to it, sort of. You do things slowly and deliberately, like a moonman. Your clothing is so puffy that if goose down were fat, you would weigh five hundred pounds. Winter elsewhere in Canada is a disappointing attenuation of thaws and freezes, of too many middle-of-the-road 20°F days. But here, the –30°F mean temperature is in little peril from warm chinooks or moist southerlies. Spring may officially arrive this month, but March on Ellesmere is winter in its purest form.

Constable Darren Malcolm of the Royal Canadian Mounted Police met me at the rough airstrip, cupped by rock walls on three sides. Our landing was textbook, but for pilots, this was the least popular strip in the Arctic. In the past, air turbulence from the cliffs tumbled approaching Twin Otters like socks in a dryer. Only one crash, but many near misses. Nowadays, nothing lands unless the wind speed is less than ten knots.

For the hundred and twenty-fifth anniversary of the RCMP, Darren was about to revive a grand tradition, and he had invited me to join him. In the 1920s and early 1930s, the RCMP sovereignty patrols covered thousands of miles each spring across the High Arctic. These were the Mounties' finest hours, and some of the best polar journeys ever. Two Mounties, in particular, stand as giants of northern travel.

With four or five local Inuit, we would snowmobile four hundred miles to Alexandra Fiord by way of Sverdrup Pass, the main non-glacier route across Ellesmere. Sverdrup Pass was the real Muskox Way of the ancient migrants. Its windblown gravel and its Hell Cleft had frustrated many explorers, who came to prefer the more hazardous but predictable route across the ice cap. Despite several attempts, no one from Grise Fiord had yet succeeded in duplicating the feat of the Paleoeskimos.

Like the first RCMP journeys, ours was a sovereignty patrol. Territorial tension between Canada and Greenland was in one of its periodic flareups, and some Inuit Rangers, a kind of local military reserve, wanted to discourage Greenlanders from hunting on the Canadian side. This was the latest chapter in an eighty-year-old dispute.

■

Darren's young family was away, and we were bacheloring it at his place—Kraft Dinner, beer, TV. It's a quiet posting for a cop. There is little to steal and nowhere to go with it. The few crimes are mainly domestic problems. Darren spent a lot of time helping around the village, just to keep in touch. "I'm beginning to sleep again at night," he said.

Grise Fiord is three hundred miles from anywhere, and that anywhere is just Resolute. Its isolation on such a lovely island seems to give it strength. There is enough federal money to employ everyone in town, although most work is part-time. One guy ploughs the airstrip; two drive the water truck. Keeping one's part of the town running may take a couple of hours a day, or one day a week. Plenty of time left to go hunting and fishing. But if you're eighteen years old and hate the outdoors, any arctic village must feel like a life sentence in the worst possible prison.

The next morning, Darren wanted to break in his new snowmobile for the long patrol, so we drove fifty miles east along the sea ice to Craig Harbour, Ellesmere's first RCMP post. By 1920, Canada had awakened to the threat of losing the arctic islands. No Canadian had even set foot on Ellesmere till 1904. No Canadian had ever touched Axel Heiberg. Canada was particularly sensitive about trespassing Greenlanders ignoring its ban on muskox hunting, to which Knud Rasmussen, the virtual emperor of northwest Greenland, fired off a letter to Ottawa calling Ellesmere a "no man's land."

The gauntlet had been thrown. In 1922, Craig Harbour was established near the southern tip of Ellesmere. It was not a popular spot. "The mountains give little protection from storms and the whole aspect of the place is bleak and forbidding," said one.

A packed snowmobile trail made the two hours to Craig Harbour less eyeball-shaking than the usual bucking bronco ride over unruly sastrugi. Today, one small house remains. From a distance, there was something poignant about this lonely hut, which the Inuit believe is haunted. Decades ago, three Greenland children died here of tuberculosis, and their spirits prompted villagers to move the house from its original position to a slightly less haunted spot nearby.

A post office sign still gives the seedy cabin an air of vague authority. One window had been broken by a polar bear and was boarded up; the rest were intact. The post looked out on the unaesthetic bulk of Smith Island. The view was Ellesmere, but mediocre Ellesmere. "It ain't no peach orchard, exactly," remarked one young RCMP officer when he saw Craig Harbour.

Inside the hut stood two double bunks upholstered with what Darren called prisoner mattresses. The hut lay near the floe edge, where belugas and narwhal blew and walrus bellowed and polar bears looked for opportunities. Craig Harbour was a good hunting camp, but signs of recent habitation were few. On a rough wooden shelf lay a fossilized

cinnamon roll and several cans of dried carrot chips that were maybe
fifty years old and had been so unpopular that they survived to become artifacts.

Before returning to Grise Fiord, we briefly visited King Edward Point,
the southern tip of Ellesmere. On a flat patch among some rocks, the
homesick Mounties had pitched their tent to watch for the ship that was
to bring them home to their peach orchards. They passed the time whit-
tling, and some of their shavings lay in crevices in the rocks. They gave
me a lugubrious feeling. The Inuit called this The Windy Place, because
of the katabatic winds that flow down from the southern ice cap. Even
on this otherwise calm day, puffs of blowing snow tinged with orange and
blue light raced southward.

■

Ten years earlier, not long after my Ellesmere travels began, sleepy Grise
Fiord endured a crisis. Residents spoke of moving back to their original
homes in northern Quebec. They also wanted compensation for having
been shanghaied to Grise Fiord. Some were sincerely upset; others
looked on it as a way to earn some fast money from the *qallunnats* down
south who had a growing guilt complex about the deeds of their fathers
and their fathers' fathers. At least, that is how one man in Grise Fiord explained it to me.

In 1993, the High Arctic exiles became a national scandal, and eventually the Canadian government apologized and gave a few million dollars in blood money. Some families tried to resettle in their ancestral
land, but almost all of them soon returned to Grise Fiord.

Forty years earlier, there had been no Grise Fiord, no Resolute. In one
of its spells of flag-planting, Canada had established (with U.S. collaboration) several arctic weather stations. It had also re-activated two
RCMP posts, including Craig Harbour. But there were no villages. Police,
scientists, military, and civilians were the four cornerstones of occupation. Canada may have won the battle for sovereignty, but the U.S.
periodically continued to test its resolve. Greenlanders also did what
they had done for centuries, dogsled to Ellesmere for its virgin hunting,
much as Lapp reindeer herders still roam untrammeled across northern
Scandinavia.

In the late 1940s, starvation had dogged Inuit communities northwest of Hudson Bay, and politicians were eager to avoid a repetition. When the Inuit at Port Harrison in northern Quebec seemed in an equally precarious position, the RCMP relocated several families to Resolute and Grise Fiord. To help these subarctic people adapt to the Far North, they also brought a few settlers from Pond Inlet on Baffin Island, where conditions were similar.

All the Inuit were volunteers, although how voluntary is open to question. In 1953, few Inuit would have had the chutzpah to resist even the gentlest prodding from a white authority figure. The architects of the relocation had a history of concern and respect for the Inuit but they failed to realize how traumatic splitting up families and tearing them from their traditional land would be. A promise to return any discontented settlers a year later also seems not to have been honored.

The establishment of Grise Fiord and Resolute was paternalistic, but that was the era. The real question is whether the move was designed to plant human flagpoles in the High Arctic, or whether it was mainly "for their own good," with sovereignty as a lesser motive. Like the Cook-Peary controversy, that debate will never go away, and there are two sides to it.

In 1953, Ray Thorsteinsson was on the beach in Resolute when the migrants got off the ship. "They were a tattered-looking bunch," he recalls, "except for the Pond Inlet people, who looked like prehistoric Eskimos, in caribou skins and with good dog teams. They weren't shanghaied at all. I'd learned the Eskimo language well, and they were happy to be here."

Nevertheless, the first winter was hard, especially for the Port Harrison people. In northern Quebec, the winter sun shone six hours a day; but in the High Arctic, night lasted from October till February. Resolute became known in Inuktitut as The Place Where Tomorrow Never Comes, and Grise Fiord was The Place that Never Melts, not the most endearing terms. They were promised great hunting, but then they were told, in essence, "By the way, see those big hairy things over there? They're called muskoxen, and you can only shoot one of them a year. You can hunt caribou, but to be honest, there aren't too many of them." Caribou hunters and fishermen thus found themselves dependent on marine mammals. Many adjusted, but others never could. A week before he died of a heart attack, the leader of the Port Harrison people climbed the hill behind Grise Fiord and looked across Jones Sound, trying to see a way home.

■

I planned to sled for two months around Kane Basin after the sovereignty patrol and I needed to prepare. Long ago, I had discovered that making a sandwich on the arctic trail meant hacking for fifteen minutes at toffee-hard peanut butter with a Swiss Army knife and laying the shrapnel between crumbly pieces of frozen bread. So I invested the afternoon at Darren Malcolm's kitchen table, making fifty-four peanut butter and jam sandwiches (one per day, with six days "lost" by working my way around the clock). The cold would preserve them for weeks, as long as I coated the bread with enough butter and peanut butter to keep the jam from soaking through. Each thousand-calorie sandwich fueled about two-and-a-half hours of sledding. The sandwiches were a kind of vegetarian seal blubber, and by the end of the afternoon, the stench of peanut butter was about as nauseating.

Our little caravan of five snowmobiles and komatiks set out early on March 30. Darkness was gone till autumn; a brief purple twilight would only last another three or four nights. It was –20° F. The sun was low enough that we didn't yet need sunglasses to avoid snowblindness.

The Greenland Inuit use dog teams, but the Canadians prefer snowmobiles. Although machines are faster, the fuel they require limits any trip to a week or so. Meanwhile, Greenlanders can stay out indefinitely, hunting seals to feed themselves and their teams.

Grise Fiord's greatest marathon snowmobile trip was in the 1960s, when several men traveled to Ellesmere's northern tip, drawing on fuel caches. It was the first modern lengthwise crossing of the island. Their route included the only known traverse of Ellesmere's most beautiful alpine pass, the Yelverton. The long glacier section made it particularly daring.

Seeglook Akeeagok's father had often spoken to him of that journey. Seeglook, the hamlet's wildlife officer, had inherited his father's wanderlust. Rather than stick to our caravan, he prowled constantly, coming back with precise forensic reports of how, for example, a two-year-old polar bear had unsuccessfully tried to kill a three-week old seal so many hours before. His curiosity about the land seemed unbounded. He was an *Innummauti*, a real Inuk, not a town Inuk.

I rode on the seat behind Darren, dressed in everything I had. It was cold. The windshield and foot warmers and heated handlebars only benefited the drivers. I was tempted to flatter myself with the thought that I was enduring effective temperatures of minus one million degrees. Then I remembered joking with my running partner back home about his obsession with this wind chill factor. His fears, like those of many other overdressed joggers, seemed fanned by the dire arithmetic of the Weather Channel, whose wind chill equivalents turned balmy days into blizzards. As a traveler I found this gauge grossly exaggerated, and scientists were beginning to agree. "It may be time to bury the wind chill index rather than to praise it," suggested one recent article.

An oversized Canadian flag snapped in the wind on the lead machine, a reminder that this was a sovereignty patrol. We were prowling for international poachers, namely the Greenlanders who had hunted Ellesmere for about a thousand years. Like all Canadian arctic villages, Grise Fiord has a polar bear quota; Greenland does not. Since the bears roam freely between countries, this was a sore point. Greenlanders could hunt seal and even some walrus on the Ellesmere side, but bears and muskoxen were untouchable.

Despite the friction, the two communities remain friendly. Student exchanges occasionally take place. Sometimes people from Qaanaaq dogsled the four hundred miles to Grise Fiord just to say hello, then sled back again. I had the sense that people in Grise Fiord were somewhat in awe of the Polar Inuit as travelers. Even Seeglook, no slouch on the trail, had heard of Nukapinguaq and regarded him with the same saucer eyes that I did.

The shadowed snow was turning deep blue, the color of my lips, by the time we stopped for the evening on Vendom Fiord. We'd covered a hundred miles. I ran another mile to warm up, making 101 for the day. An icy moon sliver hung in the purple sky. It was −38°F and everything was brittle and stiff. My nylon sled cover creased like an overstarched shirt as I peeled it back to gather my things for the night.

Up went the big white canvas tents; in went the sleeping bags; on went the Coleman stoves; then in we went. On the windblown sea ice, snow stakes were useless to hold down the tent, and I admired Seeglook's solution: six-inch nails and a hammer. After dinner, Darren and I paid a visit to our camp's equivalent of the Dorset longhouse, the social center—Seeglook's tent. We lounged like pashas on caribou rugs and sipped tea while twin stoves hissed merrily in the trench that kept cold air off the sleeping platform. A six-inch hole in the tent roof averted the carbon monoxide buildup that, some say, has killed more explorers than cold.

In the morning, one of the young guys was not feeling well and decided to return home. It may have been one of those virulent flus caused by lack of enthusiasm for the job. He had spoken mainly of television, and what a pain it was that the first decent program on Sunday was *The Simpsons*, at eight p.m.

That left Seeglook, Darren, and me, plus the two remaining Rangers, Jeffrey Qanaq, and Jarloo Kiguktak. Jeffrey was in his twenties, energetic but relaxed on the trail, the sort of guy who might have a future, even in Grise Fiord. Jarloo was a gnomish carpenter who hid his ingenuity behind a big-lipped grin. The day before, Darren had taken a corner too fast, rolling the komatik, and shattering the brittle plastic bindings of my skis, which sat on top. Later, Jarloo wired everything back together in a brilliant repair, using a heated wire to melt holes in the fragments as attachment points. The makeshift stitches survived two hard months of torque.

■

Although four countries half-heartedly laid claim to Ellesmere, Canada's claim was the least half-hearted. High Arctic sovereignty has that flavor. In calling Ellesmere a no man's land, Rasmussen was not exactly hammering a stake for his native Denmark. Otto Sverdrup banged his head against Norway's indifference for almost three decades. The United States had the weakest case but was the most aggressive, and showed its claims by persistently refusing to acknowledge the claims of others. Finally, in a kind of multi-team deal, the United States got the Virgin Islands, Denmark got Greenland, Norway got tiny Jan Mayen Island and Canada got Ellesmere and its neighbors.

It wasn't quite that simple, of course. Canada's case for ownership rested mainly on the early British expeditions, whose rights it had inherited. When other powers began to challenge this assumption, Ottawa made the right gestures and the right noises. It sent ships to stake territory anew. Most important, it set up RCMP posts.

In 1904, Canadian geologist A. P. Low built a cairn at Cape Herschel, near Pim Island, in which he left a note declaring sovereignty. (Sverdrup had already done this on northwestern Ellesmere two years earlier.) A few years later, a Greenlander mischievously demolished Low's cairn. By that time, however, Canadian sovereignty had found its one feisty advocate—the controversial Quebec ship captain, Joseph Bernier.

This greatest Canadian sailor first ran afoul of the authorities as a kid when he was caught chewing tobacco in school. He was thrashed and sent home with a board around his neck saying, "apprentice chewer." When he was a ship's boy of fourteen, his captain lashed him to the windlass to cure him of mal de mer. This drastic strategy may have worked: Later photos of Bernier show a heavyset man who had clearly been able to keep down many robust dinners, despite a lifetime at sea.

Bernier considered it his mission to win the Arctic for Canada. Often ignoring routine errands, the well-read captain sailed thirty thousand miles in quest of sovereignty, diligently seeking out old explorers' documents and replacing them with his own declarations. (One of Bernier's men, picking up on the old man's habits, showed some style of his own when he disembarked at Igloolik and shouted, "I claim this stinking island for Canada.")

Bernier had secret ambitions on the North Pole but could never quite bring himself to hijack ship and crew. He was bitterly disappointed when Low beat him to Cape Herschel, but made up for it by declaring sovereignty more often, and over more territory. He backed up practice with theory, advancing the "Eskimo pie" rule of arctic ownership, in which circumpolar countries have a right to all unclaimed lands between their east-west limits and the North Pole. He also piloted the ship that set up the first RCMP posts, including Craig Harbour.

■

As sometimes happens, cold air pooled in the valleys. The head wind burned. Ice beads grew on our eyelashes. Rime coated our parka hoods and collars like icing sugar. As the machines labored through the unpacked snow of Vendom Fiord, I gazed dreamily at the pure white hills flanking this narrow entrenchment. Now and then we stopped for tea; Seeglook roamed; Jarloo and Jeffrey tried out their new Ranger-issue GPS's, but the liquid crystal screens were frozen. As we headed inland, muskoxen galloped up improbably steep slopes out of our way. "Mountain goats," joked Seeglook.

Eventually we came to a wide prairie leading north. The snow was harder. Distant air shimmered in the afternoon sun, but by the time we stopped beside a small lake at the head of Strathcona Fiord, it was –40°F again.

Seeglook knew this unnamed lake well; he often "vacationed" here in summer, flying in by Twin Otter. He liked to roam and fish for char. The lake ice was now seven feet thick, but the angling spirit was not to be denied, and we all took turns chopping two holes in the ice using a spear with a chisel on the end.

My taste in aquatic life was more antediluvian. Strathcona Fiord was the La Brea Tar Pits of Ellesmere. Some of the weirdest things had turned up here. Fossil forests of birch and tamarack recalled a time when Ellesmere was merely subarctic. None other than Nukapinguaq had discovered a dinosaur skeleton nearby, but in a rare lapse, he couldn't find it again. Two subsequent expeditions also failed to relocate what seems to have been an ancient marine reptile. It wasn't until 1996 that the first dinosaur bones turned up in the Ellesmere area, the remains of a ninety-million-year-old, crocodile-like champsosaur.

Just across from our camp lay something almost as good—a three-million-year-old beaver pond, complete with gnawed twigs and a menagerie of supporting wildlife that included a three-toed horse and a "paleo-bunny" named *Hypolagus*. This northernmost beaver pond happened to be a thousand feet up a mountain. I could see the dark outcropping from camp. Vainly I tried to imagine what forces thrust this lowland habitat so high in the air. Scientists could look at this landscape with eyes that saw Ellesmere not as it is but as it once was. Some of them had tried to explain their vision to me, but I knew too little and my eyes could never refocus through time.

By the end of the third day, we had begun our crossing of windblown Sverdrup Pass. Only a thin dusting of snow covered the gravel. Sparks flew up from the old-fashioned steel runners of one komatik. Our snowmobiles gave us an advantage over the explorers: We could make half-mile detours in search of continuous ribbons of snow. On foot, you just drag your sled over the gravel and hope it holds up. After our daily hundred miles, we camped just before the crux of the route, the narrowing historically known as Hell Cleft.

For manhaulers, Hell Cleft is now just a picky little canyon that requires unloading the sleds a few times over high snow drifts and frozen spillways. But in the 1920s, a surging glacier completely blocked the pass and forced a long detour over sled-destroying hills. This glacier has now receded, but waterfalls still impede snowmobiles. A party from Grise Fiord the year before us had failed to make it through. In a way, Hell Cleft was a blessing, because the empty RCMP buildings at Alexandra Fiord were a tempting base for hunters. Without this obstacle, the area, now so serene, would buzz all spring with snowmobilers from Grise Fiord.

■

Many Ellesmere explorers had challenged Hell Cleft, but the greatest of them all was Alfred Herbert Joy of the RCMP. In 1929, he made the longest of his legendary patrols, an eighty-one day, eighteen hundred mile trek with Nukapinguaq to Melville Island and back. Together, they crossed nearly the entire span of the arctic islands. They made it seem effortless. It was perhaps the greatest arctic sled journey ever.

Joy emigrated from Britain and enlisted in the Force in 1909, at the age of twenty-two. In 1921 he became the point man for enforcing Canadian law on Baffin and the disputed islands. Southern justice was sometimes difficult for the natives of that era to understand. Imprisonment in a warm cell, with all the food they could eat, seemed like a strange deterrent to crime.

When Joy took charge of the High Arctic posts in 1925, the struggle for sovereignty had heated up. Donald MacMillan had just returned to his old haunts with pilot Richard Byrd, in the hope of finding new land by airplane. They pointedly did not ask Canada for permission to land on Axel Heiberg to lay caches; they asked the Norwegians instead. "Has a Canadian ever been to Axel Heiberg?" Byrd said archly, when Joy visited their Greenland base.

MacMillan's expedition never took off, so to speak, but the following year Joy and the ever-present Nukapinguaq dogsledded a thousand miles from Craig Harbour to Axel Heiberg and back. In 1927, the tireless pair covered thirteen hundred miles. In 1929, they made their greatest journey. All together, this was a tour de force of travel the Arctic had never seen.

By 1930, the patrols of Joy and the continued RCMP presence had won Ellesmere and Axel Heiberg for Canada. For the ailing Otto Sverdrup, it was a bitter defeat. He had unsuccessfully pressed Norway to do exactly what Canada had done, establish a small police force on Ellesmere. To close the deal, Ottawa paid Sverdrup $67,000 for his maps and journals, "in recognition of his work." A few months later, Sverdrup was dead.

Joy, now an inspector, left the field work to younger men but still went north with the annual supply ship in 1930, when he met Hans Krüger, and in 1931, to plan the search for Krüger with the Mounties at Bache Post. With sovereignty secured, Ottawa had begun to phase out the expensive High Arctic stations. Joy was forty-four. After seventeen years in the Arctic, a desk job loomed before him. He became engaged to a young woman, Carmel Murphy.

Like Nukapinguaq, the figure of A. H. Joy looms over Ellesmere. In the National Archives in Ottawa, I went through the 1927 Bache logbook to try to get a sense of the man—pack-a-day smoker, chocoholic extraordinaire, unparalleled traveler. I wondered how he felt to be leaving the Arctic for good. I wondered how I would feel.

On April 29, 1932, Joy arrived in Ottawa by train and checked into the Chateau Laurier, the city's grand old hotel. He was to be married the following day, but he never made that walk down the aisle. He died that night.

Rumor has it he shot himself. All the old-timers have heard this rumor, but no one can confirm it. The annals of the Chateau Laurier report nothing unusual on that day. The death certificate suggests a heart attack or stroke, but physicians of that era were not above fudging their records because of the stigma attached to suicide.

On the way north one year, I visited Joy's grave at the Notre Dame Cemetery in Ottawa. I had no idea where to find a single grave in such a large cemetery. It was Easter Sunday, and the office was closed. I expected a long and fruitless search.

To my surprise, after about fifteen minutes, I skidded to a halt. There was Joy's large black and grey headstone, "erected by his father, sisters and brothers." But they were all back in England, so he had been interred in the family plot of his fiancée. The nearby Murphys did not include a Carmel; she was probably buried elsewhere with her husband. I toyed with the idea of returning here one moonless night with a crew of Shakespearean graverobbers, to check for bullet holes in the skull. I settled for leaving a few overpriced lilies from a flower vendor at the main gate.

■

We had lost our good weather, but Hell Cleft was too narrow to admit the sun anyway. Sometimes, my arms could touch the opposing walls. We crept forward. Now and then our shovel brigade had to clear a snowdrift out of the way. We reduced the steepness of small waterfalls with our ice spear. Then Jeffrey backed up and gunned his machine up the slope while we hauled with ropes from above. Once his snowmobile was on top, we could use it to tow up the others.

We finally came to a ten-foot waterfall that had turned back the group a year ago. We took turns chiseling. Seeglook was the most artful. His blows effortlessly sheared off big hubcaps of ice. It seemed as if he just raised the spear and let it slip through his fingers. He was sculpting, not attacking. He tried to give me some pointers—"Don't make the hole too deep at first"—but my pieces remained the size of ice cubes.

"You must be a shaman," I told him, impressed.

"I'm a shaman-in-training."

Although we were both travelers, our skills were completely different, and this made Seeglook fascinating. As a walker, I was perhaps more aware of the fine points of snow. I was less conservative; he and his friends clung to familiar routes when better ones were there for the finding. He would have no interest in camping in my cold little doghouse when he could recline in the Seeglook Hilton. Yet like some Shaolin monk, he was privy to many mysteries of the trail that were beyond me.

After several attempts to finesse our snowmobiles up the falls, Jarloo radioed some Grise Fiord snowmobilers who had already reached Alexandra Fiord by Twin Otter. They came to the lip of the falls. With their horsepower from above, we eventually lifted everything over.

To avoid a second canyon, we took the explorers' detour over the hills. It was a torture of gravel. I'd never seen so much. The hills looked like mine tailings. Ugly country. The austere ice cap on the other side of the valley, so white and gentle, beckoned like a vision of paradise.

The wind picked up suddenly after the height of land. Sverdrup called this a cow-storm, a gale so strong it blows the horns off cows. It was not a weather wind, but an avalanche of air rolling down from the ice cap. Happily it was at our backs. We drove at the same speed as the wind, and Jarloo's Canadian flag hung limply, strange sight. For once, the wind chill was no factor. I thought of those perfect sledding days, when a light tailwind moved at exactly my speed. No air resistance. Warm face.

At the end of the pass, the bare green ice of the Flagler River looked waxed and polished by Zambonis. Somehow the snowmobiles found traction but the komatiks jackknifed crazily.

By now it was midnight. The early April twilight was soft but not deep. No more stars for five months. We'd been going for twelve hours, and we were still three hours from Alexandra Fiord. Everyone was tired. I was tired too, and fatigue made me nervous. I reminded Jarloo of the polynya ahead. Thin ice was so rare that an inattentive crew could easily overlook it. In the days of Joy, one man fell through but Nukapinguaq yanked him out by the hair before the current swept him under the ice.

But today, the polynya was frozen solid. Our caravan hooked around the Knud Peninsula, and the wind abruptly died. Darren and I sped along, trying to keep up with the more experienced drivers. At two a.m. we pulled into Alexandra Fiord. The five white houses with blue trim signaled a northern RCMP post.

■

Alexandra Fiord was opened in 1953, after the ever-pesky Americans started making vague noises again: "Hey, how about building an airstrip for long-range nuclear bombers on Ellesmere?" After the hiatus of World War II, it also seemed a good time to remind Greenlanders who held the deed to this patch of permafrost. The post stayed open ten years. Afterwards, scientists used the buildings. The RCMP began to control use in the 1980s after the first tour groups began squatting. These are the only shelters on Ellesmere, indeed, some of the only ones in the Arctic, that are normally locked.

My friends prowled outer Buchanan Bay for two days without discovering any tracks from the Greenlanders' dogteams. The Inuit kept far away from Camp Clay. One night on the trail, I had told them about the Greely disaster, and my ghost stories had never had a more receptive audience. Two years later, they were still avoiding Pim Island.

After everyone left for Grise Fiord, I sledded twenty miles north to the older Bache Post, "by far the most pleasant and attractive place in the eastern Arctic," according to Joy. As the world's northernmost post office, it used to receive the letters to Santa Claus. Thousands of them found their way here.

The post lay near the foot of a tan cliff that extended for miles along the Bache Peninsula. In summer, a feeble stream, trickling under rocks, supplied drinking water. The buildings were gone but plenty of eloquent garbage from that golden age of the RCMP remained: a wooden crate of dog food, another of Christie's biscuits ("Purest of all Pure Foods"), and even a box of paperbacks that had helped the Mounties endure the long winter. Moisture had glued some of the pages together, giving new meaning to the term pulp fiction, but considering that the books had sat outside for seventy years, they were in good shape. Most were Edwardian society novels, with characters such as Lord Fisher and Mr. Asquith and chapter openings such as "The loveliest mouth in France turned into a distracting smile. . . ."

Perhaps Sergeant Henry Stallworthy himself curled up by the oil stove with one of these page-turners. Stallworthy took over the post in 1930. Although the sovereignty patrols were over, Krüger's disappearance that year gave the lanky Englishman a chance to make one last magnificent journey for the Force. His circumnavigation of Axel Heiberg has never been repeated. He also made several other long treks that his reports modestly present as neighborhood ambles.

But Stallworthy was more than the sum of his patrols. His arctic career began in the Yukon, then he quit the RCMP to try prospecting. He reenlisted in 1923 and was posted to Chesterfield Inlet, on Hudson Bay. He immediately loved the Arctic and its people. "All the glory and honor the Mounties have in the North is due, absolutely, to the Eskimo guides."

In 1926, on sick leave after a bout of pneumonia, he met his future wife, Hilda Austin, on a skating rink in Jasper, Alberta. He was despondent: They were not going to send him north that summer. The next period of his life is sketchy, but by the time he left for Bache in 1930, he and Hilda had established a correspondence romance.

Mail came just once a year in Bache, at best. In 1932, ice blocked the supply ship, and Stallworthy had to remain there an unscheduled third year. He survived on walrus meat, read about lovely mouths in France, and wondered if Hilda had lost patience. She hadn't. Stallworthy's letters on his way south in 1933 are those of a gallant swain who has made up his mind to settle down. "I know now that, above all, you matter more to me than anything in my life."

His commitment to the RCMP weakened with his attachment to Hilda. He was furious when the fox furs he collected on his own time were confiscated under a new ruling. "Every time I took a fox out of a trap, I thought—there's another chair or something for our home. Maybe the wheel of a new car."

The Krüger search had made the thirty-eight-year-old sergeant's reputation. With Joy dead, he was now the ranking arctic expert within the Force, and he was up for the illustrious King's Police Medal. "Personally, I don't think I deserve the honor," he wrote, although he lobbied hard to get it. But the medal eluded him, perhaps because when he had boarded the northbound ship in 1930, he had been caught with alcohol in his luggage, contrary to regulations.

He and Hilda quickly married after his return in 1933. Tragedy struck almost immediately. After a near-fatal ectopic pregnancy, Hilda could no longer have kids. Stallworthy was grief-stricken. "Why have I done this to you?" he cried at her hospital bed.

Stallworthy performed one more tour of arctic service. He told Hilda that he couldn't get out of it, but his feelings must have been mixed. To avoid a repetition of the Krüger disaster, he was to guide an expedition of young Oxford students to Ellesmere. Leaving Hilda with his parents in England, Stallworthy sailed north in 1934, where he reunited with Nukapinguaq, now nearing the end of his expedition career. The age of exploration on Ellesmere was itself coming to a close. Nukapinguaq and Stallworthy helped the Britons over the learning curve, and their dogsled journeys to Lake Hazen and the ice caps beyond were uneventful. Stallworthy's notes on bidding at bridge decorate the journal of this adaptable man.

After Stallworthy retired from the RCMP, he and Hilda started a tourist resort on Vancouver Island. Despite all his time alone in the Far North, Stallworthy was a people person. Hilda was sharp and opinionated, while he kept a quiet, wry style. Even grey-haired and frail, his lanky six-foot-two figure and square jaw recalled the great Mountie whose long, spidery legs ate up the arctic miles. Shortly before his death in 1976, after a vigorous letter-writing campaign by Hilda, he received the Order of Canada from the Queen for his northern patrols.

As I stood at the empty shell of Bache Post, I couldn't help comparing the two, Joy and Stallworthy. Joy flared like a meteor across the arctic sky and burned up in the southern atmosphere. Uncompromising, magnificent, he left a legend behind him. Stallworthy was graceful, multi-dimensional. A family photo taken near the end of his life shows the incorrigible old coot lying down in a flower bed, holding up a chrysanthemum he has just plucked for Hilda, who stands over him, fists on hips, looking faux-vexed. He has the smile of a man who had achieved serenity.

Serenity was a long way off for me. I wasn't sure I wanted it. Banging my head against the wall of life was such fun. I had planned to move on that night, but I liked the feel of Bache, so I set up my tent on a bit of flat ground, and looked out over the ocean, and admired its many views.

Epilogue

The ancient Greeks deemed a region severe if it was so cold that the inhabitants had to wear pants. What would they have thought of Ellesmere? Forget the togas, boys. That May around Bache, it dropped one night to −44°F, and frost catkins reappeared in my tent. A week later a brief hurricane struck, riding weird clouds above the ice cap. It was the only true white-out I'd ever experienced, when earth and sky vanished and I was left swimming in skim milk. I could lean back into the wind as onto a soft pillow, without falling. I stopped sledding just to play with the wind, and to let it play with me. Some places, like revenge, are best enjoyed cold.

It was a long, rich spring. My Ellesmere journeys had begun in Buchanan Bay, and I continued to discover new things, but now I walked with the measured step of one who knew what he was looking for. Wonder and curiosity were my companions.

If I regretted anything, it was that I had never found the blood brotherhood of the trail that had so enriched some of the old-timers. What I would have given to have flown with Weldy Phipps when he crashed his Piper Super Cub at Fort Conger, then wired the radio back together with artifacts. To have toasted Geoffrey Hattersley-Smith with Amundsen's rum from Cape Richardson. Imagine a Vulcan mind meld with Renee

Wissink, or waiting out a three-day storm in a Logan tent with the entertaining geographer John England. To have shared an igloo with Nukapinguaq, or a pound of chocolate with A. H. Joy. To dog the steps of the eccentric Russell Maris, a British doctor and amateur botanist who hikes the island wearing a tie and eating rock tripe and lots of questionable food that he carries in a beat-up schoolbag. To have been with Peter Schledermann on Skraeling Island when he unearthed the Viking chain mail and watched his expressive hands flutter with excitement, like Wing Biddlebaum's in the great Sherwood Anderson story. Sometimes I wanted to embrace every inch of Ellesmere's 76,600 square miles.

In some ways, sharing the experience had been easier for past generations. They were doing their jobs; work throws together a lot of personalities, and some become friends. But in the company of modern adventurers, I felt as if we were all jostling for a piece of the island. Expeditioners who became outfitters or corporate lecturers. Scientists who longed to become filmmakers. Adventurers trumpeting their minor journeys as landmarks in human achievement. Professionals and would-be professionals. Peary's spirit—and I'm not blameless here—animates a lot of the adventure on the island. Everyone is on the watch for Dr. Cook.

I kept coming back to the difference between mountaineers and polar travelers. While rivalry existed among climbers, there also seemed to be a deep bond forged by mutual dependency. The climbing rope was a constant reminder that people were connected and needed each other. But in the Arctic, a solo traveler can do most anything that a team can. A very few sledging expeditions were held together by more than the glue of convenience. An aloofness separates most polar equals.

At the same time, I was surprised by how much I learned from the tourists whose trips I sometimes shared. As a destination, Ellesmere does not attract the same crowd that wants Mount Everest on its list of trophies. Despite its scenery, it is too horizontal, too understated. For many, it is another few bars in a running medley of the world's wild places. They enjoy it and when they leave, they never look back, just as I have never looked back on Nepal, a destination that has enraptured many.

But for others, one extreme journey on Ellesmere Island connects them to the place forever. They return almost every year. Many have jobs, families, outwardly conservative lives. But their social circle vacations in Hawaii while they proudly hump sixty-pound packs in a place where it snows in July. The Arctic becomes part of their persona. One wonderful fellow who lost part of his big toe to frostbite considers it a badge of honor that connects him to the old explorers. Someone who didn't belong on Ellesmere would simply sue the outfitter.

■

I did my roaming, then set up camp at Alexandra Fiord and waited to go south. Two months were my limit; beyond that, I couldn't sustain the intensity. Travel then became a form of temporary residence. My epiphanies came on the move.

I built a snow wall so I could sit outside and watch the midnight sun without being chilled by the evening breeze from the Twin Glaciers. I'd recently taken to carrying music with me, and I often looked across the fiord toward Bache Post with Beethoven's *Ninth* crashing in my ears. The "Ode to Joy" seemed particularly appropriate.

It was almost summer. The twitter of snow buntings filled the air. I was again in tune with the big, slow rhythm of the land. I could sit peacefully and watch a woolybear caterpillar as it crept along a sun-warmed rock, meticulously keeping out of the shade. In half an hour, it covered twelve inches.

Tourists and scientists were arriving. A geologist I knew offered me a lift out. Hurriedly, I dismantled my camp and threw everything into the Twin Otter, then took a seat at the rear.

As we flew west across Jokel Fiord, the evening light modeled the world below. Nunataks erupted like cold stone meat from white bones. The Stygge Glacier was a symphony of ice, I could hear it. It ended in the living ice cap, which spread on toward infinity, a choppy white sea interrupted by pools of unimaginable calm.

I was glad that piles of gear blocked the aisle of the airplane. Otherwise, out of habit, I would have gone up front to photograph from the co-pilot's seat. It would have spoiled everything. This was the closest I had ever come to seeing God. It was awful, serene, lovely, violent, unutterably ancient. The vision lasted half an hour, then the ice cap abruptly gave way to a brown openness. Ellesmere was earth again.

We landed in Resolute around two a.m. Warm sunlight fell on the drab gravel like a Midas touch. Gathering my gear, and feeling completely lost, I wondered where to go.

Glossary

Bully beef tins: Resembling jumbo cans of corned beef, these tins held the preserved meats of nineteenth-century expeditions. A common find around historic sites.

Cairn: Pile of rocks left by explorers on hilltops and other visible locations as a letter box, proof that they have passed that way or to mark a supply depot.

Climbing skins: Strips of fur fastened underneath skis for better traction. Used going up hills and while pulling sleds. As Olaus Magnus explained in 1555, "the hairs, like bristles or the spines of a hedgehog, rise on end, and by the wonderful power of Nature keep the planks from sliding backwards."

Floeberg: Little-used term coined by Nares but useful for describing a pressed-up, eroded piece of old sea ice.

Iceberg: Usually much bigger than a floeberg and made of fresh water ice. Icebergs come from glaciers that reach the sea. Icebergs are commonly pictured in open water, but for most of the year they're frozen in.

Ice cap: Expanse of permanent ice from which glaciers issue. On Ellesmere, the ice caps begin near sea level on the north coast and at around 2,500 feet elsewhere, and are up to 100,000 years old.

Ice floe: Flat piece of floating sea ice.

Ice foot: Shelf of sea ice that clings to the shore at the high tide line. Often a good path for traveling.

Ice shelf: Kind of a super-ice foot, a blend of glacier and sea ice attached to the north coast of Ellesmere in several places. Ice shelves periodically break away to form ice islands, which can be miles in diameter.

Kamiks: Sealskin boots with uppers of ring seal and soles of tougher bearded seal. Still the best footwear for walking in the arctic spring.

Katabatic winds: Strong winds from heavy, cool air avalanching down a mountain.

Komatik: Inuit sled, formerly of driftwood and bone, now wood shoed with hard plastic runners. May be pulled by either dogs or snowmobiles. High Arctic komatiks are about twelve feet long.

Lead: Open crack in sea ice caused by pressure.

Nunatak: "Piece of land" in Inuktitut. It is the part of a mountain that sticks above an ice cap.

Parcoll: Type of semi-permanent arctic building, usually tube-shaped, with a solid frame, and an insulated fabric shell. Quonsets, Jamesways, and weatherhavens are similar structures.

Polar oasis: Informal name for an area of local warmth. Ellesmere's four oases—Eureka, Lake Hazen, Tanquary Fiord, and Alexandra Fiord—enjoy a few 60° to 70°F days a year. A more typical July day is 45°F.

Polynya: Region where currents keep the sea open much of the year. Ellesmere has three or four small polynyas and one, the North Water, that is the size of Switzerland.

Sastrugi: Hard, wind-sculpted snow resembling frozen whitecaps. Usually just a few inches high.

Serac: Obelisk of glacier ice. Seracs are ticking time bombs, falling unpredictably.

Tidal ice: Disturbed ice along the edge of the shore. Varies from a slight buckling around small tides to an impenetrable barrier of giant ice blocks.

Selected Reading

The Arctic has no roguish Sir Richard Burtons, no dreamy W. H. Hudsons. Instead, it is top-heavy with government employees like Nares merely seeking to advance their careers. They do not write the best books.

The Antarctic has fared slightly better. Apsley Cherry-Garrard's *The Worst Journey in the World* is the best polar book ever written and its last page is great literature. Robert Scott's diary during his final days almost makes one forget that the tragedy was of his own making; truly, "nothing in his life became him like the leaving of it." Sara Wheeler's wonderful *Terra Incognita* (1997) puts a human face on Antarctica and imbues it with a humor lacking among arctic adventurers, who tend to take their icy calling very seriously. By contrast, the literary value of Amundsen's *The South Pole*, written by the greatest of all polar travelers about his most famous triumph, lies on a par with droning essays on the Treaty of Utrecht.

The subarctic has a few minor classics like *Sleeping Island*, but the farther north one goes, the more barren the prose. It is hard to know which of Ellesmere's prominent explorers was the poorest writer, Greely, Nares or Sverdrup. The romantic explorers, Cook, Peary, and Kane, are only slightly more engaging. Even the multi-talented Nansen is a scholar, not a scribbler.

Polar exploration books, in fact, are identical to most of the adventure tales found on the shelves of today's camping shops. Someone does something interesting, or at least well-publicized, and produces a forgettable book about it for a small audience sold on the public profile of the expedition or personally interested in sailing, or Brazil, or whatever.

Only four types of exploration books transcend niche literature to become mainstream:

1. Tragedy. e.g. *The Lure of the Labrador Wild.* "Incompetence is a literary asset in arctic matters," wrote Vilhjalmur Stefansson. To experience great misadventure, you must either capitalize on your window of innocence or keep putting yourself in unfamiliar environments. It's too late for me as a polar traveler, but I could still have hair-raising adventures by photographing Cape buffalo or observing volcanic eruptions, about which I know nothing.
2. Rivalry/Controversy. e.g. North Pole.
3. Celebrity. Good as it is, *Seven Years in Tibet* is a classic because of Heinrich Harrar's inside look at the life of the young Dalai Lama.
4. Literature. e.g. *Arabian Sands.*

Stefansson, one of the last arctic explorers, may have been the best writer—he's clever, ironic, erudite—but his lack of spirituality largely neutralizes the style. He's calculating and worldly-wise when we long for a dash of the mad dreamer. The very shallowness that made him a man of the hour deprived him of being a man for the centuries.

These days, Farley Mowat's arctic books are often dismissed as half-fiction, but standards of nonfiction have changed. Traditional nature writing often featured a mixture of fact, personal anecdote, and tall tales. When I was researching a book on cougars, biologists were as skeptical about R.D. Lawrence's experiences in *The Ghost Walker* as David Mech was when I asked him about *Never Cry Wolf.* I, too, had been exasperated by Mowat's half-hearted research in *The Polar Passion,* but accuracy was not his job. Mowat is best at making people passionate about things they know nothing about, which is harder than being accurate.

Barry Lopez's *Arctic Dreams* struggles with dense prose. "You can't read much of it at a sitting," everyone says, but this 325-page essay on science, history, and the northern landscape remains the best book on the Arctic. Ecotourists are immediately recognizable in arctic airports by their new Gore-Tex jackets and paperback copy of *Arctic Dreams.*

Despite such exceptions, what George Rice wrote at Fort Conger in 1883 remains true today: "There is very little charm to arctic literature, and there are few books on the subject that one not interested or engaged in arctic work would read."

I can buy a second-hand copy of *Macbeth* or *The Brothers Karamazov* for the price of a cappuccino, but badly written explorers' tomes cost their weight in titanium. Nares material is especially valuable; his *Voyage to the Polar Sea* costs almost a thousand dollars. Edward Moss's *Shores of the Polar Sea*, whose illustrations make it the loveliest of all Ellesmere books, is also the most expensive, typically three thousand dollars a copy. The Parliamentary papers on the Nares expedition cost slightly less but are even more desirable to the ghost-hunter. The volume with the sledging journals, in particular, is second in usefulness only to a trip to Cambridge.

Such collectors' items were beyond my budget, so I either photographed them page by page or, when able, photocopied them. Most are in the rare book rooms of university libraries, which restrict copying to a few pages. But some libraries have not yet reassessed the value of certain old books and still loan them out.

Most of the arctic books below are out of print but can be found in libraries or purchased through second-hand specialists such as High Latitude near Seattle (highlatitude@prodigy.net) or Aquila Books in Calgary (aquila@cadvision.com), or through an online consortium such as Abebooks.

General Arctic

Taylor, Andrew. *Geographical Exploration and Discovery in the Queen Elizabeth Islands.*
> Published in 1955, this all-in-one history is still easy to find second-hand. It includes even obscure explorers such as Krüger and Björling, and their routes. Its portability makes it the ideal companion for a High Arctic trip.

Dunbar, Moira and Greenaway, Keith. *Arctic Canada From the Air.*
Another little-known old volume of exploration by a pair of geographers with a lust for history. Its black-and-white aerial photos give ideas for dozens of potential new routes.

Holland, Clive. *Arctic Exploration and Development.*
An indispensable reference encyclopedia of every arctic expedition up to 1915.

Polar Record.
This academic periodical out of Cambridge, England is to polar history what the *New England Journal of Medicine* is to cure and disease: first word on the latest news. Obscure expeditions, new wrinkles on old polar tragedies, all detailed and footnoted and bibliographed. Fertile ground for travelers seeking historical themes.

Chapter One: Into the Void

Anderson, J. R. L. *The Ulysses Factor.*
Anderson discusses the drive for adventure by examining several well-known explorers and their motivations.

Zweig, Paul. *The Adventurer.*
Similar to *The Ulysses Factor,* but more literary: In Zweig's model, Edgar Allen Poe, Robinson Crusoe, and Nietzsche represent idealized types of adventure better than celebrity sailors and mountaineers. Along with Wilfrid Noyce's *The Springs of Adventure,* these are the three "whys of adventure" books.

Chapter Two: Raw Fear

Bruemmer, Fred. *The Polar Bear.*
Bruemmer is better known as a photographer, but years of research went into this words-and-pictures book, and it shows.

Chapter Three: Getting Away with Murder

Harper, Kenn. *Give Me My Father's Body.*
  Unrelated to Peeawahto or murder, but shows how Peary and his school treated their native helpers as commodities.

Chapter Four: The Horizontal Everest

Bryce, Robert. *Cook and Peary, The Polar Controversy Resolved.*
  Unlike most accounts, this book places truth above partisanship and sets the right tone for a modern reappraisal of these two explorers: Cook was a nice guy, Peary was insufferable, both were lying. However, the 1,133 pages demand a lot of commitment.

Chapter Five: Dance of the Sea Ice

Mitchell, Edwin Valentine, editor. *The Pleasures of Walking.*
  A great collection of old essays on walking.

Sverdrup, Otto. *New Land.*
  Invaluable for the Ellesmere traveler, but nothing you'd want to read for pleasure.

Chapter Six: Life in the Freezer

Brandenburg, Jim. *White Wolf.*
  Magnificent photos of a pack of wolves near Eureka, with text on his observations.

Mech, David. *The Arctic Wolf.*
  Ten years after the *National Geographic* article with Brandenburg, Mech's photography has greatly improved, but it is still the natural history that makes this book fly.

Chapter Seven: Inanimate Things

Guttridge, Leonard F. *Ghosts of Cape Sabine.*
Guttridge has never been to the Arctic and so overlooks several key issues in the tragedy, but the research of this 80-year-old amateur historian is otherwise so thorough that you can ignore the other Greely books. This is the one worth reading.

Chapter Eight: The Ken Dryden Factor

Liljequist, Gösta. *High Latitudes.*
A survey of Swedish polar expeditions, it includes the only detailed account of the Björling tragedy in English.

Chapter Nine: Inside the Arctic Triangle

Barr, William. *Polar Record.* June, 1990.
A scholarly investigation of Hans Krüger by the world's foremost polar historian.

Chapter Ten: Shores of the Polar Sea

Carpenter, Kenneth J. *The History of Scurvy and Vitamin C.*
Published in 1986 but already the classic work on this "explorers' disease."

Chapter Eleven: On High Alert

Lee, Robert Mason. *Death and Deliverance.*
The story of the Boxtop 22 crash. Detailed, although told somewhat from the outside.

Gray, David. *Alert: Beyond the Inuit Lands.*
Commissioned by the Department of National Defence, this is an accurate but uncritical look at life in the world's northernmost settlement. For diehards only.

Chapter Twelve: They, the People

Malaurie, Jean. *The Last Kings of Thule.*
A classic tale of living and traveling with the Polar Inuit of northwest
Greenland in the 1950s and how the following twenty years changed
their way of life. Malaurie also compiled a little-known CD of local
music, *Chants et Tambours Inuit,* that includes Sakaeunnguaq's song
about his famous father, Nukapinguaq.

Marie-Rousselière, Guy. *Qitdlarssuaq: The Story of a Migration.*
A scholarly but readable account of the visionary, amoral shaman.
Some libraries also have Renee Wissink's fine article on his Qitdlarssuaq Expedition, which appeared in the November/December 1987
issue of *Equinox* magazine.

Schledermann, Peter. "Eskimo and Viking Finds in the High Arctic."
National Geographic, May 1981.
The story behind the find of a career. Schledermann's 1996 book,
Voices in Stone, reviews Inuit prehistory in light of his Ellesmere work.

Chapter Thirteen: Tours de Force

Commissioner's Report, RCMP, 1924-1934.
Published annually, the so-called "Blue Books" summarized a year in
the life of the Royal Canadian Mounted Police, district by district. I
first read them for the detailed patrol reports of Joy and Stallworthy,
but it was impossible to overlook cops and robbers issues in other
parts of the country—arrests for witchcraft and "furious driving," and

hot pursuit of straw bondsmen, Prussian blue Ford sedans, absconding paramours, illicit worm and drip stills, and the wily trafficker Dack Fun. Note: The Mounties always got their man, but finding these obscure little volumes may be difficult.

Index